ROUTLEDGE LIBRARY EDITIONS BROADCASTING

Volume 31

SATELLITE TECHNOLOGY IN EDUCATION

SATELLITE TECHNOLOGY IN EDUCATION

Edited by
JOHN K. GILBERT,
ANNETTE TEMPLE
AND
CRAIG UNDERWOOD

LONDON AND NEW YORK

First published in 1991 by Routledge

This edition first published in 2024
by Routledge
4 Park Square, Milton Park, Abingdon, Oxon OX14 4RN

and by Routledge
605 Third Avenue, New York, NY 10158

Routledge is an imprint of the Taylor & Francis Group, an informa business

© 1991 J.K. Gilbert, A. Temple and C. Underwood

All rights reserved. No part of this book may be reprinted or reproduced or utilised in any form or by any electronic, mechanical, or other means, now known or hereafter invented, including photocopying and recording, or in any information storage or retrieval system, without permission in writing from the publishers.

Trademark notice: Product or corporate names may be trademarks or registered trademarks, and are used only for identification and explanation without intent to infringe.

British Library Cataloguing in Publication Data
A catalogue record for this book is available from the British Library

ISBN: 978-1-032-59391-3 (Set)
ISBN: 978-1-032-62976-6 (Volume 31) (hbk)
ISBN: 978-1-032-62987-2 (Volume 31) (pbk)
ISBN: 978-1-032-62981-0 (Volume 31) (ebk)

DOI: 10.4324/9781032629810

Publisher's Note
The publisher has gone to great lengths to ensure the quality of this reprint but points out that some imperfections in the original copies may be apparent.

Disclaimer
The publisher has made every effort to trace copyright holders and would welcome correspondence from those they have been unable to trace.

Satellite Technology in Education

Edited by
John K. Gilbert
Annette Temple
Craig Underwood

London and New York

First published 1991 by Routledge
11 New Fetter Lane, London EC4P 4EE

Simultaneously published in the USA and Canada
by Routledge
a division of Routledge, Chapman and Hall, Inc.
29 West 35th Street, New York, NY 10001

© 1991 J.K. Gilbert, A. Temple, and C. Underwood

Typeset by LaserScript Limited, Mitcham, Surrey
Printed and bound in Great Britain by
Billings & Sons Limited, Worcester

All rights reserved. No part of this book may be reprinted or reproduced or utilized in any form or by any electronic, mechanical, or other means, now known or hereafter invented, including photocopying and recording, or in any information storage or retrieval system, without permission in writing from the publishers.

British Library Cataloguing in Publication Data

Satellite technology in education.
   1. Great Britain. Education. Use of communications satellites
   I. Gilbert, John *1940–* II. Temple, Annette *1953–* III. Underwood, Craig *1961–*
371.335

ISBN 0–415–02376–9

Library of Congress Cataloging-in-Publication Data

applied for

Contents

List of figures	vii
Notes on contributors	ix
Foreword *R. Gibson, lately Director-General,* *British National Space Centre*	xii
List of abbreviations	xv

	Part I Satellite systems	1
1	Amateur radio, science and technology satellites *M.N. Sweeting*	3
2	Earth observation satellites *P.A. Vass and R.F. Thomas*	38
3	Telecommunications satellites *G. Groom*	62

	Part II Satellites and the teaching and learning of subjects	77
4	Geography and environmental science *Keith Hilton*	79
5	Satellites and language teaching *Brian Hill*	91
6	Science *Craig Underwood*	103
7	Information technology and satellites *John Gilbert and Annette Temple*	128

Contents

Part III Satellites and sectors of the educational systems   143

8   Schools and teacher education
    Annette Temple   145

9   Higher and continuing education
    B. Groombridge   156

Part IV The realization of potential   169

10   Resource systems for education
    J. Stevenson   171

11   Copyright and other legal issues
    G. Crabb   193

12   Research and development on satellites in education
    John Gilbert   205

    Index   219

List of figures

3.1	Growth of Intelsat satellites	63
3.2	Schematic diagram of Intelsat IV	67
3.3	Transponder frequency plan and beam switching	68
6.1	A typical UoSAT-2 telemetry frame	117
6.2	UoSAT-2 navigation magnetometer telemetry	119
6.3	UoSAT-2 solar-array current	120
6.4	UoSAT-OSCAR II: whole-orbit data plot for the z-axis navigational magnetometer	122
6.5	UoSAT-OSCAR II: whole-orbit data plots	123
6.6	Whole-orbit data plot of radiation intensity	124
10.1	The convergence of resources	175
10.2	A framework for learning	179
10.3	Followers as part of a circle	182

List of tables

2.1	Technical characteristics of the main meteorological satellites	41
2.2	Technical characteristics of the first generation of Landsat satellites	46
2.3	Technical characteristics of NASA's experimental satellites launched in 1978	48
2.4	Technical characteristics of Landsats 4 and 5 and SPOTs 1, 2 and 3	52
3.1	Summary of the Eutelsat satellites	75
3.2	Technical criteria of the Astra satellites	76
4.1	Examples of linking geographical concepts to pupil use of Landsat MSS: the Jacaranda kits	83
7.1	Uses of microcomputers in school science	133
10.1	Relations between learners and learning resources	172
12.1	Subject areas in which satellite work is pursued	211
12.2	Satellite systems from which data was received by schools	212
12.3	Types of activity being pursued in satellite-related work	212

Notes on contributors

Roy Gibson is Special Adviser to the Director General of INMARSAT, the marine navigation organization. He has spent over twenty years in the space industry, including thirteen years with the European Space Agency where he was Director General for six years. He holds a Visiting Professorship at the University of Southampton.

Martin Sweeting is Director of Satellite Engineering at the University of Surrey and Technical Director of Surrey Satellite Technology Ltd. In 1974 he established a satellite tracking station at the University of Surrey and led a team of researchers at the University through the design, construction, test, launch and orbital operation of the UK's first, and subsequent, low-cost spacecraft (the UoSAT series). He is a member of the British National Space Centre's Space Technology Requirements Board.

Pam Vass is a director of Earth Observation Sciences and has been involved with satellite remote sensing since the mid-1970s. She was instrumental in the establishment of the promotional programme and user documentation service at the UK National Remote Sensing Centre. She is currently working on technical and user documentation for the next generation of earth observation satellites with a particular interest in micro-based interactive documentation for educational purposes.

Richard Thomas, who has a background in geographical sciences, joined Earth Observation Sciences in 1987. He is currently based at the National Remote Sensing Centre, where he is responsible for documentation and promotional activities.

Geoff Groom, after several years of involvement with the maintenance and operation of radio systems, joined the staff of the British Telecom International College where he is responsible for the establishment of

Contributors

microwave and satellite training. He has consulted and lectured internationally on satellite communications.

Keith Hilton is currently Head of Geography at Chester College. Until 1986 he was a lecturer at the University of London Institute of Education where his research interests lay in the field of remote sensing in geographic education. He is Chairperson of the Geographical Association's Satellite Remote Sensing Working Group and a member of the Education and Training Group of the National Remote Sensing Centre. He has been involved in the production of a number of educational remote sensing products, including 'The Earth Below', 'Spaceview UK' and 'Cheshire from Space'.

Brian Hill is currently Professor and Head of The Language Centre at Brighton Polytechnic. The wide range of courses at the Centre make regular use of satellite-transmitted programmes from all over Europe. He has directed several research investigations into the use of television, including satellite-transmitted programmes, in education.

Craig Underwood is currently a research fellow with the UoSAT project at the University of Surrey. He graduated in physics and computer science from the University of York in 1982 and, after taking a PGCE course, taught at Scarborough Sixth Form College until 1986.

John Gilbert has been Professor in the Department of Science and Technology Education at the University of Reading since 1988. With a background in chemistry he spent six years as a school teacher before moving into educational research at the University of Surrey.

Annette Temple is Director of the Dyfed Satellite Project. A graduate in physics, she taught in schools, during which time her interest in satellites evolved.

Brian Groombridge is Professor of Adult Education at the Institute of Education, University of London. He was formerly Head of Educational Programme Services at the Independent Broadcasting Authority. He is President of EUROSTEP – the Association of European Users of Satellites for Education and Training – and Chairman of SPACE-Satellite Programmes for Adult and Continuing Education at the University of London.

Jim Stevenson has been Head of Educational Broadcasting Services at the BBC and is currently Chief Executive of the Educational Broadcasting Services Trust. In over twenty years in broadcasting he has held many posts, including Head of Programmes at the Open University. From 1985 to 1988 he was Chairman of the International Advisory Council of Project SHARE – Satellites for Health and Rural Education – and is actively involved in national and international broadcasting developments, particularly those in the field of distance and open learning.

Geoffrey Crabb has been with the National Council for Educational Technology for over sixteen years and provides a copyright consultancy service for educational users. He is also concerned to ensure that government departments and rights owners are aware of the needs of education and training.

Foreword

R. Gibson

In January 1988, there were about 340 man-made satellites in orbit around the Earth. The majority have, of course, been launched by he USSR and the USA, but recent years have seen a considerable increase in the number of countries not only willing to purchase satellites but also capable of designing, building and launching them. Although satellites have continued to grow in size and complexity, an even more startling advance has been made by the development of manned laboratories in space.

Unfortunately, this book is being published at a time when UK space activities are passing through one of their familiar black periods. Government expenditure, it has been announced, will not be increased. This has happened before and it ought to be instructive to note that, happily, UK governmental reticence has not significantly retarded European space development. The UK declined to join the original Ariane programme on the grounds that Europe did not need its own launch vehicle, and made only a token contribution to Europe's first manned space programme Spacelab. The Ariane launch vehicle has won general approval and much success since then, and European ministers (other than the UK's) agreed in November 1987 that it was timely to start development on Ariane 5. Similarly, experience gained from Spacelab paved the way for Europe to participate in the US space station programme, and ministers have also agreed to develop the Columbus programme as Europe's contribution to the international station – again without the UK.

Sad though UK absence is, European and other ambitious space programmes will go ahead. The only sensible course to take is to learn how to exploit these new programmes internationally. The fact that the UK aerospace industry will have no share in their production – indeed, the UK's contribution to the overall budget of the European Space Agency (ESA) will sink to around 5 per cent compared with a GNP share of over 16 per cent – must not deter other communities in the UK from evaluating the future possibilities of space technology. Space

Foreword

development will continue and the pace will quicken – even without UK financial support – and the time needed to know how best to use the facilities is almost as great as the production time for the hardware.

There are, of course, lessons for UK industry and UK university space groups to learn from the UK government's present attitude, but that is a separate subject. The purpose of this book is to explain the ways in which spacecraft can be helpful in education, and the UK can afford to feign indifference to the fact that the spacecraft will be largely provided by other nations. It would be compounding stupidity on stupidity for us to believe that the UK government's reluctance to increase space funding was a valid judgement on the value of space activities to the UK as a whole. In fact, these national considerations – born of the UK government's continued reluctance to increase expenditure on space – are equally applicable to a large number of other countries who wish to benefit from the possibilities opened up by space technology, but which themselves lack the appropriate industrial and technological capacity.

Whether we like it or not, space developments will have an ever-increasing effect on the daily lives of us all, and there is no better place for this to be realized than in education. It is my hope that in the coming decade students of all ages will become increasingly exposed to the possibilities opened up by space technology. The students themselves, as I have observed them, do not lack enthusiasm and it is always a stimulating experience to talk to young people about space programmes. They exhibit a freshness of approach that is exactly what is needed, for example, to take advantage of microgravity experimentation; they have much less difficulty in imagining the consequences than have many of the older specialists. Nor are they afraid of the excitement and challenge which so many fields of space activity offer.

Our problem is not with the student but with the older generations. Thinking in space terms requires jettisoning many conventional ideas, and some of the concepts are not immediately accessible to the newcomer. Hence the value of this present book. It aims to set out some of the available space 'tools' and relate them to specific areas of teaching. There has not so far been a successful introduction to the subject, and I am sure that the appearance of this volume will stimulate others to fill in the gaps.

The essential message that we must try to convey is that space activities are not simply of interest and value to a few oddballs who wish to play toy trains with public money. On the contrary, the effects are relevant to and will increasingly influence many areas of our lives, both professional and private. It has been foolish in the past to oversell the advantages to be gained from space: there are some things that can best be achieved using space technology, and others where alternative

Foreword

methods are more appropriate. It is no miracle cure for our ills. The justification for making it more accessible to the younger generation lies in the inevitability that space will enter more and more into human activities. A knowledge of space and an understanding of its potential are going to be as important as understanding how to use computers. There is, let us admit it, more adventure and stimulation to be gained – at least for most of us – from understanding and being associated with space activities than in wrestling with the complexities of the controls on a microwave oven!

For all these reasons, and also because I believe that a well-informed educational community would have the power to convert future governments to see the value of public investment in space, I am greatly honoured to be associated with this publication. The editors and authors deserve our praise and our support, particularly at this time when UK governmental attitudes to space show that it is very low on the official list of priorities. I am delighted that they have not allowed this to discourage them.

Space techniques can already be a significant aid in teaching many subjects, and we need to ensure that this valuable application of space technology is not neglected. One important function of all national and international space organizations, including the British National Space Centre, is to ensure that educational needs are not forgotten. This becomes even more important in a country where the national space programme is small. I hope that this book will remind both space and education authorities that educational exploitation is not tarred with the same brush as the large and expensive space infrastructure programmes which have critics not only in the UK but also in the USA. Here is an area where benefits can be demonstrated at a very moderate cost – and we need not mention that the whole thing can be fun as well.

List of abbreviations

ADCS	attitude determination, control and stabilization
AMSAT	Amateur Satellite Organization
AOR	Atlantic Ocean Region
APT	automatic picture transmission
AVHRR	advanced very high resolution radiometer
BCR	battery charge regulator
BNSP	British National Space Project
BPSK	binary phase-shift keying
CAL	computer-assisted learning
CATV	cable television
CCD	charge-coupled device
CEPT	Conference of Postal and Telecommunications Authorities
DBS	direct broadcasting satellite
DCE	digital communications experiment
DCP	data collection platform
DRAM	dynamic random access memory
DSI	digital speech interpolation
DSR	digital store and readout
EBU	European Broadcasting Union
ECS	European Communications Satellite
EDAC	error detection and correction
EIRP	effective isotropic radiated power
ELB	emergency location beacon
EOSAT	Earth Observation Satellite Company
ESA	European Space Agency
ETM	enhanced thematic mapper
FDMA	frequency division multiplexing access
GTO	geostationary transfer orbit
HACE	higher, adult and continuing education
HCMM	heat capacity mapping mirror
HE	higher education
ICSC	Interim Communications Satellite Committee

Abbreviations

IHU	integrated housekeeping unit
INSET	in-service training
IOR	Indian Ocean Region
JARL	Japanese Amateur Radio League
MCS	maritime communications subsystem
MOP	Meteosat Operational Programme
MSC	Manpower Services Commission
MSS	multi-spectral scanning system
NERIS	National Educational Resource Information Service
NOAA	National Oceanic and Atmospheric Administration
NRSC	National Remote Sensing Centre
OC	Open College, UK
OU	Open University, UK
PCM	power-conditioning module pulse code modulation
PDM	power distribution module
PKM	perigee kick motor
POR	Pacific Ocean Region
PSK	phase-shift keying
QPSK	quadratic phase-shift keying
RAL	Rutherford-Appleton Laboratory
RBV	return beam vidicon
SES	Société Européene des Satellites
SMS	Satellite Multiservices System
TBEF	transborder educational flow
TIR	thermal infrared
TIROS	thermal infrared observation satellite
TM	thematic mapper
TOVS	IROS operational vertical sounder
TRIST	TVEI-related in-service training
TTNS	The Times Network for Schools
TVEI	Technical and Vocational Education Initiative
VITA	Volunteers in Technical Assistance
VSAT	very small aperture terminal
WARC	World Administrative Radio Conference

Part I
Satellite systems

Chapter one

Amateur radio, science and technology satellites

M.N. Sweeting

Introduction

The exploration of space has fired the imagination of generations since early man gazed and pondered on the stars and moon. The dawn of the 'space age', with the launch of Sputnik-1 from the USSR on 4 October 1957, heralded an explosive development of sophisticated technology stimulated by the desire to reach and utilize 'space'. The impact of that technology now touches our individual daily lives at every turn – whether it be communications, computers or meteorology. The spacecraft required to achieve orbit, operate in the hostile environment of space and provide us with the services we now take for granted have become increasingly large, complex and, above all, expensive. Space has become synonymous with large budgets, long time-scales and international agencies – it may therefore come as a surprise to find that a highly successful low-cost 'small' space programme has been running in the background for more than twenty-five years and is responsible for over twenty-five satellites in orbit!

No sooner had the USSR launched Sputnik-1, followed later by Explorer-1 launched by the USA in 1958, than radio amateurs began to ponder upon the possibility of a small earth-orbiting satellite to support amateur radio communications.

Amateur radio

Guglielmo Marconi was the first self-proclaimed 'radio amateur', pioneering a new technology with crude tools but a powerful imagination and a determined will to succeed. Radio communications developed rapidly to support commercial, civilian and military needs; however, alongside the 'professional', there remained a body of technical enthusiasts who continued the challenge of developing imaginative low-cost solutions to radio communications problems, often working in attics, basements or the garden shed! These so-called 'radio amateurs', who

Satellite systems

had been allocated what were thought to be useless short wavelengths for experiment, came from all walks of life – some were engaged in professional engineering and science, while others came from completely non-technical backgrounds and were satisfying a basic interest in communicating with like-minded individuals world-wide.

Radio amateur operators quickly discovered that the sort wavelengths allocated to them were far from 'useless' and demonstrated long-distance communications using very low powers by bouncing radio wave signals around the world using the ionosphere. The ability to achieve world-wide communications, using relatively simple and inexpensive equipment, catalysed the growth of amateur radio as both a technical challenge and a means of establishing international friendships. With 'necessity being the mother of invention', radio amateurs working within domestic resources have made repeated technical contributions to the professional radio community. It was from within this community of technical enthusiasts that amateur radio communications using low-cost earth-orbiting satellites was born.

The history of amateur radio satellites

When Sputnik-1 was launched on an unsuspecting world, the amateur radio community was best placed to track its orbit and receive its radio beacon signals – transmitting on 20 MHz short wave. Soon afterwards, imaginative radio amateurs began to consider how they might participate in this new era. A group of radio amateurs in the USA, keen on using short-range VHF, formed a team to build a small satellite from which they could eventually relay VHF radio signals beyond their normally limited horizons. This group became Project OSCAR (orbiting satellite carrying amateur radio). In 2 years, working in their own time, the group constructed OSCAR-1, a simple spacecraft weighing only 10 lb and transmitting a repetitive signal (dit dit dit dit dit dit) at 140 mW and 145 MHz at a speed depending on the internal temperature of the satellite. OSCAR-1 was launched on USAF Discoverer-36 on 12 December 1961 from the Vandenberg Air Force Base, California. The satellite was ejected from the rocket using a simple spring and remained in orbit for 22 days before burning up in the earth's atmosphere. During that short time, more than 570 radio amateurs in twenty-eight countries forwarded over 5,000 observations to Project OSCAR concerning radio wave propagation through the ionosphere, the satellite's orbit and its thermal behaviour. OSCAR-1 clearly demonstrated that radio amateurs were capable of designing, building, tracking and analysing data from low-cost simple satellites using readily available inexpensive equipment. Although this first amateur satellite was very elementary compared with later OSCARs, it firmly established the basic philosophies governing the amateur satellite programme that followed:

1   imaginative low-cost solutions to satellite construction;
2   satellite tracking and reception using inexpensive equipment;
3   direct participation by radio amateurs world-wide;
4   space science, communications, engineering and education.

OSCAR-2 repeated the earlier success but with improved telemetry. However, these first amateur satellites were in low orbits, were short-lived and provided no communications relay functions. OSCAR-3 became the first amateur communications satellite carrying a multiple-access VHF transponder, relaying voice and Morse code transmissions from over 1,000 radio amateurs from twenty-two countries during its 18 day mission. It also carried a small number of early solar cells to back up the on-board battery.

OSCAR-4 suffered a launch vehicle failure and was placed in the wrong orbit; however OSCARs 5, 6, 7 and 8 steadily developed amateur satellite communications using inexpensive equipment at 29 MHz, 145 MHz and, finally, 435 MHz. These satellites carried increasingly comprehensive telemetry systems to monitor the performance of the satellite throughout its lifetime, and more sophisticated linear transponders supporting international amateur radio communications. Placed into higher longer-lived earth orbits, these satellites provided an ideal opportunity for schools and colleges world-wide to participate in space experiments – in many cases stimulated and encouraged by radio amateurs.

The USSR launched their first amateur radio satellites, RS-1 and RS-2, into a 2,000 km orbit in October 1978 and later, in 1981, launched a cluster of six amateur satellites (RS-3 to RS-8) together on one vehicle! In 1982, two small amateur satellites (Iskra or 'spark'), built by aeronautical students of the Moscow Aviation Institute, were launched from the Salyut-7 space station into short-lived low earth orbit. The Soviet satellites have carried analogue transponders operating at 21, 29 and 145 MHz, with telemetry beacons and a 'ROBOT' to respond automatically to Morse code enquiries. The latest Soviet amateur communications transponders, RS-10 and RS-11, were mounted on-board housekeeping functions with the 'host' satellite.

The first two satellites, UoSAT-OSCAR-9 (UoSAT-1) and UoSAT-OSCAR 11 (UoSAT-2), constructed by the University of Surrey in the UK and launched by NASA, carried a wide range of technology and scientific and educational experiments to complement the linear amateur communications transponders on other amateur satellites. UoSAT-2. launched in 1984, included the first digital transponder

Satellite systems

providing store-and-forward communications to amateur radio operators world-wide through regional 'gateway' stations.

In 1986 Japan launched FUJI-OSCAR-12, carrying both analogue and digital transponders, into a 1,200 km orbit inclined at 57°. The digital transponder operates using a packet radio communications protocol and provides both real-time and bulletin board digital communications.

The latest amateur radio communications satellites operate in a highly inclined eccentric elliptical orbit (close to the 'Molniya' orbit used by the USSR). This orbit configuration provides much improved communications coverage by 'seeing' almost half the earth when the spacecraft is moving slowly around apogee, and AMSAT-OSCAR-13 (AO-13), launched in July 1988, carries several sophisticated linear, and one digital, transponders covering VHF, UHF and SHF. AO-13 is a complex spacecraft with on-board propulsion systems, an integrated housekeeping unit, and attitude determination and control facilities – a major technical achievement and a far cry from OSCAR-1.

A wide range of amateur satellite missions are being planned for the future. Several small digital store-and-forward communications satellites (UoSAT-D and AMSAT-NA MICROSTATs) were launched into low earth orbit on Ariane in 1989; UoSAT-E, which accompanied these, carried further spacecraft engineering, space science and in-orbit technology demonstration experiments. Enhanced Molniya-orbiting satellites are planned for the early 1990s, and, the design for the first geostationary amateur communications satellite is on the drawing board.

Operational amateur communications satellites

In 1990 there were five amateur radio satellites operational in orbit: UoSAT- OSCAR-11 (UoSAT-2), FUJI-OSCAR-12 (JAS-1), AMSAT-OSCAR- 13, RS 10 and RS 11.

Each satellite carries different payloads with differing mission objectives, between them supporting amateur radio communications, science, technology and space education. Several of these spacecraft are described in summary below; however, the reader is referred to the bibliography at the end of this chapter for more detailed information on these and other amateur satellites.

AMSAT-OSCAR-13 (Germany–USA)

The AMSAT-OSCAR-13 amateur radio communications satellite was launched on the first Ariane-4 flight in July 1988 as part of the development and qualification of the new launcher. Ariane successfully placed three spacecraft into geostationary transfer orbit (GTO): METEOSAT-P2 (700 kg), Panamsat (1,220 kg) and AMSAT-OSCAR-13 (150 kg).

AMSAT-OSCAR-13 is a third-generation OSCAR amateur radio communications satellite, developed under the AMSAT programme as a joint project of AMSAT-NA and AMSAT-DL with significant assistance from several affiliated international AMSAT groups.The satellite weighs 135 kg and has a design lifetime of 5 years. The first such satellite, AMSAT Phase 3A, was lost during the launch failure of Ariane L02 on 23 May 1980. The second, AMSAT-OSCAR-10, was successfully launched on Ariane L6 on 16 June 1983. After 3 years of operation in orbit, the spacecraft suffered from radiation damage to the on-board computer as a result of its being placed in an incorrect final orbit following minor damage to the perigee motor during separation from the launcher.

AMSAT-OSCAR-13 operates several transponders in the amateur satellite service.

Mode B:	Uplink	435.420 – 435.570 MHz
	Downlink	145.975 – 145.825 MHz
	General beacon	145.812 MHz
	Engineering beacon	145.985 MHz
Mode JL:	Uplink 1	1269.620 – 1269.330 MHz
	Uplink 2	144.425 – 144.475 MHz
	RUDAK up	1269.710 MHz
	Downlink 1	435.715 – 436.005 MHz
	Downlink 2	435.990 – 435.940 MHz
	RUDAK down	435.677 MHz
	General beacon	435.651 MHz
Mode S:	Uplink	435.601 – 435.637 MHz
	Downlink	2400.711 – 2400.747 MHz
	Beacon	2400.325 MHz

Spacecraft description

The spacecraft structure is based around a three-pointed star, with solar array panels on each side facet. A perigee kick motor (PKM) is mounted within a central thrust cylinder, and communications antennas are mounted on the top facet.

Power system Solar arrays generate 50 W initially, falling to about 35 W after 3 years' service, depending on radiation damage. Two on-board Ni-Cd batteries, the primary rated at 10 A h and the auxiliary rated at 6 A h, solar power for operation during eclipse. Power regulation is provided by a battery charge regulator (BCR).

Satellite systems

Attitude control and stabilization The spacecraft spins on its z axis at 10–60 rev min^{-1}, with its attitude and spin rate adjusted magnetically by generation of torque through interaction of on-board pulsed electromagnets (magnetorquers) and the local geomagnetic field. Spacecraft attitude determination and spin rate detection are made using two sun sensors (cross slits) and an earth sensor with inputs to the on-board computer (IHU).

On-board computer – integrated housekeeping unit The spacecraft is controlled by a microcomputer based around the RCA-1802 microprocessor running a multi-tasking operating system, with 32 kbyte of error-correcting (i.e. 48 kbyte total) Harris HS–6564RH radiation-hardened memory. The integrated housekeeping unit (IHU) provides all housekeeping telemetry and telecommand functions.

Propulsion The on-board PKM comprises a liquid-fuelled bi-propellant rocket engine with a thrust of 400 N and specific impulse of 293 s, giving a δ_v with the 142 kg spacecraft of 1480 m^{-1}s. The fuel used is Aerozine-50, which is a 50 per cent blend of unsymmetrical dimethyl hydrazine (UDMH) and hydrazine with nitrogen tetroxide (N_2O_2) as an oxidizer. This is a hypergolic (self-igniting) fuel, pressurized by helium at 400 bar high side and 14 bar low side.

FUJI-OSCAR-12 (Japan)

The first amateur satellite built in Japan, FUJI-OSCAR-12 (JAS-1), was not the first contribution by Japan to the amateur satellite programme. AMSAT members in Japan (JAMSAT) had designed and built a UHF–VHF transponder for a previous OSCAR satellite (OSCAR-8).

FUJI-OSCAR-12 (FO-12) was conceived in 1980 as a joint project between JAMSAT and the Japanese Amateur Radio League (JARL). The spacecraft was to be built by NEC of Japan, whilst the analogue and digital transponder were to be built by JAMSAT volunteers. In August 1986 FO-12 was launched successfully by a Japanese H1 rocket into a 1,500 km circular earth orbit inclined at 50°.

FO-12 operates one digital and two analogue transponders in the amateur satellite service.

Analogue

Mode JA: Uplink   145.900 – 146.000 MHz
          Downlink 435.900 – 435.800 MHz (inverting, 1W RF)
          Beacon   435.795 MHz (CW and PSK, 100 mW RF)

Digital

Mode JD:	Uplink 1	145.850 MHz (bi-phase FM)
	Uplink 1	145.870 MHz
	Uplink 3	145.890 MHz
	Uplink 4	145.910 MHz
	Downlink	435.910 MHz (NRZI-PSK, 1 W RF)
	Beacon	435.910 MHz (PSK, 1 W RF)

Spacecraft description

The FO-12 spacecraft is a twenty-six-sided obicular structure with solar array panels on each facet.

Power system Silicon solar cells (979 mounted on the facets) generate 8.5 W to power the housekeeping systems and transponders. Power is stored in an on-board 6 A h Ni-Cd battery for peak and eclipse operations. Power conditioning is provided by a BCR and three power regulators.

Attitude stabilization The spacecraft contains permanent magnets which cause it to align itself along the earth's magnetic field around the orbit.

On-board computer – integrated housekeeping unit The spacecraft telemetry and telecommand housekeeping functions are provided by the on-board computer comprising an NSC800 with 256 kbyte of dynamic random access memory (DRAM) which also supports the digital transponder MAILBOX.

RADIO-SPORT-10 and RADIO-SPORT-11 (USSR)

This Soviet amateur radio transponder system, carried on board Cosmos-1861 in June 1987 into a 980 km orbit inclined at 83° supports a wide range of amateur radio communications using both HF and VHF links. RS-10 and RS-11 are almost identical except with regard to frequency translation. Each uses three frequency bands in various combinations to achieve five distinct modes of operation in addition to their ROBOT transponders.

RS-10 Analogue

Mode A:	Uplink	145.860 – 145.900 MHz
	Downlink	29.360 – 29.400 MHz
Mode K:	Uplink	21.160 – 29.400 MHz

Satellite systems

Mode T:	Downlink	29.360 – 29.400 MHz
	Uplink	21.160 – 21.200 MHz
	Downlink	145.860 – 145.900 MHz
	Beacons	145.903, 145.857, 29.403, 29.357 MHz

RS-10 ROBOT

	Uplink	21.120, 145.857 MHz
	Downlink	29.403 MHz

RS-11 Analogue

Mode A:	Uplink	145.910 – 145.950 MHz
	Downlink	29.410 – 29.450 MHz
Mode K:	Uplink	21.210 – 21.250 MHz
	Downlink	29.410 – 29.450 MHz
Mode T:	Uplink	21.210 – 21.250 MHz
	Downlink	145.910 – 145.950 MHz
	Beacons	145.953, 145.907, 29.453, 29.407 MHz

RS-11 ROBOT

	Uplink	21.130, 145.830 MHz
	Downlink	29.403 MHz

Spacecraft description

RS-10 and RS-11 are hosted on Cosmos-1861. They share common power and housekeeping functions with the primary payload and little is known about their configuration. Telemetry is sent mainly in Morse code and represents various status indicators and measurements made on the transponders. The ROBOT responds to Morse code signals transmitted by amateur radio stations on earth and replies giving an acknowledgement of the contact with a serial number.

Satellites for amateur science, engineering and education

The amateur radio community has pioneered the development of small cost-effective spacecraft and associated engineering techniques. As traditional commercial, scientific and military satellites become increasingly large, complex, lengthy and, above all, expensive, considerable interest has grown in a complementary small, low-cost, rapid-response satellite programme. A demand for relatively small light-weight quick-response missions has grown rapidly since 1986 to pursue modest scientific objectives, evaluate the effect of the space environment on new technologies in orbit, provide resilient military service and support a broad-based space education programme. The aerospace industry also needs experienced engineers to design, build, test and operate spacecraft – large and small. Today's schoolchildren will become tomorrow's university students and, eventually, future spacecraft engineers, and so it is important to introduce young people to space technology in an exciting and stimulating manner by involving them directly in space experiments and training.

British universities have long been involved in space, traditionally focusing on space science and concentrating on the development of sophisticated detectors, instrumentation, data processing and analysis. The provision of the host spacecraft and the associated spacecraft engineering has been left largely to industry. The development of scientific payloads for inclusion in satellites entails solving many engineering problems and developing significant engineering skills, but these have been considered largely by-products of the primary scientific objective. Until very recently, no UK university had focused on spacecraft engineering as a research topic in its own right.

The UoSAT satellite programme

Complementary to the low earth- and Molniya-orbiting amateur radio communications satellites are a series of small inexpensive satellites aimed specifically at amateur science, space education and spacecraft engineering research. These spacecraft (UoSAT-OSCARs) have been designed, built and operated in orbit by a team at the University of Surrey.

It all began in 1974 when a group of radio amateurs at the University of Surrey tracked AMSAT-OSCAR-6 and, when its batteries began to fade after 4 years in orbit, set up a simple control station to prolong the life of the satellite through careful supervision of transponder operation. Monitoring the spacecraft battery voltage during use by amateur radio stations over Europe, the Surrey ground-station de-activated the analogue transponder on OSCAR-6 whenever the batteries became depleted to allow them to recharge using power from solar cells mounted on the exterior of the satellite. By close control over the scheduling of the transponder to prevent excessive discharging of the satellite's batteries, the useful lifetime of OSCAR-6 was prolonged to in excess of 4.5 years.

The concepts of an amateur radio satellite specifically devoted to scientific, engineering and educational objectives in the Amateur Satellite Service (AMSAT) rather than primarily amateur radio communications developed from the experience gained through this activity at the University of Surrey. Thus the University of Surrey Satellite (UoSAT) Programme was born. In addition to educational objectives, the UoSAT Programme was formulated to transfer the unique experience of AMSAT in 'cost-effective spacecraft engineering techniques' into the professional aerospace industry, with the goal of providing low-cost spacecraft for in-orbit technology demonstration of new devices or technologies prior to their inclusion in large and costly spacecraft.

The UoSAT-1 satellite

The first University of Surrey satellite, UoSAT-1, was designed and built at the University and launched by NASA in 1981. UoSAT-1 was created by a small group of university researchers, supported by UK industry and research establishments, and its highly successful operation in orbit encouraged Surrey to establish spacecraft engineering research and space education as legitimate university activities. Further, the UoSAT-1 mission generated very considerable interest from academic, technological, industrial and commercial quarters in the use of inexpensive satellites for a number of space applications hitherto considered either impracticable, uneconomic or simply the preserve of large-budget projects.

UoSAT-1 was launched on 6 October 1981 by a Delta 2910 rocket accompanying the NASA Solar Mesosphere Explorer Mission into a 560 km polar sun-synchronous earth orbit. UoSAT-1 established the fundamental objectives of the UoSAT Programme.

1. To investigate the feasibility of, and the problems associated with, the design, construction, test and launch of a relatively small and inexpensive yet sophisticated spacecraft capable of a significant contribution to the industrial engineering, scientific, educational and amateur radio communities.
2. To stimulate and promote a greater awareness of and interest in space engineering and science in schools, colleges and universities by direct active participation in the satellite experimental programme. The satellite engineering and experiment data are transmitted in such a manner that they are readily received not only by professional ground stations but also by simple low-cost amateur ground terminals.
3. To broaden the scope of the Amateur Satellite Programme by catering for the interests of the amateur experimenter/scientist.
4. To evaluate the use and performance of novel technologies, spacecraft system architecture and cost-effective spacecraft engineering techniques to provide a lower-cost entry level into space activities.

This programme established the University of Surrey as a centre of excellence in spacecraft engineering and space education.

UoSAT-1 was constructed by a team of research engineers at the University of Surrey, and took 30 months and £250,000 to design, build and test ready for launch. Shortly after separation from the Delta launch vehicle, the spacecraft primary VHF downlink was switched on and telemetry data were received at the control station in Surrey. The satellite's first transmissions were also monitored by hundreds of radio amateurs around the world. Since then, many thousands of radio amateurs, school, college and university groups, and other interested individuals in many countries have participated in the technical challenge of receiving, decoding and analysing the housekeeping and experimental data transmitted by the spacecraft. In 1990 it re-entered the earth's atmosphere and was destroyed.

UoSAT-1 spacecraft description

The UoSAT-1 spacecraft comprised engineering subsystems which support experimental payloads – although, in several cases, the engineering subsystems themselves had experimental features. The spacecraft was constructed from a square-section central core supporting rigid top and bottom honeycomb panels. Solar cells were mounted on further honeycomb panels on all four sides of the structure, enclosing a basic cuboid of dimensions 73.5 cm x 42.5 cm x 42.5 cm. Two stacks, each of two module boxes of dimensions 23.5 cm x 17.6 cm x 4.0 cm, were mounted on the outside of each face of the central core. A 'wing' extended the base of the spacecraft symmetrically by 18 cm on each side in the x axis to permit the mounting of the 2.4 and 10.4 GHz antennas, one on each side of the launcher attach fitting which was in itself mounted in the centre of the bottom plate. The navigation magnetometer was mounted on this wing above the 10 GHz antenna. The gravity-gradient boom, deployment motor and charge-coupled device (CCD) camera were mounted within the centre column whilst the Geiger detectors and scientific magnetometer were mounted on the top (+z facet).

Spacecraft engineering subsystems The engineering subsystems comprised the following: power sources, storage, conditioning and distribution; telemetry and telecommand; attitude determination, control and stabilization; RF communications (transmitters, receivers and antennas).

The experimental payload modules comprised technology experiments, space science experiments and space education experiments.

Technology experiments:
  two on-board computers (RCA 1802, F100);
  three-axis navigation magnetometer;
  static and dynamic CMOs memories;

gravity-gradient stabilization;
single-axis magnetorquer;
Solarex high-efficiency solar cells;
two-dimensional array CCD camera.

Space science experiments:
three-axis multi-range flux-gate magnetometer;
20 keV and 40 keV particle counters;
phase-referenced beacons on 7, 14, 21, 28 MHz;
radio beacons on 2.4 and 10.4 GHz.

Space education experiments:
downlink data formats were home computer compatible;
VHF–FM downlink transmissions for low-cost reception;
synthesized speech Digitalker experiment;
easily decodable spacecraft telemetry and experiment data.

The design and construction of a satellite is only part of a spacecraft programme; subsequent operation of the satellite once in orbit may indeed prove as demanding and expensive. Once the spacecraft has been launched and placed in orbit, the only access to and influence over its activities that the designers and operators left on earth have is through the telemetry and telecommand radio links furnished by the ground control station. The interpretation of telemetry data from, and interactive control over, a complex machine 500–2,000 km away moving at 7.5 km s^{-1} in a hostile radiation environment is quite demanding!

Three data downlinks operating at 145.825, 435.025 and 2401 MHz were available from UoSAT-1. These employed audio-frequency shift keying–phase modulation (AFSK–PM) of 1,200/2,400 Hz synchronous tones, and had been specifically designed for reception using low-cost ground terminals. The data sources available to these downlinks were telemetry (ASCII/Baudot/Morse code), on-board computer (OBC) (serial ports/Digitalker) and CCD camera. The data source was selected according to a pre-programmed weekly schedule under the automatic control of the Diary operating system implemented on the spacecraft OBC. Data transmitted by the spacecraft were normally sent asynchronously as a series of 7 bit ASCII characters together with one start bit, one even parity bit, and two stop bits. The usual transmission speed was 1,200 bit s^{-1}, although the rate could be varied if required. The information can be displayed on a standard computer terminal.

The digital downlink provided a number of data formats, including a plain text bulletin providing general space news to radio amateurs and experimenters throughout the world. Other formats included telemetry, Digitalker, OBC status messages and whole-orbit data, and CCD camera image data.

Telecommand subsystem The telecommand system provided for the remote control over the on-board subsystems and experiments, without which the spacecraft was of little practical use. The telecommand system comprised two uplink receivers at VHF and UHF and two data demodulators of the commands specified. There was also a parallel input–output port to the spacecraft's OBC for autonomous control of spacecraft operations in addition to serial data links with the OBC and the F100 experimental computer. Thus two modes of control over the spacecraft were available: direct real-time control over the satellite's functions via transmissions from a ground command station; indirect stored-program control executed by the OBC according to a Diary of command sequences loaded in advance from the ground command station.

Telemetry subsystem Also essential for effective use of the spacecraft is the telemetry subsystem. Sixty analogue telemetry channels and forty-five digital status indicators were available for transmission via the VHF, UHF or SHF downlinks in a variety of formats to cater for a wide range of user ground terminal facilities. By the end of the first year in orbit (1982), the low-speed ASCII, BAUDOT and Morse code options were used less frequently and were replaced by increasing use of 1200 bit s^{-1} ASCII as inexpensive personal microcomputers became widely available. With the advent of these powerful microcomputers, real-time processing of telemetry data became increasingly practicable, attractive and resilient against transmission-induced errors of considerable importance.

The original telemetry format produced by the hardware was designed for easy visual processing on a simple visual display unit (VDU) and did not possess any error coding or any individual frame identification:

AMSAT 10101 10000 00100 10000 01110 00111 10001 10101 00000
AMSAT 10101 10000 00100 10000 01110 00111 10001 10101 00000
00380 01370 02661 03481 04059 05046 06027 07056 08040 09033
10512 11357 12000 13089 14002 15432 16000 17487 18467 19572
20523 21061 22659 23000 24000 25000 26104 27483 28600 29544
30435 31040 32283 33000 34003 35378 36434 37460 38529 39539
40855 41000 42674 43000 44171 45001 46000 47528 48541 49509
50569 51073 52702 53295 54990 55000 56000 57535 58532 59535

The OBC was used to modify the standard telemetry frame to include a series of checksum digits (one for each channel) to provide for transmission error detection (but not correction). This format was similar to that used subsequently by UoSAT-2 and provides a method of validating the various parameter values:

Satellite systems

UoSAT-1 84051701 12923 COMPUTER GENERATED TELEMETRY
00380B01370502661303481E040598050467060273070564 08040C0903 39
10512711357112000313089314000515000416000717487D18467C1957 28
20523621061422659A230001240006250007261041 27483A28600C2954 4E
30435131040632283833000034000735 3378A364346374606385295395 395
40855C41000542674443000744171745001046000247528C48541C49509 1
50569F5107305270225329585499015500005600035753515853 2959535 F

The OBC did not have access to the forty-five digital status indicators provided in the original telemetry format, but did insert a software clock–calendar for frame identification. This innovation, entirely due to the flexible architecture of the spacecraft and the availability of a reprogrammable OBC, greatly enhanced the value of telemetry data from UoSAT-1 and, by making the format compatible with UoSAT-2, simplified reception and analysis.

On-board computer subsystem The primary OBC was based around an RCA CDP1802 microprocessor with 16 kbyte of DRAM. A number of input–output ports provided direct access to the spacecraft telemetry and telecommand subsystems, allowing autonomous control of the spacecraft by the OBC. In addition, the OBC had direct high-speed links with the magnetometer and radiation experiments to allow rapid data acquisition yielding fine time resolution data. The 16 kbyte of DRAM program memory had error detection and correction (EDAC) circuits that automatically detected and corrected 'soft' errors induced in the memory cells by energetic particles, e.g. cosmic rays. The OBC could also access the CCD camera memory (32 kbyte) for image processing and additional data storage.

Commencing with initial very simple checkout software, followed by more complex but single-operation programs, leading on to limited multi-operation software packages and finally using a modified version of the Diary multi-tasking operations software originally developed for UoSAT-2, the OBC played an increasingly important role in the orbital operation of UoSAT-1. UoSAT-1 ran daily experiments on a weekly schedule completely automatically under OBC control relying on only periodic software and schedule updates from the Surrey ground-station supporting:

- automatic downlink and experiment schedules;
- computer-generated error-coded telemetry;
- news and schedules bulletins;
- operations and OBC status messages;
- whole-orbit data surveys;
- Digitalker experiments.

The secondary spacecraft computer was based around an F100L 16 bit microprocessor and 16 kword (128 kbit) of static CMOS RAM. This computer was used extensively during the first 6 months of orbital operation of UoSAT-1 for extended telemetry surveys. However, the VLSI CMOS memory devices failed in March 1982. The computer was decommissioned and its responsibilities were taken over by the primary (1802) OBC.

Power subsystems Primary power generation for UoSAT-1 was from four solar arrays mounted on the body of the spacecraft which delivered an average of 25 W when fully illuminated. Ten General Electric prismatic Ni–Cd rechargeable cells, connected in series, formed a 14 V battery of 6.4 A h nominal capacity and were charged when the spacecraft was in sunlight. This provided sufficient power to run the subsystems and experiments during peak load demands and eclipse periods.

Two BCRs (primary and back-up) were responsible for accepting the 35 V supplies from the solar arrays and charging the battery. The power conditioning module (PCM) regulated the 12–14 V battery bus supply to provide stable +10 V, +5 V and −10 V supplies for powering the spacecraft systems and experiments. The power distribution module (PDM) switched the various regulated and unregulated power supplies to all spacecraft systems and experiments, executing commands which it received from the telecommand system.

Whole-orbit surveys of telemetry via the OBC were used routinely to monitor the power budget of the spacecraft and ensure that the batteries were not abused through deep discharge. The battery was divided into two five-cell packs, mounted on opposite sides of the spacecraft −z facet 'floor'. Care was taken to ensure that differences in temperature (and hence terminal voltage) were minimized by maintaining a z axis spin.

UoSAT-1 was placed into a 550 km polar sun-synchronous orbit; however, at this low altitude the effect of the earth's residual atmosphere was to cause the orbit to decay at a significant rate and thus to loose sun synchronism. This changed the orbital eclipse period and had a profound effect on the spacecraft power and thermal budget. As the orbit altitude decayed, the orbit plane processed around towards 6 a.m. − 6 p.m. with the result that the spacecraft was in sunlight throughout the orbit with no eclipse. This provided a healthier power budget for the on-board systems and minimized the cycling of the battery, thus extending its operational lifetime.

Attitude determination, control and stabilization The spacecraft attitude and dynamics of motion were determined using a simple sun-presence detector and measurements of the earth's known magnetic field as seen by the satellite. The navigation magnetometer was a

Satellite systems

three-axis flux-gate device mounted on the spacecraft wing above the 10 GHz antenna. This magnetometer was monitored via the spacecraft telemetry system and provides low-resolution attitude data. The sun-presence detectors were simply solar cells, mounted on the top and bottom (+z and -z) panels of the spacecraft, with their output monitored via the telemetry system to resolve the up–down ambiguity of the spacecraft around the geomagnetic field.

A single-axis magnetorquer – a coil of wire energized to act as an electromagnet – was built into the x axis of the spacecraft, wound around the inside of the main spacecraft body. The field created interacted with the earth's magnetic field to produce a torque which tended to rotate the spacecraft rather like a compass needle, thus providing control over the spacecraft dynamics.

The spacecraft was designed to be gravity-gradient stabilized, with the $-z$ facet ('bottom') pointing at the centre of the earth (nadir), by extending a light-weight Be–Cu boom from the 'top' (+z facet) of the spacecraft. The boom resembled a steel tape measure, was preformed to become tubular once it had been unrolled and could extend some 12 m in length. The boom carried a 2.5 kg mass on the far end in which a high-resolution magnetometer sensor was mounted; this, in conjunction with the spacecraft body at the other end, created a dumbbell configuration which naturally lined up with the earth's gravitational field so that one end pointed downwards. It was, however, bi-stable!

The spacecraft was manoeuvred, using the single-axis magnetorquer under interactive OBC–ground-station control to process the z spin angular momentum vector, so that the z axis was aligned towards the geocentre as the spacecraft came over the North Pole and into range of the Surrey ground-station. There was some concern that the six coaxial cables feeding the tip-mass magnetometer might become tangled and prevent the boom from deploying properly, and so the data from the magnetometer in the tip-mass on the boom were monitored via the OBC during deployment to detect any undue bending. After approximately 1.2 m of boom extension, the magnetometer data indicated a rapid departure from the z axis, indicating that the cables had snagged, causing the boom to bend severely, and further development was stopped under ground command. Even with only 1.2 m extension of the boom, the spacecraft remained gravity-gradient stabilized for several days; however, liberation rapidly built up and eventually caused the spacecraft to fall out of gravity lock. After repeated attempts over several weeks to clear the jam, the boom and tip-mass were finally rewound back to the top (+z) surface of the spacecraft and the satellite was spin stabilized instead. However, the experience with UoSAT-1 provided an essential foundation for the successful gravity-gradient stabilization subsequently achieved with UoSAT-2.

Payload experiments

In addition to the engineering experiments, UoSAT-1 carries several payload experiments aimed at the scientific and educational communities.

Radiation experiment Two Geiger particle detectors, one measuring electrons with energies above 20 keV and the other measuring electrons with energies above 40 keV (or protons with ten times these energies), were mounted on the top of the spacecraft to provide real-time and stored-survey information on solar activity and auroral events, particularly in the region of the auroral 'oval' around both the North and South Poles. The radiation experiment was particularly useful for monitoring the activity of the sun (solar storms lead to a dramatic increase in electron precipitation at the altitude of UoSAT-1), and so data from the experiment were recorded in whole-orbit data surveys carried out by the OBC on a regular basis. The thin mica window of the 20 keV Geiger tube shattered during launch, and only the 40 keV tube was operational.

The radiation monitor experiment on UoSAT-1 provided a useful general survey instrument in support of the more elaborate particle–wave experiments on the UoSAT-2 spacecraft. The real-time data available via the spacecraft telemetry, supported by the routine whole-orbit data surveys, were particularly useful for identifying geomagnetic disturbances and solar flares, and their effect on radiowave propagation.

Charge-coupled device camera experiment The aim of the CCD camera experiment flown on UoSAT-1 was to provide engineering quality pictures of the earth to assess simple low-cost satellite-borne imaging techniques. The CCD array used on this spacecraft was an early development device, and the image quality was not up to that available from the National Oceanic and Atmospheric Administration (NOAA) or Meteosat meteorological spacecraft; however, the CCD imager on UoSAT-1 was in regular use on a weekly basis, and yielded some quite good images of the Mediterranean and the limb of the earth.

The experiment was based on a two-dimensional CCD array manufactured by GEC (type MA 357) with an imaging area of 385 x 288 pixels. Light incident on the CCD generated electric charges which were collected in a matrix of light-sensitive storage sites. The time interval over which the charges were collected was known as the 'integration time', and was under ground-station control via the command system. The charges were read, digitized and stored one by one into the associated memory.

UoSAT-1 images (256 x 256 pixels per image) were stored in 32 kbyte of RAM as 4 bit words, i.e. as one of sixteen intensity or 'grey' levels. The image was transmitted to the ground at 1,200 bit s^{-1} and could be received using a standard 2 m frequency modulation (VHF AFSK FM) receiver and a simple monostable type decoder which extracted the data and clock from the synchronous FSK signal. The frame synchronization and line codes could be detected and the correct data stored and displayed using straightforward logic designs.

Digitalker experiment The synthesized speech experiment aroused considerable interest amongst the educational communities because of its ease of reception using inexpensive hand-portable NBFM receivers. The Digitalker was controlled by the OBC using a parallel port, through which data were sent resulting in a series of spoken messages. The speech synthesizer was able to 'speak' telemetry and experiment data in a limited English vocabulary of around 140 words which were transmitted via the VHF downlink. This experiment was intended for simple demonstrations of satellite communications in schools using the very minimum of equipment – a low-cost VHF–FM receiver and a whip antenna are all that is required.

Calibration equations were used to convert the raw telemetry data into commonly used units. A total of nineteen channel numbers could be programmed into a speech sequence with a 400 Hz and 80 Hz tone used to signify the start of each message, of which the following is an example.

This is Digitalker on UoSAT-1 in space.
The time is 13:54 and 10 seconds.
Number 01 is 220 milliamperes.
Number 13 is 444 volts etc.
Please QRX and check numbers again.

Such was the interest shown in this experiment, especially by schools, that a similar but enhanced Digitalker experiment was placed in UoSAT-2.

SHF beacons experiment Two microwave beacons on 2.401 and 10.47 GHz on UoSAT-1 were intended to encourage the study of SHF propagation from the spacecraft at low elevations and also to stimulate the development of inexpensive microwave satellite ground terminals by radio amateurs. The 2.401 GHz beacon was activated routinely until 1986 when SHF experiments were taken over by the UoSAT-2 spacecraft 2.4015 GHz beacon (UoSAT-2 provided improved earth coverage as a result of its gravity-gradient stabilization). Telemetry data were gathered using the UoSAT-1 2.4 GHz beacon at the Surrey ground-station and several radio amateur stations.

The 10.47 GHz beacon was only activated upon demand since tracking and reception of this beacon from a satellite in low earth orbit presented quite a technical challenge!

HF propagation experiment Phase-referenced beacons on 7.050, 14.002, 21.002 and 29.502 MHz were included on UoSAT-1 to study HF propagation phenomena. The operational performance of these was degraded by the non-deployment of the gravity-gradient boom, which also acted as an HF antenna, and only the 21 MHz and 14 MHz beacons were continuously operational – transmitting Morse code. The 21 MHz beacon, and latterly the 14 MHz beacon, were used extensively in the amateur radio community to study below-the-horizon propagation phenomena.

Orbital lifetime of UoSAT-1 in low earth orbit The orbital parameters of spacecraft in low earth orbit (below about 600 km) are significantly affected by aerodynamic drag caused by the tenuous remnants of the upper atmosphere. The effect of this drag is to remove kinetic energy from the satellite, causing it to fall towards earth, which in turn increases the orbital velocity, resulting in higher drag and faster orbital decay. The lifetime of a satellite with a perigree height of 300 km or less is thus of the order of a few months; however, for satellites with heights much greater than 300 km it is of the order of many years. Predicting the precise orbital lifetime of satellites is a difficult problem, primarily because of the unpredictability of the density of the upper regions of the earth's atmosphere. The density of these regions is not uniform around the orbit because the atmosphere is non-spherical, and can vary quite rapidly by an order of magnitude depending on solar activity. None the less, an estimate of the orbital lifetime of the satellite is useful, although the results may be only approximate.

UoSAT-1 was placed into a circular polar sun-synchronous orbit at a mean height of 554 km in October 1981. The initial estimate of orbital lifetime was in the region of 4 years before the spacecraft was expected to re-enter the denser parts of the earth's atmosphere and burn up. Since launch, the orbital height of UoSAT-1 dropped to 484 km; however, the rate of decay has been slower than anticipated during the period 1984–6, resulting in a revised life expectancy of approximately a further 7 years. Since the orbit inclination has changed little, the reduction in orbital height has caused the orbit to be no longer sun-synchronous. The orbit plane, originally at 45° to the sun line (3a.m.–3p.m.) drifted significantly towards 80° (i.e. nearer 6a.m.–6p.m.). This had a profound effect on the power budget (beneficial), the thermal equilibrium (warmer, but not unduly) and the daily ground-station visibility patterns.

Satellite systems

The orbital operation of the UoSAT-1 spacecraft was an example of triumph over adversity, as a result of both a flexible space- craft systems architecture and the perseverance of the operations team. Working within constraints placed by spacecraft performance, imaginatively reconfigured systems, supported by advanced software developed originally for the later UoSAT-2 mission, resulted in highly successful orbital operations continuing an active experimental programme 6 years after launch. UoSAT-1 orbital operations provided the basis of experience from which the UoSAT-2 mission was created, and have established spacecraft engineering research as an important activity at the University of Surrey.

The UoSAT-2 satellite

Two years experience of operating UoSAT-1 in low earth orbit, following the launch of the spacecraft in October 1981, provided the Surrey spacecraft team with considerable first-hand insight into the problems and potential of low-cost satellite missions. Therefore it was natural that plans for a second enhanced spacecraft should begin to take shape early in 1983.

UoSAT-B (to become UoSAT-2 upon successful launch) was catalysed dramatically in July 1983 by two main factors in addition to the above general desire to develop further the UoSAT-1 concept:

1 the urgent need to fly a proof-of-concept digital store-and-forward communications experiment prior to a planned dedicated PACSAT communications satellite;
2 an unexpectedly early launch opportunity identified with NASA because of the need to replace the ailing Landsat-4 earth resources satellite.

The launch opportunity was confirmed in late September 1983, and scheduled for 1 March 1984 – only 6 months ahead! By retaining the same fundamental design philosophy and system architecture that had been developed and proved for UoSAT-1, whilst undertaking a complete subsystems redesign and incorporating totally new more complex payloads, it was decided that it should just prove possible to design, fabricate, assemble, integrate, test and prepare UoSAT-2 for launch within the 6 months available.

Mission objectives

The overall objective of the UoSAT-2 project was to develop further the cost-effective spacecraft engineering initiative pioneered by the earlier UoSAT-1 spacecraft launched in 1981, and to continue to promote amateur science and space education. Building on these, the specific mission objectives were as follows.

1. Cost-effective spacecraft engineering research: study the potential of, and the problems associated with, relatively small inexpensive satellite systems and evaluate novel technologies during extended exposure in orbit to the space environment.
2. Satellite communications: investigate the use of small satellites in low earth orbits for global store-and-forward digital communications, with particular emphasis on inexpensive portable ground terminals for use in remote areas where no telecommunications infrastructure exists.
3. Space education: stimulate further the space education programme directly involving schools, colleges, universities and the amateur radio community already catalysed by UoSAT-1.
4. Space science: support several modest scientific studies associated with auroral physics and 'space dust' particle statistics to demonstrate the potential of small satellites to contribute worthwhile science on a limited budget.

Mission overview

Guided by the mission objectives and constrained by the extremely short development time-scale before launch, the UoSAT design team identified a complement of spacecraft systems and payload experiments. Indeed, many of the spacecraft engineering subsystems were themselves (or included) experimental technology elements, whilst still having to satisfy mission critical reliability considerations.

Spacecraft engineering

The primary interest of the UoSAT team at Surrey is in spacecraft engineering research and space education, including the following.

- Spacecraft operations autonomy – the potential of high-performance spacecraft at low cost – is greatly enhanced by increased spacecraft and ground-station autonomy. Careful and effective management of the spacecraft's resources are necessary to optimise the mission and require a flexible spacecraft systems architecture supported by significant on-board intelligence. Research into, and the development of, these facilities can only be done effectively in conjunction with a 'live' spacecraft in orbit tackling real-life problems as they occur.
- VLSI technology: spacecraft autonomy, imaging and digital store-and-forward communications in particular are reliant on advances in VLSI microcircuit design and fabrication to provide the

necessary on-board intelligence. The performance of recently developed VLSI devices throughout long-term exposure to the space radiation environment in orbit is not well known but is essential for reliable spacecraft design and operation. Distributed amongst several spacecraft subsystems and experiments, 350 kbyte of CMOS RAM devices and two different microprocessors were designed to provide in-orbit data over the lifetime of the satellite.

- Battery technology: rechargeable batteries to provide power to the subsystems and experiments during the regular and lengthy periods that spacecraft spends in eclipse represent expensive items whose long-term performance may ultimately limit the operational lifetime of the spacecraft. Inexpensive satellites need to be able to use inexpensive batteries, and so a suitable low-cost commercial production cell was identified and qualified in collaboration with AMSAT and Volunteers in Technical Assistance (VITA) for inclusion on UoSAT-2.

- Attitude stabilization: to be able to support worthwhile payloads, inexpensive satellites must also be able to provide low-cost yet precise attitude determination, control and stabilization (ADCS) facilities. The exact requirements will vary from mission to mission; however, accurate earth pointing is required for many applications envisaged for such satellites. Gravity-gradient stabilization, enhanced by active deliberation, was identified as a potentially useful technique since it uses no moving parts (except the initial deployment of a boom) and no depletable resources. Experimentation with advanced active gravity-gradient control algorithms can only be done in orbit. Inexpensive attitude sensors are also needed to support and assess the active control studies and provide information on spacecraft orientation and the dynamics of motion for payload experiments.

- Earth imaging: medium resolution (1–2km) imaging of the earth's surface is of considerable interest for meteorological and climatological studies. The prototype CCD camera on board UoSAT-1 demonstrated the feasibility of providing such a service using a small low-cost spacecraft. Further development of the camera system used on UoSAT-1 was necessary to assess fully the potential of inexpensive earth-imaging satellites.

- Space education the UoSAT-1 mission generated very considerable interest within schools, colleges, universities and amongst the amateur radio community world-wide. The University of Surrey and NASA attached very considerable importance to providing a stimulating educational resource capable of supporting direct participation in satellite experiments throughout the educational spectrum. Direct participation in space experiments has proved to be a very powerful educational tool and can only be achieved if the data reception and display equipment is inexpensive and the engineering and experiments data are wide ranging and informative. The Digitalker speech synthesizer on board UoSAT-1 proved most effective in encouraging an initial entry into space technology for many younger students at minimum cost and complexity, and it was proposed to expand this capability on UoSAT-2, whilst the more advanced experiments and demonstrations used the digital telemetry transmissions.

Experimental payloads

In addition to the spacecraft engineering topics, the UoSAT Unit is also interested in satellite communications and in providing a platform for modest space science experiments. Therefore UoSAT-2 supports the following collaborative experimental payloads: store-and-forward digital communications; auroral particle–wave studies; space dust studies.

Although the UoSAT-2 project was managed, technically and financially, by the University of Surrey as an independent venture, several external groups were invited by to participate in the mission and contribute payload elements of mutual interest.

- VITA, an overseas development organization based in the USA which supports field workers in developing countries by acting as a source of expertise on a wide range of topics, has experienced considerable difficulties in maintaining effective and timely communications between the field workers, who are often working in areas where no telecommunications infrastructure exists, and predominantly US-based technical experts. A previous study, involving the UoSAT Unit, had identified digital packet store-and-forward communications techniques using inexpensive satellites in low earth orbit as a possible solution to VITA's communications problems. A satellite (PACSAT) dedicated to providing such a service to VITA and its geographically dispersed field workers was proposed in 1982, but it relied on VLSI memory and processor technology as yet unproven in the space environment. Further, the operational performance and viability of the proposed communications system was unclear, and so a 'proof-of-concept' digital communications experiment (DCE), funded by VITA, was included on UoSAT-2 to evaluate the necessary technology and operational potential of such a system.
- AMSAT, the international Amateur Radio Satellite Satellite Service, supported VITA in a volunteer capacity with much of the design and

construction of the DCE. AMSAT volunteers also assisted in the procurement and testing of the spacecraft's Ni–Cd battery cells and in negotiations with NASA concerning launch arrangements. The UoSAT spacecraft downlink transmissions are placed within internationally agreed frequency allocations for AMSAT since the spacecraft supports amateur radio communications via the DCE as well as space education and technology research.

- The Science and Engineering Research Council, although unable to support the development of the spacecraft itself, collaborated via the Rutherford–Appleton Laboratory (RAL) on particle–wave studies in the auroral regions through the provision of flight-spare instruments from the AMPTE-UKS mission. These instruments were intended to provide a reference in low earth orbit for the studies of the magnetosphere to be carried out by the AMPTE spacecraft scheduled for launch some 5 months later.
- Sussex University contributed a particle–wave correlator to analyse data from the RAL instruments.
- Kent University contributed a small space dust experiment, designed and built by final-year undergraduate students, to study the presence of small particles and micrometeorites in low earth orbit.

UoSAT-2 spacecraft systems

The fundamental philosophy and architecture adopted for the systems design and fabrication of UoSAT-1 had been demonstrated to be both effective and sound, as it had proved particularly capable of supporting evolutionary operations requirements and resilient against failures. Thus, with considerable enhancements to avoid the limitations experienced with UoSAT-1, a similar philosophy and systems architecture was adopted for UoSAT-2.

Fundamental to the philosophy of failure resilience on-board UoSAT spacecraft is the concept of 'redundancy through alternative technology' rather than through the duplication of circuits and components. Thus a failure due to either a design or component shortcoming is not circumvented by simply switching over to a redundant duplicate (which might well exhibit the very same shortcoming) but rather to a completely different circuit using a completely different design and component technologies where the chance of repeating the shortcoming is greatly reduced. In order to be able to use this technique, however, the spacecraft systems architecture must be designed with this philosophy in mind from the outset – it is clearly only possible to employ escape routes if they have been provided in the first place. It so happened that this philosophy of failure resilience was put to the test within hours of launch of UoSAT-2!

Amateur radio, science and technology satellites

Therefore central to the spacecraft systems architecture is the communications network between the subsystems and experiments within the spacecraft itself. There are numerous communications architectures that could be employed based on formal networks; however, their individual performance under wide-ranging operational environments is difficult to predict with accuracy and within a very limited time-scale. The experience gained with UoSAT-1 had demonstrated the basic reliability and predictability of a partially interconnected architecture or 'spider' network, where nearly every subsystem or experiment was connected to another in some way wherever appropriate.

Spacecraft engineering subsystems

Although many represented or contained experiments themselves, spacecraft engineering subsystems are required to provide the essential services in support of the payload experiments.

Mechanical structure The spacecraft structure is similar to that of UoSAT-1, with a square-section central thrust column core supporting honeycomb panels with rigid tops and bottoms. Solar cells are mounted on further honeycomb panels on all four sides of the structure, enclosing a basic cuboid of dimensions 35.5 cm x 35.5 cm x 58.5 cm. Two stacks, each of two module boxes of dimensions 23.5 cm x 17.6 cm x 3.1 cm, are mounted on the outside of each face of the central core. A 'wing' extends the base of the spacecraft symmetrically by 16 cm on each side in one axis to permit the mounting of two SHF helical antennas, one on each side of the launcher attach fitting which is itself mounted in the centre of the bottom plate. The primary VHF–UHF antenna system is also mounted on the underside of the wing around the attach fitting. The magnetometer and space dust experiments are mounted on top of this wing, one on each side. The gravity-gradient stabilization boom motor, Ni–Cd battery and CCD camera experiment are mounted within the central column, whilst the top plate supports the Geiger detectors, multi-channel electron spectrometer and power supply, six digital sun-angle sensors, a twin-beam earth horizon detector and the deployable gravity-gradient tip-mass.

Power subsystems Four solar arrays, comprising 1248 high-efficiency silicon solar cells of dimensions 2 cm x 2 cm manufactured by the Solarex Corporation, are attached to the four sides of the spacecraft. Each array is capable of supplying up to about 1 A at 28 V when fully illuminated.

Satellite systems

UoSAT-2, in a low sun-synchronous earth orbit, experiences lengthy eclipse periods of around 30 min out of each 90 min orbit. Unlike spacecraft in geostationary orbit, UoSAT-2 is powered primarily from its on-board battery, which is recharged during the sunlit portion of each orbit. The battery is not composed of expensive space-qualified cells, but rather the best cells selected from 150 commercial grade cells which had undergone stringent testing by AMSAT–VITA collaborators in Canada. Therefore these cells form a most interesting experiment on the performance of low-cost batteries in space. The battery is charged from the solar arrays via two BRCs with one primary unit and one back-up. The BRCs accept the 28 V supplies from the solar arrays (and a similar supply from the umbilical connector during ground check-out) and charge the battery as required depending on the current drain, the battery voltage and the array temperature.

The PCM regulates the 12–14 V battery bus supply using switched-mode power regulators to provide +10 V, +5 V and −10 V supplies for powering the spacecraft systems and experiments. The PDM switches the various regulated and unregulated power supplies to all the spacecraft systems and experiments, depending on the commands which it receives from the telecommand system. Each switch has an individual current foldback facility so that a faulty module is allowed to draw no more than a pre-determined current before it it latched off, necessitating a power-down under positive command before resetting.

Telecommand subsystem The telecommand system provides remote control over the spacecraft's functions in orbit and comprises three uplink receivers, three data demodulators, a command detector and 108 command latches. The receivers operate in the 144, 438 and 1268 MHz amateur radio satellite service frequency allocations. A command detector scans the three receivers according to a priority system and, upon detection of a valid set of command instructions, passes the data contained therein to the relevant latch.

The 112 command latches drive the power distribution system, the remaining spacecraft systems, the downlink data multiplexers and the experiment functions. A parallel input–output port to the spacecraft OBC is provided for autonomous control of spacecraft operations, and additional serial data links with the OBC and the DCE provide failure resilience.

Telemetry subsystem Telemetry data provide general engineering or housekeeping information concerning the state of the spacecraft and the numerous on-board experiments and subsystems, e.g. temperature, voltages and currents.

The basic output format of the UoSAT-2 telemetry system has sixty analogue channels digitized to three decimal digits and a further 96 binary status points encoded into hexadecimal digits. These are presented together with a real-time clock–calendar for frame identification and the satellite identification 'UoSAT-2'. A checksum digit is also added to each channel to allow for detection of transmission errors. A programmable dwell facility has been added so that up to 128 channels can be output in rotation, combined with clock times and line feeds or frame headers in any combination. Telemetry data are transmitted as asynchronous ASCII at 300, 600, 1,200 or 2,400 bits s^{-1}.

Radio frequency communications subsystems Three downlinks transmitting at 145.825, 435.025 and 2401.5 MHz, employing AFSK–PM and binary phase-shift (BPSK) modulation, are provided on UoSAT-2. Any combination of telemetry or experiment data can be routed to each of the downlinks independently. The 145.825 MHz VHF downlink on UoSAT-2 is similar to the one flown most successfully on UoSAT-1; however, the modulation index (to UoSAT-2) has been increased in order to ensure optimum reception on most inexpensive NBFM receivers. The 435.025 MHz UHF downlink is a completely new design which generates its frequency standard from a phase-locked synthesizer system. As a result, the d.c. to RF efficiency is much improved over that achieved with UoSAT-1. In addition to AFSK–PM, BPSK modulation is a switchable option.

Associated with the three downlink channels are three uplink channels at VHF, UHG and SHF to support uplink of telecommand instructions, uplink of OBC software and data, and store-and-forward communications traffic.

The VHF and UHF uplink receivers and downlink transmitters all share a common antenna system similar to that used for UoSAT-1. The antenna, in the form of four phased canted turnstile monopoles, is fed via a four-port hybrid network and operates on both its fundamental (VHF) and its harmonic overtone (UHF). The four-port hybrid network provides a high degree of isolation between the uplink receivers and the adjacent downlink transmitters. Considerable difficulty has been experienced with UoSAT-1 in maintaining a sufficient degree of isolation, and substantial 'desensing' of the command receiver from the adjacent downlink transmitter resulted. The antenna and hybrid feed system was redesigned and carefully matched on UoSAT-2 with the result that the orbital performance is greatly improved and the satellite's communications systems are able to support full duplex operation on both VHF and UHF. The SHF antennas comprise three-turn helixes.

Attitude determination, control and stabilization subsystems Attitude control commonly represents one of the most complex and costly of satellite subsystems, and therefore useful low-cost satellites require inexpensive attitude determination, control and stabilization mechanisms. Gravity-gradient stabilization techniques were explored in the 1960s and then largely abandoned owing to the imprecise results. The availability of greatly increased on-board computing power on UoSAT-2, compared with these early satellites, and its used in supporting complex control algorithms providing active deliberation employing magnetorquers makes gravity-gradient stabilization attractive once again. This technique requires a minimum of moving parts (a boom that it deployed once only), uses no depletable resources (magnetorquers are powered from the solar arrays) and can provide useful earth-pointing precision.

Magnetorquers – coils of wire energized to act as electromagnets – are built into all six faces of the spacecraft, wound around the edges of the honeycomb panels supporting the solar cells and the top and bottom plates. The magnetic fields created interact with the earth's magnetic field to produce a torque which tends to rotate the spacecraft. The magnetorquers can be commutated under OBC control with the changing geomagnetic field vector around the orbit so as to be able to control completely the dynamics of motion of the spacecraft.

In order to achieve and maintain precise earth pointing, the orientation and dynamics of motion of the spacecraft have to be determined and monitored. This is done through a number of attitude sensors using the sun, the earth's horizon and the local geomagnetic field vector. A three-axis flux-gate magnetometer, developed from the one flown on UoSAT-1, provides continuous attitude information by resolving the components of the geomagnetic field at the satellite which can then be compared against a known (computed) geomagnetic field model. Six digital sun-angle sensors, developed at the University of Surrey, are mounted around the top plate to provide complete 360° coverage around the z-axis and ±60° along it. A twin-beam infrared earth horizon sensor is mounted on the top (+z facet) of the spacecraft to provide periodic attitude cross-references with the other sensors.

On-board computer subsystem The OBC is based on an RCA 1802 microprocessor and has been designed to automate spacecraft operations in orbit, gather data from and control the on-board experiments, and provide redundancy to a number of modules on the spacecraft. To satisfy these requirements, the OBC has access to many modules via parallel interfaces, and to some of the others and the receivers and transmitters via serial connections. In addition, a real-time clock and total of 48 kbytes of DRAM for data storage. The Digitalker speech synthesizer is housed in the OBC and has two read-only memories (ROMs) containing over 550 words used for educational experiments such as 'speaking' telemetry.

A multi-tasking Diary software operating system is implemented on the UoSAT-2 OBC, which enables tasks to be activated in a regular sequence or as defined by a real-time clock-calendar facility. The OBC can issue commands (subservient to ground control) to the spacecraft subsystems and experiments. It also has direct access to the telemetry system and can store selected channels away in the memory over the course of an orbit, or several orbits, to be downlinked later. This facility enables telemetry data to be collected whilst the spacecraft is out of range of ground-stations, thus yielding a more complete picture of the spacecraft's operations and characteristics than can be gathered from just a 12 min visible 'pass'. In principle, any number of telemetry channels can be monitored by the OBC in this way – the amount of data collected is limited only by the size of memory available to the OBC.

Payload experiments

The payload experiments on UoSAT-2 cover satellite communications, auroral particle–wave studies, earth imaging, space dust studies and space education.

Store-and-forward digital communications experiment The DCE was designed and built by AMSAT and VITA groups in the USA and Canada. The DCE is included on UoSAT-2 to demonstrate the concept of store-and-forward digital communications from a low earth-orbiting satellite, and to provide a test-bed for hardware and software for a planned operational digital store-and-forward satellite PACSAT supporting communications to field and relief workers in remote areas. In store-and-forward communications, instead of using a transponder to communicate with stations that can 'see' the satellite simultaneously, a message is stored in the satellite's memory and is later retrieved by another station. By using a satellite like UoSAT-2, such messages can be transferred between any two points on earth – usually in under 6 h – and the UoSAT-2 polar orbit provides excellent coverage of polar regions out of range of geostationary communications spacecraft. In addition, the DCE provides systems level redundancy through interfaces with the telemetry and telecommand systems. The DCE is based around an NSC-800 CPU and 128 kbyte of CMOS RAM, and uses two serial ports which can receive data from and transmit to the RF communications system and the OBC.

The DCE was commissioned early in 1986 and 'gateway' ground-stations have been established in Washington, DC (USA), Dallas, TX (USA), Los Angeles, CA (USA), Guildford (UK), Adelaide (Australia), Auckland (New Zealand), Chelmsford, MA (USA), Karachi (Pakistan) and Lahore (Pakistan). These stations also link into their regional terrestrial VHF packet radio networks to connect to many thousands of

Satellite systems

stations in the amateur radio community. These stations provide an invaluable traffic-handling experiment for the DCE.

Earth-imaging experiment The aim of the earth-imaging CCD experiment flown on UoSAT-2 is to explore the feasibility of providing medium-resolution images of land, sea and cloud formations using simple low-cost techniques. However, the CCD array used on UoSAT-2 is not yet able to match the image quality currently available from the NOAA and Meteosat meteorological spacecraft.

The CCD camera is a redesigned version of the experiment flown on UoSAT-1. Indeed, the CCD array at the centre of the camera is the same type as used before, although the later batches of this sensor are substantially improved over the early one used three years previously. The analogue electronics surrounding the array have also been greatly improved. The active area of 384 x 256 pixels is digitized into 7 bit (128 grey levels) and stored in 96 kbytes of static CMOS RAM in the digital store and readout (DSR) experiment. The DSR is then responsible for the picture readout, adding addresses and error correction and detection information as required. The variable video amplifier gain and integration period of the CCD camera provide the latitude required to image both land details and also auroral features; the latter are of interest in conjunction with the particle detector experiments.

Because of the limited time period of any one satellite pass and the large amount of data to be transmitted per image (96 kbyte), the image data are generally transmitted at 4,800 bit s^{-1} AFSK/PM using the UHF downlink.

Particle–wave experiment Three Geiger detectors (RAL), each with different electron energy thresholds, and a multichannel electron spectrometer from the AMPTE mission are mounted on the top of the spacecraft to serve as a near-earth reference for magnetospheric studies. These have been used concurrently with the Viking spacecraft mission in orbit and for ground-based studies of the ionospheric D, E and F regions being pursued with riometers and EISCAT. Data are available to professional scientists and radio amateurs either in real time or, for more detailed analysis, from stored measurements over both polar auroral regions. The modulations imparted to particles, as a result of wave–particle interactions in the magnetosphere on auroral field lines, can be observed by a particle correlator experiment (University of Sussex) designed around an NSC-800 microprocessor. The measurements can be identify the wave modes responsible for accelerating electrons into the auroral beam and will also identify wave modes which limit the further growth of the auroral beam.

Digital store and readout experiment The DSR provides a central mass data storage facility on board the spacecraft, accessible to the CCD imager, the particle–wave experiment or the OBC, and outputs data in an addressed error-coded format for transmission. The DSR has two banks of 96 kbytes with an 8 bit CMOS memory which can be used as either two separate banks or as one contiguous 192 kbyte bank. The DSR formatting inserts frame and data block addresses together with codes. The EDAC codes can be turned off to produce a direct readout of data in the memory. The data can be output at 1,200, 2,400, 4,800 and 9,600 bits s^{-1}.

Space dust experiment The space dust experiment (similar to that flown on Giotto) was built by a group of final-year undergraduate students at the University of Kent. It has a dielectric diaphragm which, when punctured by a large particle, discharges the capacitance associated with it, thereby indicating the impact. In conjunction with a piezo-crystal microphone which detects the impact of particles of smaller size, correlation techniques can yield a measurement of the momentum of the incident particle.

Speech synthesizer experiment As with UoSAT-1, the synthesized speech experiment on UoSAT-2 has aroused a great deal of interest, particularly from young children in schools. The OBC drives the Digitalker, resulting in a series of spoken messages.

The speech synthesizer is able to 'speak' telemetry and experiment data in a limited English vocabulary of around 550 words (held in two ROMs). There are also two 'voices' available; one has an English accent, and the other an American. This experiment is intended for simple demonstrations of satellite communications in schools using a minimum of equipment – a low-cost VHM–FM receiver and a whip antenna are all that is required.

Orbital operations with UoSAT-2

UoSAT-2 was launched by Delta-174 from the Vandenberg Air Force Base, Limpoc, CA, into a 700 km 97.5° polar sun-synchronous earth orbit alongside Landsat-5 at 17:59 GMT on 1 March 1984. However, after successful activation of the spacecraft on initial orbits, communication was lost. Ten weeks after loss of signals from UoSAT-2, the station in Greenland confirmed reception of the microwatt signal from the spacecraft SHF local oscillator! This observation confirmed the basic operation of the spacecraft battery and that the orbit parameters provided by the NORAD radar were indeed correct. Armed with this information, spacecraft operators then concentrated on attempting to communicate with the spacecraft through the redundant UHF uplink and on the second day command instructions successfully reactivated the VHF downlink and telemetry was received once more from UoSAT-2.

The telemetry data received indicated that the spacecraft was in good health, and diagnostics quickly located the problem. It appears that a few hours after launch a logic gate and its associated diode, resistor or capacitor in the VHF uplink data detector circuit failed – thus effectively severing the VHF uplink communications channel to the telecommand system or OBC, preventing the execution of commands. The redundant UHF channel had always been working correctly; however, recovery operation had concentrated on using the primary VHF uplink and, during the occasions that the UHF uplink was tried, the spacecraft antennas had been pointing away from earth! The VHF uplink data could be re-routed around the failed components using the serial interfaces to either the OBC or the DCE to provide a 'bypass' – the DCE was used initially, whilst the OBC was used to commission the spacecraft subsystems and experiments. The installation of the bypass function restored the spacecraft communications to full capacity and the failure had no further impact on the mission. Once the spacecraft had been gravity-gradient stabilized and the software for routine OBC operations written, the OBC took over the bypass function from the DCE as an interrupt-driven background task. Following restoration of communications with the spacecraft, the engineering subsystems were thoroughly checked out and commissioned.

Digital communications experiment   The DCE provided the initial data bypass function until the OBC Diary software had been completed. Store-and-forward communications using the DCE commenced in January 1985, and now support international 'gateway' stations in the UK, USA, Australia, New Zealand, Pakistan and Antarctica serving many thousands of amateur radio stations via local terrestrial VHF packet radio links.

Particle–wave experiment   The particle–wave experiment has been used successfully for numerous surveys in the auroral regions. In November 1986, a joint experiment was undertaken with the Swedish Viking spacecraft when the Viking and UoSAT-2 orbit planes were coincident. The UoSAT-2 particle–wave experiment was used as in low earth orbit to measure the acceleration of particles along the geomagnetic field lines in between Viking at 15,000 km and UoSAT-2 at 700 km. The Geiger detectors have experienced some problems because of the low temperatures experienced on the $-z$ facet of the spacecraft.

CCD imaging experiment   The CCD camera experiment has only recently been activated and preliminary results highlighted the difficulties experienced in obtaining correct 'exposure' settings of CCD integration time and video amplifier gain. Early images appeared to be either over- or under-exposed and were followed by a series of images taken over the earth's terminator and moving gradually into sunlit areas. These images proved to be ambiguous, since attitude manoeuvres were also in progress on the spacecraft and this affected camera pointing. Further tests are under way now that the spacecraft is maintained accurately earth pointing.

Speech synthesizer experiment The Digitalker speech synthesizer, under the control of the Diary software operating system in the OBC, has been used regularly in support of the Education Experiments Day on UoSAT-2 each Wednesday specifically aimed at schools. During 1988, the Digitalker was used to provide communications support to the Trans-Polar Ski Expedition travelling from the USSR to Canada via the North Pole.

Space dust experiment The space dust experiment was activated shortly after launch and experiment data have been available through the telemetry digital status channels transmitted routinely on the VHF downlink.

UoSAT-2 has been used to provide a highly flexible in-orbit test-bed for a number of studies associated with spacecraft engineering, space science and communications which have been carried out for several space agencies. These studies have focused on:

1 statistical occurrence radiation-induced single-event upsets in VLSI CMOS devices (ESA–ESTEC);
2 studies of digital store-and-forward communications using low earth-orbiting satellites (Swedish Space Corporation);
3 studies of low-cost spacecraft attitude determination, control and stabilization for small spacecraft (Desking Inc.);
4 spacecraft systems studies for T-SAT (UK SERC);
5 development of cost-effective spacecraft techniques (SUPARCO);
6 auroral particle–wave interactions (UK SERC, RAL, University of Sussex).

UoSAT experimenter communities

A survey carried out in 1987 identified over 1,000 amateur radio stations in forty-three countries world-wide actively receiving data directly from UoSAT-2. These stations vary greatly in resources and complexity from simple receivers, omnidirectional antennas and the cheapest of microcomputers to computer-driven VHF–UHF tracking antenna systems

Satellite systems

using high-performance data decoders, powerful microcomputers and graphics yielding sophisticated data displays and analysis. A dozen of the most advanced stations in the amateur satellite service have established digital gateway stations linking the UoSAT-2 to the terrestrial VHF amateur radio packet networks that now cover most developed countries, thus providing international digital communications to thousands of amateur radio stations.

The two UoSAT spacecraft provide a unique resource to the educational community as they allow direct participation in space experiments in orbit at very low cost and with minimum complexity. Around 900 schools, colleges and universities in the UK alone use UoSAT satellites to support 'live' classroom demonstration of orbital physics, laws and dynamics of motion, geomagnetic field studies, radiation studies, data handling, validation and analysis, spacecraft design and operation, and receiver and antenna design and operation. The ability to participate directly in a space programme has fired the imagination of many schoolchildren and brought to life otherwise rather 'dry' or academic topics whilst also providing exposure to realistic practical problems associated with advanced technology.

Conclusions

For more than twenty-five years, the amateur radio community, through AMSAT has pioneered cost-effective solutions to a demanding technological challenge, whilst providing world-wide analogue and digital communications by satellite and promoting space education using the simplest of inexpensive equipment. The imagination and determination of radio amateurs has complimented the more traditional long-term extremely expensive commercial and international projects which have limited direct involvement in space activities to only the most committed and wealthy of agencies or organizations. In particular, the UoSAT Programme has created an opportunity for many to participate directly in space experimentation at minimal cost and complexity, whilst also providing professional opportunities for new ideas, technologies and experiments to be flown and to yield results within sensible time-scales.

Acknowledgements

Many people and organizations contributed to the success of the international amateur satellite programme and it is clearly impracticable to acknowledge them all individually. Special thanks are, however, due to NASA, MacDonnell Douglas Aircraft Corporation, NASDA, Ariane

Space and the ESA who have provided the essential launch support needed by the Programme.

Bibliography

Bonsall, C.A. and Moore, R.G. NUSAT-1 – The First Ejectable Getaway Special. *Get Away Special Experimenters Symposium, Goddard Space Flight Centre, October 1985*, NASA, Greenbelt, MD, pp. 87–8.

Connors, D. The PACSAT Project. *Proceedings of the 2nd ARRL Amateur Radio Computer Networking Conference, San Francisco, CA, 1983*, ARRL, Newington, CT.

Davidoff, M.R. *The Satellite Experimenter's Handbook*, American Relay League, Newington, CT, 1984.

Gilbert, J.K. and Sweeting, M.N. Satellites in education – a strategy paper, University of Surrey, Guildford, 1986.

Limebear, R.W. and Broadbent, R.J. *AMSAT-UK Technical Handbooks (UO-9, UO-111, AO-10, FO-12, AO-13, RS-10/11)*, AMSAT-UK, London.

Sweeting, M.N. AMSAT – United Kingdom Telecommand Centre, *Telecommunications, Journal of the International Telecommunication Union*, October 1977.

Sweeting, M.N. The University of Surrey AMSAT Telecommand Centre, *Journal of the Radio Society of Great Britain* 54, 524–7, 1978.

Sweeting, M.N. UoSAT – Britain's first amateur radio spacecraft?, *Radio Communication*, 54, 230–1, 1979.

Sweeting, M.N. The amateur space program, *Journal of the British Interplanetary Society*, 32, (8), 142–7, 1979.

Sweeting, M.N. UoSAT – Britain's first amateur scientific spacecraft, *Journal of the Radio Society of Great Britain*, 55, 230–1, 1980.

Sweeting, M.N. The University of Surrey amateur scientific and educational spacecraft – UoSAT, *Journal of the Radio Society of Great Britain*, 57, 134–5, 1981.

Sweeting, M.N. The University of Surrey amateur scientific and educational spacecraft – UoSAT, *Telecommunications, Journal of the International Telecommunication Union*, March 1981.

Sweeting, M.N. UoSAT – an investigation into cost effective spacecraft engineering, *Journal of the Institute of Electronic and Radio Engineers*, 52 (8/9), 363–78, 1982.

Sweeting, M.N. The UoSAT spacecraft programme – experimental results and future plans, *Proceedings of the AMSAT–USA Space Symposium, Dallas, Tx, November 1986*, AMSAT–NA, Washington, DC.

Sweeting, M.N. *UoSAT Spacecraft Data Booklet*, University of Surrey, Guildford, 1986.

Traynar, C.P. The development of a satellite-borne earth imaging system for UoSAT, *Radio and Electronic Engineer*, 52 (8/9), 398–402, 1982.

Chapter two

Earth observation satellites

P.A. Vass and R.F. Thomas

Satellites in orbit around the earth provide an unrivalled vantage point from which to observe, measure and monitor the atmosphere, oceans and land surfaces. Since the first monochrome images were transmitted from the weather satellite TIROS-1 in 1960, the application of the technology, which has come to be known as remote sensing, has increased the range of information which can be collected from spaceborne platforms.

To those new to the field of remote sensing, the terminology, the many acronyms and the large number of different satellites must be very confusing. In this chapter we shall concentrate on outlining the main types of civilian satellites for earth observation, leaving the application and use of the collected data in education activities to other authors. For more details on the background to remote sensing, its principles, the techniques of data and image processing, and the wide range of application areas, the reader is referred to a number of excellent text books.[1-9] However, it is necessary to explain a few points, such as how a sensor works, how the data are received by the satellite and transmitted to the ground etc.

A sensor on board a satellite is sensitive to a particular range of wavelengths within the electromagnetic spectrum. Our remote sensors, i.e. our eyes, are responsive to visible light and a spectral band of 0.4–0.7 μm (1 μm = 10^{-6}m), while other instruments record information in the ultraviolet, visible, infrared and microwave regions.

Sensors are of two types. Passive sensors, like our eyes, record the energy reflected or emitted from the earth, while active sensors generate a radar pulse and record its echo. The information (data) collected by the satellite is also of two types, either recorded in a one-dimensional data stream, such as an atmospheric temperature profile, or a two-dimensional image in a digital or photographic format. A photograph from space requires the return of the camera to earth for the film to be processed, relying on manned missions such as the US Space Shuttle. Therefore most satellite pictures are correctly referred to as digital images, in that they are numerical representations of the imaged area. Such imagery, which is built up in lines as the satellite moves across the earth's surface, has several important advantages over space photography: it can be transmitted as electronic signals to the ground, and can be manipulated and enhanced by computers and image-processing systems to provide a valuable source of information that is becoming increasingly familiar to many users.

All satellites must transmit their data to the earth through a suitably equipped ground station; these range from simple devices for receiving some types of meteorological data to very sophisticated systems for the reception of microwave imagery. If there is a receiving station in range the data can be transmitted virtually as they are recorded – for some satellites this is the only option. For others with tape recorders, the information can be stored on magnetic tape for playback later to a data centre. However, the recorders have often been the first element to fail and emphasis is now being placed on establishing networks of communication satellites for the transmission of data from remote sensing satellites to the ground.

There are two principal types of orbit – geostationary and polar orbiting – for unmanned remote sensing spacecraft. At an altitude of 35,900 km the speed of the satellite in geostationary or geosynchronous orbit is the same as the earth's rotation and thus the satellite appears fixed above the same point. A polar orbit takes the satellite over or near the North and South Poles and most commonly the orbit is sun synchronous with the satellite maintaining a constant relationship with the sun, while the earth spins below. On each satellite orbit, which views a swath of the surface, the earth rotates below the satellite and coverage of the globe is obtained by successive orbits.

In very general terms remote-sensing satellites fall into one of two categories based on their primary application, i.e. whether they are used in the study of meteorology (metsats) or of the earth's resources. Thus in this chapter we follow this division, dealing first with the metsats and then with the land and ocean satellites. Within this classification the metsats are further divided by orbit type (as described above), and the earth resources satellites by sensor capabilities and mission status. Sensors can be described in terms of three types of resolving powers – spectral resolution (number and sensitivity of sensing channels), spatial resolution (fineness of detail that can be sensed) and, in relation to the satellite, temporal resolution (how frequently an area is sensed). These terms are discussed more fully elsewhere, but, where possible, each of the satellite systems described here is summarized in terms of these characteristics.[8,10] In general we move from the low spatial and high temporal resolution of the meteorological satellites to the higher spatial and high temporal resolution of the meteorological satellites to the

Satellite systems

higher spatial and lower resolution of the meteorological satellites to the higher spatial and lower temporal resolution of the earth resources satellites. The spectral resolution of a particular sensor depends on the application for which the instrument was developed. Mission status can be broadly divided into three phases – experimental, semi-operational and operational – and these can be seen to match the three decades of the 1970s, the 1980s and the 1990s.

Meteorological satellites

Meteorological applications of remote-sensing data are met by a network of geostationary satellites providing a broad view of global weather patterns and polar-orbiting satellites collecting a wide range of more detailed environmental data.

Geostationary meteorological satellites

Data collected by geostationary satellites have contributed significantly to the increased confidence associated with the medium-range weather forecasts and provide information on:

1 height and type of cloud cover, and sea and cloud surface temperatures;
2 distribution of water vapour in the upper troposphere;
3 the earth's radiation and energy balance, and wind direction and speed by assessment of cloud movements.

In addition such data are increasingly used for non-meteorological studies, including the monitoring of regional vegetation changes, particularly in response to drought, mapping major soil and vegetation boundaries, evaluating biomass, hazard monitoring, and evaluating ocean currents, areas of upwelling and sea ice.

US GOES programme

In 1966 and 1967 NASA included a spin-scan camera on two communication satellites demonstrating the acquisition of a picture of the earth every 20 min. These experiments led to the development of an operational programme with the launch in 1974 of the synchronous meteorological satellite (SMS 1). In 1975 the programme, owned and operated by the National Oceanic and Atmospheric Administration (NOAA), was renamed GOES (Geostationary Operational Environmental Satellite).[11,12] Since then NOAA has launched further GOES satellites, the most recent in 1989. A new generation of US

Earth observation satellites

geostationary satellites (GOES-Next) is under development with an expected launch date in 1990.

The primary sensor on the current series is a visible and infrared spin scan radiometer (VISSR) atmospheric sounder (VAS). The VAS has eight visible channels and six thermal sensors that detect infrared radiation in twelve spectral bands. A filter wheel is used to achieve the selection of the spectral bands, which have central wavelengths between 3.9 and 15 mm. The spatial resolutions is 1 km in the visible and 7 or 14 km in the infrared depending on the detectors used. Data are acquired routinely every 30 min day and night in the infrared and during daylight only in the visible. To maintain an operational GOES system NOAA moves the satellites to different locations as information requirements change. The characteristics of the current GOES satellites are summarized in Table 2.1

Table 2.1 Technical characteristics of the main meteorological satellites

	Meteosat	*GOES*	*NOAA/AVHRR*
Orbital parameters			
Orbit	Geostationary (above the equator)	Geostationary (above the Equator)	Near polar, sun synchronous at an inclination of 98.8°
Altitude (km)	35,900	35,900	833–870
Repeat cycle	Data acquisition every 30 min	Data acquisition every 30 min	12
Sensor details			
Wavebands (μm)	0.40–1.10	12 spectral bands with wavelengths between 3.9 and 15μm	0.58–0.68
	5.70–7.10		0.73–1.10
	10.50–12.50		3.55–3.93
			10.30–11.30
Spatial resolution (at nadir) (km)	Visible: 2.4	Visible: 1	Visible: 11.5–12.5
	Infrared: 5.0	Infrared: 7 or 14	Infrared: 1.1

Meteosat (European Space Agency)

Meteosat is the geostationary satellite launched by the European Space Agency (ESA) and positioned at the intersection of the Greenwich meridian and the Equator over West Africa (see Table 2.2).[13] Meteosat-1

Satellite systems

was launched in 1977 and failed in November 1979, to be followed in 1981 by the launch of Meteosat-2. Meteosat has three primary tasks:

1   To acquire data in three wavebands every 30 min
     visible and near infrared (0.4–1.1 µm);
     middle infrared, water vapour obsorption band (5.7–7.1 µm);
     thermal infrared (TIR) (10.5–12.5 µm).
    The spatial resolution varies with waveband and latitude from 2.5 km in the visible and 5 km in the water vapour and TIR bands in the tropics to 4 km and 8 km respectively for temperature areas.
2   To distribute image data and other meteorological information.
3   To collect and relay information from various data collection platforms (DCPs), such as land stations, ocean buoys, ships, aircraft, balloons and other satellites.

Following the launches of Meteosats 1 and 2, which are termed pre-operational satellites, in June 1988 ESA launched a prototype (P2) to provide continuity of data supply to the European meteorological services until the launch of the first satellite in the operational series. The Meteosat Operational Programme (MOP) aims to provide further continuity until approximately 1995, with launches in 1989 (MOP-1), 1990 (MOP-2) and 1991 (MOP-3).[14]

Japan and India

Other geostationary meteorological satellites are operated by Japan and India. In 1977 Japan launched GMS-1, also known as Himawari 1, followed by GMS-2 in 1981 (operated for six months) and GMS-3 in 1984 (currently operational) over the western Pacific at 140°E. The Japanese Meteorological Agency plans to have a new satellite system operational by 1989, with GMS-4 under development and two further satellites under consideration.[15] To date, India has launched two geostationary satellites combining the functions of telecommunications relay, direct broadcast and weather imaging.[16] Insat 1A was operational for only 5 months in 1982 and was replaced prior to its failure by Insat 1B launched by the Space Shuttle. Insat 1C, which was to be launched by the Shuttle in 1986, now awaits an Ariane launch and will be followed by Insat 1D, the last in this generation, in 1989 or 1990.

Polar-orbiting meteorological satellites

The US polar-orbiting meteorological satellites have had a relatively long history and now, unlike most other earth observation missions, are regarded as genuinely operational, with a number of spacecraft guaranteed for launches well into the 1990s.[17]

TIROS and ESSA satellites

The first polar-orbiting satellite purpose-built for the collection of weather data was launched by NOAA in 1960 and was known as TIROS-1 (Television and Infrared Observation Satellite). Ten TIROS satellites were launched in the period 1960–5. Orbit configurations of the first eight satellites restricted data acquisition to tropical and subtropical regions. In 1966 the TIROS satellites restricted data acquisition to tropical and subtropical regions. In 1966 the TIROS operational system was designed to provide routine daily observations on a worldwide basis with satellites passing close to the poles. Nine ESSA (Environmental Science Services Administration) satellites were launched between 1966 and 1969. Even-numbered ESSA satellites provided direct transmission of their image data to ground receiving stations by automatic picture transmission (APT), and the odd-numbered satellites stored their data on tape recorders, transmitting it later to receiving stations in the USA.

ITOS series

In 1970 the third generation of polar-orbiting meteorological satellites was launched with the Improved TIROS Operational System (ITOS) combining direct APT transmission and on-board data storage for the collection of daytime imagery (visible and TIR) and night-time (TIR only). The ITOS satellites were the first to be named after their operators NOAA.

TIROS-N series

The fourth generation, completing the development of a polar-orbiting environmental satellite system, is the TIROS-N series. The first satellite in the series was launched in 1978 and was followed by NOAA-6 in 1979 and NOAA-7 in 1981 and then the Advanced TIROS-N series: NOAA-8 in 1983, NOAA-9 in 1984 and NOAA-10 in 1986. It should be noted that, although the programme is still known as TIROS, the individual satellites are called NOAA. At the present time NOAA has an undertaking to maintain two operational satellites, the current ones being NOAA-10 and NOAA-11. At a height of approximately 830 km and an orbital separation of 90° each satellite views both the night and day sides of the earth twice every day, crossing the Equator at 07.30 a.m. and 07.30 p.m. and at 2.00 a.m. and 2.00 p.m. local time respectively. These satellites acquire, broadcast and record environmental information on the earth's cloud cover, surface and atmospheric temperatures,

Satellite systems

humidity, water–ice moisture boundaries, the distribution of ozone, the heat budget, and proton and electron fluxes.[12]

There are two primary sensors on board. The advanced very high resolution radiometer (AVHRR) is a five-channel instrument with an optimum resolution of 1.1 km (see Table 2.1 for a summary of the technical characteristics of the AVHRR). Its main applications are in weather forecasting, cloud delineation, snow and ice monitoring and sea surface temperature measurements, but the data are also used for a variety of other studies such as mapping marine oil pollution, monitoring volcanic eruptions and assessing vegetation vigour on an international scale. The TIROS operational vertical sounder (TOVS) is a three-instrument system consisting of a twenty-channel high-resolution infrared sounder (HIR/2) with a 17 km resolution used to measure vertical temperature profiles, water vapour and total ozone content, a three-channel stratospheric sounding unit (SSU) with 147 km resolution for measuring stratospheric temperatures and a four-channel microwave sounding unit (MSU) with 109 km resolution used to obtain atmospheric soundings in cloudy areas.

NOAA intends to launch further satellites (NOAA-K, NOAA-L and NOAA-M) identical with the current ones and eventually to continue providing these data services via similar instrumentation on board the polar platforms of the Space Station programme.[14]

Nimbus series

In parallel with NOAA's TIROS series, NASA operated seven Nimbus satellites with the aim of developing and flight testing advanced sensors for the study of the atmosphere and other applications and to provide data for meteorological research. Numerous sensors were flown during the series, recording data in the visible, infrared and microwave. Perhaps the most well-known sensor was the coastal-zone colour scanner on Nimbus-7 (see later).[18]

Earth resources satellites

The use of an orbital platform to acquire imagery of the earth's surface was first recognized in the 1960s during the manned Mercury, Gemini and Apollo NASA missions. This pioneering work led to the development of an experimental series of satellites to evaluate the utility of images collected from an unmanned satellite. The first such satellite, now known as Landsat 1, which was launched in 1972, offered the advantages of readily available and inexpensive imagery recorded at regular intervals. A series of subsequent launches has given a near-continuous service, which many users coming to rely on such data.

Earth observation satellites

The years since 1972 have seen major sensor developments; for example, in the Landsat series from an original 80 m resolution four-channel multispectral scanner system (MSS) to a seven-channel thematic mapper (TM) with improved ground resolution (30 m for the visible, near-infrared and middle-infrared bands), spectral sensitivity and the introduction of a thermal sensor. With the transfer of the Landsat series from NASA first to NOAA and then to a consortium of commercial organizations, this type of satellite remote sensing is now deemed semi-operational.

An important milestone occurred in 1986 with the launch of SPOT-1 and the introduction of linear arrays of sensors which can be pointed to obtain stereoscopic images or to increase the frequency of coverage of a particular area. Another feature of the SPOT programme is its underlying philosophy of operating as a commercial system scheduled to provide a continuous service for around 12 years, allowing users to confidently develop their applications into the 1990s.

In this second half of the chapter we describe the various satellites, past, present and future, launched for the study of the earth's land and ocean areas. The section is divided broadly into three parts based on the 1970s, the 1980s and the 1990s as the science and technology has moved from an experimental nature to a more operational status.

Experimental missions (the 1970s)

Landsats 1, 2 and 3

The American Landsat 1 was the first satellite designed to collect data about the earth's surface and resources. Three satellites, initially called the Earth Resources Technology Satellites (ERTS) launched by NASA and operational almost continually between 1972 and 1983, comprised the first generation of the Landsat series. Through being able to observe large areas and provide repetitive data an entirely new way of monitoring and analysing the earth's surface was made available to scientists and environmental workers.[19, 20]

All three satellites were launched (1972, 1975 and 1978) into a sun-synchronous near-polar orbit at an altitude of about 900 km (±30 km). Such an orbit ensured potential coverage of almost the entire surface of the earth (between 82°N and 82°S) every 18 days. When two satellites were operational they were positioned 9 days apart to allow a more frequent data acquisition capability. A summary of the technical details of the satellites is given in Table 2.2.

Satellite systems

Table 2.2 Technical characteristics of the first generation of Landsat satellites

	Landsats 1 and 2	*Landsat 3*
Orbital parameters		
Orbit	Near polar, sun synchronous	Near polar, sun synchronous
Altitude (km)	919	919
Inclination (deg)	99.09	99.09
Repeat cycle (days)	18	18
Sensor details		
RBV waveband(s)[a] (μm)	0.475–0.575 (80m)	0.505–0.750 (40m)
	0.580–0.680 (80m)	
	0.690–0.830 (80m)	
MSS waveband(s)[a] (μm)	0.50–0.60 (80m)	0.50–0.60 (80m)
	0.60–0.70 (80m)	0.60–0.70 (80m)
	0.70–0.80 (80m)	0.70–0.80 (80m)
	0.80–1.10 (80m)	0.80–1.10 (80m)
		10.40–12.50 (120m)

Note: [a] Resolution (in metres) in parentheses

The payloads consisted of two sensors: return beam vidicon (RBV) television cameras and a four-band multi-spectral scanning system (MSS).

Three RBV cameras, sensitive to the blue–green (0.475–0.575 μm), yellow–red (0.58–0.68 μm) and red–near–infrared (0.69–0.83 μm) wavelengths and numbered bands 1, 2 and 3 respectively, were used on Landsats 1 and 2. As a result of technical problems there were few data from those systems. Two identical RBV panchromatic (0.505–0.72 μm) cameras on Landsat 3 proved more successful, but even though the RBV resolution was improved from 80 m to 40 m, the spectrally and radiometrically superior MSS was still the preferred sensor.

The MSS line scanner recorded data for a ground area of 85 km x 185 km in four wavebands (bands 4, 5 6 and 7) between the green and near-infrared parts of the spectrum at a ground resolution of about 80 m. The MSS on Landsat 3 had an additional band recording in the TIR (10.4–12.6 μm) and a spatial resolution of about 237 m, but this failed shortly after launch. The sensed data from both the RBV and MSS sensors were either transmitted directly to specially equipped ground stations or stored on tape recorders for later transmission to data centres in the USA.

Applications of Landsat data have been widespread in many fields, including geology, mineral and petroleum exploration, forestry and agriculture, hydrology, coastal processes, land use and land cover, mapping environmental changes, resources inventories and pollution monitoring.

Seasat

Seasat, although only operational for 106 days in 1978, produced a wealth of unique information by providing the first opportunity to acquire, receive, process and analyse data from a space-borne synthetic aperture radar (SAR).[21] Primarily designed for oceanographic objectives, the satellite had a circular orbit at an altitude of 800 km.

Seasat carried five sensors: an L-band (23.5 cm) SAR producing images with a nominal ground resolution of 25 m over swaths 100 km wide to monitor surface wave fields and polar sea ice (see Table 2.3 for further details); a radar scatterometer (SASS) to measure wind speeds and directions; a scanning multi-spectral microwave radiometer (SMMR) to measure sea temperatures, wind speeds, rain rate, liquid and water vapour content of the atmosphere, and ice conditions; a visible and infrared radiometer to image ocean and coastal features and to measure sea surface temperatures.

Seasat is best known for its SAR images and its capability of observing the earth in all weather conditions, day or night. SAR products have been used in a wide range of earth resources projects including oceanographic monitoring, ice mapping, geological mapping to detect lineaments, faults, fractures, folds etc., hydrological studies and drainage network analysis, vegetation mapping and soil moisture studies. Seasat data will play an important role in the next few years in the lead up to the microwave satellites of the 1990s (see ERS-1, Radarsat etc.) as the processing and interpretation of such data are markedly different from the now familiar optical imagery.

Heat Capacity Mapping Mission

The Heat Capacity Mapping Mission (HCMM) was launched by NASA in April 1978 and operated until September 1980.[22] Data were acquired by a two-channel scanning radiometer in the visible and near infrared (0.5–1.1 mm) and in the TIR (10.5–12.5 mm). The near-circular low orbit (620 km) provided coverage of the earth's surface between 85°N and 85°S with a 16 day repeat cycle. The satellite passed over the mid-latitudes of the northern hemisphere at 1.30 p.m. and 2.30 a.m. local time allowing measurements to be taken at the time of maximum variation to determine the thermal inertia of the ground surface. The orbit resulted in night–day coverage patterns at least once every 16 days, at approximately 12 hour intervals for tropical latitudes between 20°N and 20°S and the mid-latitudes above 35°.

Satellite systems

Table 2.3 Technical characteristics of NASA's experimental satellites launched in 1978

	HCMM	*Experimental mission* CZCS	*Seasat*
Orbital parameters			
Orbit	Circular, sun synchronous	Near polar, sun synchronous	Nearly circular
Altitude (km)	620 (540 km for last 6 months of operation)	955	790 ± 50
Inclination (deg)	97.6	99.3	108 nominal
Repeat cycle (days)	16	6	152
Sensor details			
	Visible/IR, 0.5–1.1μm Thermal; 10.5–12.5μm	Band 1 0.43–0.45μm Band 2 0.51–0.53μm Band 3 0.54–0.56μm Band 4 0.66–0.68μm Band 5 0.70–0.80μm Band 6 10.50–12.50μm	SAR Frequency, 1.275 GHz Wavelength, L-band 23 cm Polarization; HH
Spatial resolution (m)	600	800	25 in four look directions
Swath width (km)	716	1,800	100 on one side of the spacecraft

With a scan angle of ±60°, imagery of a swath 720 km wide was recorded. A large overlap between adjacent tracks allowed coverage of any given point on six consecutive days and nights within the 16 day repeat cycle. The satellite did not carry tape recorders and therefore data were only collected in real time, when in the receiving range of certain ground stations. As a result coverage exists only for Europe, mainland USA and Alaska, southern Canada, northern Mexico and eastern Australia.

The main objectives of the HCMM programme were to conduct research into the feasibility of using day–night thermal infrared data for discriminating rock types and mineral resource location, measurement of plant canopy temperatures to determine evapo-transpiration and water stress, measurement and monitoring of soil moisture changes, mapping natural and man-made thermal effluents, detection of thermal gradients in water bodies, mapping and monitoring snow fields for water run-off prediction and measuring the effects of urban heat centres.

Nimbus-7 was launched in October 1978 to conduct a variety of experiments in oceanography, meteorology and pollution control.[18] Its main earth resources sensor was the coastal zone colour scanner (CZCS), a six-channel multi-spectral line-scanner optimized for use over water, which was operational until late 1984. Imagery with a spatial resolution of 800 m and a swath width of 1,836 km was recorded in the blue, green, red, near infrared and TIR (see Table 2.3 for a summary of the technical characteristics of the satellite and the CZCS). The swath width ensured that successive orbit coverage overlapped, providing at least one per daytime pass over every point on the earth.

The major objectives of the CZCS experiment were to establish optimum characteristics for mapping and measuring suspended materials and other water phenomena, improve scientific knowledge of marine ecosystems, evaluate existing fisheries and potential grounds, experiment with real-time data acquisition for rapid assessment and define requirements for future ocean-monitoring instruments.

Bhaskara 1 and 2

In the long-term planning of the Indian space programme the realization of operational capabilities in space remote sensing was a high priority.[16,23] The Bhaskara programme, conceived around 1975, provided an intermediate step towards obtaining an operational system for India. It consisted of two experimental satellites launched in 1979 and 1981. Both payloads included a slow-scan vidicon television camera system operating in the visible (0.54–0.65 µm) and near infrared (0.75–0.96 µm) at a spatial resolution of 1 km and a multi-frequency passive microwave radiometer (19, 22 and 31 GHz).

A comprehensive data utilization programme involving a number of academic and government organizations was established to demonstrate the potential of space remote sensing data. The television data have been used for land cover and geolithological mapping on a 1:2 million scale, mapping forests, flooded areas and snow cover, and monitoring drought-prone areas. The radiometer data were used for sea-state studies and for estimating water vapour and liquid water content in the atmosphere.

Experimental satellite stations

Manned satellite stations provide a useful platform for remote-sensing instrumentation, particularly for evaluating experimental sensors, including prototypes of those being designed for future satellite

Satellite systems

missions. In addition, manned missions allow the acquisition of high-resolution photographic data.

Skylab

Skylab, launched by NASA during 1973 and 1974 into a near circular orbit 435 km above the earth's surface, carried an Earth Resources Experiment Package (EREP) comprising three types of camera, an infrared spectrometer, a thirteen-channel multi-spectral scanner, a microwave radiometer–scatterometer and an L-band radiometer. The camera systems took over 35,000 photographs, some of which still represent a unique information source because of their high spatial resolution (20 m) and the large range of solar angles under which the imagery was acquired.

Space Shuttle

The Space Shuttle programme was to play two roles in remote sensing: the launch of unmanned satellites, such as Landsat, and the deployment of packages within the orbiter vehicle, such as OSTA and Spacelab.

The OSTA package, named after the NASA Office of Space and Terrestrial Applications, consisted of a collection of sensors. In 1981 an L-band synthetic aperture radar known as SIR-A (Shuttle imaging radar) was flown and in eight hours collected analogue data for an area of 10 million km^2 of the earth's surface, including many regions almost continuously covered by cloud which were imaged for the first time.[24] In 1984 SIR-B acquired digitally processed imagery at selectable incidence angles of between 15° and 60°, allowing its evaluation for a wide range of different applications. Unfortunately problems with the link used to transmit data to the ground receiving station resulted in acquisition of 20% of the planned data; however, this amounted to an area of more than 6 million km^2. A photographic payload, the Large Format Camera (LFC), was flown on the same mission as SIR-B.[25] Although plagued by extremely poor weather conditions over North America and Europe, some remarkable photographs on colour, colour infrared and two types of monochrome film were acquired at various points around the world.

An Ocean Colour Experiment (OCE) – an eight-channel multi-spectral scanner – was flown in 1981, and produced 3 km resolution imagery in eight very narrow bands from the blue to the near infrared for a swath width of 550 km. A modular opto-electronic multi-spectral scanner (MOMS), the first push-broom scanner in space, was flown on the Shuttle in 1983 and 1984.[26] It was planned that future systems would develop stereo imaging and extend the spectral sensitivity towards the middle infrared and the TIR (currently limited, in satellites, to line-scanners).

Earth observation satellites

The other remote-sensing package carried on the Space Shuttle was ESA's Spacelab which had a large exterior pallet to carry a number of sensors to be operated with the Shuttle flying upside down with its doors open. The first Spacelab mission in 1983 carried the Metric Camera Experiment, a modified aerial survey camera to evaluate the cartographic capabilities of high-resolution monochrome and colour infrared photography in space.[27]

The Space Shuttle programme came to a tragic halt in January 1986 with the loss of Challenger and its crew. One proposed science package anticipated to be flown in 1991-2 will be an X-band SAR (joint German and Italian project) together with NASA's L- and C-band SAR system. The three SARs will be combined in two missions with a 6 or 18 month interval to maximize the interpretation of seasonal effects.

Semi-operational satellites (the 1980s)

Landsats 4 and 5

The second generation of the Landsat series was initiated in July 1982 with the launch of Landsat 4. In addition to the conventional multi-spectral scanner the payload included a thematic mapper (TM) which recorded data in seven wavebands with a resolution of 30 m in the visible, near and middle infrared bands and 120 m in the TIR band.[12,20,28] Unfortunately, power supply problems terminated the reception of TM data in February 1983. Landsat 5 was launched in March 1984 with a 3 year lifetime, but was still operating satisfactorily at the end of 1987.

The lower orbital configuration (705 km) of this series of Landsats creates a 16 day repeat cycle, with a time interval between adjacent tracks of 7 days, in contrast with the 18 day repeat of Landsats 1-3 with a 1 day interval between adjacent tracks Both the MSS and TM data for each scene cover a surface area of approximately 170 km along track by 185 km across track. The satellites travel from north to south on the dayside of the earth and then northward for the night-time portion of each orbit.

The MSSs on Landsats 4 and 5 are similar to those on the earlier Landsats, but with the four spectral bands identified by a new numbering scheme (bands 1-4 rather than 4-7/8), although the spectral coverage remains unchanged. The TM offers improved radiometric sensitivity over the MSS with 255 rather than 64 grey levels to measure the intensity of the radiation in each discrete waveband. The TM acquires data in seven spectral bands, four of which are located in parts of the spectrum not sensed by the MSS. The bands were carefully chosen for sensitivity to certain natural phenomena and to minimize the attenuation of surface energy by atmospheric water (Table 2.4).

Satellite systems

Table 2.4 Technical characteristics of Landsats 4 and 5 and SPOTs 1, 2 and 3

	Landsats 4 and 5	*SPOTs 1, 2 and 3*
Orbital parameters		
Orbit	Near polar, sun-synchronous	Near polar, sun-synchronous
Altitude (km)	705	830
Inclination (deg)	98.2	98.7
Repeat cycle (days)	16	26
Sensor details		
Waveband(s)[a](μm)	MSS	Multi-spectral mode:
	0.50–0.60 (80m)	0.50–0.59 (20m)
	0.60–0.70 (80m)	0.61–0.68 (20m)
	0.70–0.80 (80m)	0.79–0.89 (20m)
	0.80–1.10 (80m)	
	TM	Panchromatic mode:
	0.45–0.52 (30m)	0.51–0.73 (10m)
	0.52–0.60 (30m)	
	0.63–0.69 (30m)	
	0.76–0.90 (30m)	
	1.55–1.75 (30m)	
	10.40–12.50 (120m)	
	2.08–2.35 (30m)	
Swath width (km)	185	60–80

Note: [a] Resolution (in metres) in parentheses.

The first three Landsats relied on tape recorders to store data until the satellite passed within range of a ground-station, but these were often the first component to fail. It was therefore decided that Landsats 4 and 5 would utilize data relay satellites, which would consist of two geostationary satellites plus an in-orbit spare transmitting data to a centralized ground receiving station in White Sands, NM. However, this plan has not yet been totally fulfilled. TDRS-East (41°W) was launched in April 1983 and after some initial problems reached its correct height in October of that year; however, TDRS-West (171°E), after a launch delay of a year, was lost in the Challenger disaster in January 1986. Although there is a network of Landsat receiving stations around the world, not all have been upgraded to receive TM data.

Landsats 1–5 were developed by NASA, but with a remit to undertake primarily research activities; the responsibility for Landsat MSS and TM data passed to NOAA in 1982 and 1984 respectively. The latter year also saw the US Department of Commerce start the transfer of Landsat from the public to the private sector. In September 1985 NOAA assigned operational control to the Earth Observation Satellite Company (EOSAT) to continue the operation of Landsats 4 and 5 and the launch and control of Landsats 6 and 7. The commercialization of remote-sensing satellites had started.

SPOTs 1, 2 and 3

The development of the SPOT (Système Pour l'Observation de la Terre) satellite by the French in collaboration with Belgium and Sweden introduces several new features and concepts to satellite remote sensing.[29] It is the first to include a linear array sensor and employ push-broom scanning techniques. Rather than using a scanning mirror, each pixel across a scan line is viewed by an individual detector. These detectors form a linear array which is moved forward by the motion of the satellite without the need for moving parts within the sensor. The system is also the first to have steerable optics, i.e. the instrument can 'look' to one side or the other of the satellite ground track. Among the possibilities introduced by this facility of off-nadir viewing is that of increased revisit coverage at intervals ranging from one to several days and the recording during successive passes of stereoscopic pairs of images of a given area. SPOT-1 was launched on 22 February 1986 into a near-polar sun-synchronous orbit at an altitude of 830 km. The next two satellites will be identical with SPOT-1. SPOT-2 has been built and is on hand to replace SPOT-1 when required, and SPOT-3 will be prepared for a launch in the early 1990s. The technical characteristics of the satellites are summarized in Table 2.4.

Another important feature of the SPOT system is its commercial, rather than experimental, nature from the outset. The technical facilities associated with the satellite and image reception and processing are complemented by a marketing organization, SPOT Image, which handles the world-wide promotion and sale of SPOT satellite imagery through a network of authorized distributors.

The payload of SPOT-1 consists of two identical, but independent, imaging instruments (Haute Résolution Visible (HRV)). Each HRV is designed to operate in either of two modes: 10 m resolution panchromatic mode (0.51–0.73 µm); 20 m three-channel multi-spectral mode (0.5–0.59 µm, 0.61–0.68 µm and 0.79–0.89 um). The width of the observed swath varies between 60 km for nadir viewing and 80 km for extreme off-nadir viewing.

Satellite systems

The fine resolution and unique viewing capabilities of revisit and stereoscopy make SPOT data suitable for a wide variety of applications, for example:

- Geology: stereoscopic imagery at 1:50,000 facilitates the identification of terrain and the detection of geochemical and structural anomalies – a useful tool in the exploration of oil and minerals;
- Regional and Urban Studies: SPOT data can be used in land cover studies, in the analysis of damage caused by natural phenomena, such as flooding, and by town planner, who regularly need to monitor trends in land use;
- Cartography: topographic maps can be prepared at scales of 1:50,000 and even 1:25,000 and the imagery is particularly useful as an aid in the updating of existing maps.

Japan's MOS series

In February 1987 Japan launched its first remote-sensing satellite, the Marine Observation Satellite, (MOS-1).[30,31] The payload consists of:

- two push-broom multi-spectral electronic self-scanning radiometers (MESSRs) with 50 m ground resolution in four visible and near-infrared bands (0.51–0.59 μm, 0.61–0.69 μm, 0.73–0.8 μm and 0.8–1.1 μm) providing imagery with a swath width of 100 km for studies of sea surface colour, vegetation, land use etc.:
- a visible and thermal infrared radiometer (VTIR) with a 900 m ground resolution and swath widths of 1500 km in the visible (0.5–0.7 μm) and 2,700 m in the water vapour absorption band (6–7 μm) and in two split windows in the TIR (10.5–11.5 μm and 11.5–12.5 μm);
- a passive microwave scanning radiometer (MSR) with 32 km and 23 km resolution in the 24 GHz and 31 GHz frequency bands respectively.

Simultaneously acquired MESSR and VTIR data will permit large-scale monitoring applications. As there are no tape recorders on MOS-1, ground-stations are required to acquire data out of range of the Japanese Earth Observation Centre.

India's remote-sensing satellites

IRS-1A represents India's first in a series of operational remote-sensing satellites that will serve user needs for natural resources information. Launched in March 1988, the satellite was placed in a polar sun-synchronous orbit at an altitude of about 900 km with a repeat cycle of

22 days.[16,23] It carries two linear imaging self-scanned sensors (LISS) providing imagery in the visible (0.45–0.52 μm, 0.52–0.59 μm and 0.62–0.68 μm) and near infrared (0.77–0.86 μm). LISS-1 provides data with a spatial resolution of 73 m and a swath width of 148 km, and LISS-2 provides data with a spatial resolution of 36.5 m and an overlapping swath width of 145 km, realized by the combined swath of two LISS-2 sensors.

Satellites of the 1990s

The long lead times involved in the design, development and other prelaunch phases of a satellite's life often mean that political and economic, as well as technical, factors result in delayed or even cancelled launches for some proposed satellites and sensors. Even a list of the proposed launches for the 1990s would be extremely lengthy. Therefore in this section we concentrate on three aspects: the satellites which continue a current series (Landsat and SPOT), the new era of microwave satellites (ERS-1, JERS-1, Radarsat) and the concept of an international space station. However, it is interesting to note that a growing proportion of the developments are from countries other than the USA.

Landsats 6 and 7

In mid-1987 EOSAT announced plans to fly new sensor payloads on Landsat 6, with a planned launch date in 1989 and an orbit configuration the same as Landsats 4 and 5.[32] The primary sensor will be an enhanced thematic mapper (ETM) incorporating the multi-spectral capabilities of the TM and an additional 15 m panchromatic (0.5–0.9 μm) band.

The payload will also include a wide field sensor (Sea WiFS) to provide ocean colour data with thermal capacity and land data spectrally compatible with TM data. The data will have a 500 m ground resolution and a swath width of 1,500 km providing coverage every other day. The selection of visible and near-infrared bands addresses both chlorophyll and pigment absorption values, as well as water optical properties and suspended sediment measurements. The two TIR bands (0.5–11.5 μm and 1.5–12.5 μm) will provide continuity for AVHRR data users and provide the data in conjunction with ocean colour data from the same instrument, which was previously only available on separate NASA–NOAA missions. The data will be collected for about 40 min during each orbit and transmitted in real time or recorded on tape recorders. It is expected that research and commercial uses in marine transportation, fishing and mining/exploration will be able to improve short- and long-term operations using downlinked data or maps created from recorded Sea WiFS data.

Satellite systems

A proposed modification to the ETM sensor is the addition of five TIR bands (3.53–3.93 μm, 8.2–8.93 μm, 8.75–9.3 μm, 10.2–11 μm and 11–11.8 μm) with spatial resolutions of 120 m for the first band and 60 m for the others. Geoscientists and specialists in hydrology and vegetation sciences have defined applications for TIR data including the evaluation of ground-water resources, global volcanic activity, snow cover, flood and erosion studies, and crop yield.

It is hoped that the launch of Landsat 7 in the 1990s will introduce a new concept of a large modular long-lived expandable spacecraft, to be known as OMNISTAR, which can be retrieved or repaired at Shuttle orbit to carry scientific payloads in addition to the Landsat mission instruments.

SPOTs 4 and 5

The intention with the second-generation satellites (SPOTs 4 and 5) is not only to ensure continuity of data supply but also to introduce a number of enhancements, including an additional 20 m resolution channel in the mid-infrared (between 1.5 and 1.7 μm), a new imaging instrument with a resolution of about 1 km in the four HRV bands and a field of view of almost 2,000 km, and replacement of the 10 m panchromatic mode by a sampling of the 0.61–0.68 μm band at 10 m intervals to ensure excellent geometric registration between the 10 m (panchromatic) and 20 m (multi-spectral) data.[29]

ERS programme

ERS-1 (ESA Remote-Sensing Satellite), with an expected launch data in 1990, is to be the forerunner of a series of European remote-sensing satellites to become operational in the 1990s.[33] The ERS-1 mission will be concerned with the monitoring of ocean and ice and with all-weather high-resolution imaging over the ocean, coastal regions and land. The ERS-1 spacecraft will utilize a multi-mission platform, based on the SPOT satellite, with a payload of the following remote-sensing instruments.

Active microwave instrument (AMI) This instrument consists of a C-band (5.3 GHz) radar capable of operating as an SAR or a wind scatterometer. In SAR operation two recording modes will be possible with observations of either a full 100 km swath (image mode) or regularly spaced 5 km x 5 km vignettes (wave mode). In the image mode the SAR will operate for a maximum duration of 10 min per orbit and data will only be acquired for areas within the reception zone of specially equipped ground-stations. In the wave mode these limitations are avoided and the data collected of the vignettes every 200 or 300 km will be stored on board for subsequent transmission. The SAR image mode an wind scatterometer share elements of AMI hardware and therefore cannot be operated simultaneously. However, the SAR wave mode and wind scatterometer can be interleaved.

Radar altimeter The radar altimeter is a Ku band (13.5 GHz) nadir-pointing active microwave sensor for measuring echoes from ocean and ice surfaces. It has two measurement modes for ocean and ice areas. Over the ocean it will be used to measure significant wave height, wind speed and topographic data relating to ocean currents, the geoid and tides, and over ice it will be used to determine ice sheet surface topography, ice type and sea–ice boundaries. Land surface elevations and the levels of lakes, marshes and rivers will also be obtainable.

Along-track scanning radiometer and microwave sounder (ATSR/M) This device is an experimental infrared imaging radiometer with two passive microwave channels to provide measurements of sea surface temperatures (SST), cloud-top temperatures, cloud cover and atmospheric water vapour content. The ATSR with a swath width of 500 km, a spatial resolution of 1 km and a radiometric resolution of 0.08 K, uses similar infrared channels (1.6, 3.7, 10.8 and 12 μm) to the NOAA AVHRR sensors but with enhanced accuracy due to a conical scanning technique and improved black-body calibration sources. The microwave sounder operates at 23.8 and 36.5 GHz within a 20 km footprint and will contribute to the accuracy of the ATSR SST measurements, especially in difficult atmospheric conditions.

Japanese remote-sensing satellites

To complement the MOS series of satellites, Japan will launch an Earth Resources Satellite in 1991.[34] It has much in common with the ESA's ERS-1, including its acronym (thus the Japanese satellite is to be known as JERS-1), with an SAR as its primary sensor. However, the SAR on JERS-1 will operate in the L band, permitting useful comparisons if the satellites are operational at the same time. JERS-1 will also carry a high-resolution (18 m) seven-channel passive radiometer.

Further in the future, Japan plans to launch the Advanced Earth Observation Satellite (ADEOS) carrying an ocean colour and thermal sensor and a more developed form of passive radiometer on JERS-1. It is also hoped to carry sensors supplied by other countries with the data transmitted by a Japanese data relay satellite system.

Satellite systems

Radarsat

After several fundamental changes to the payload of Canada's first remote-sensing satellite, Radarsat, to be launched in the mid 1990s, it will be a single-sensor satellite carrying only a C-band SAR. Currently deleted from the original proposed payload are a scatterometer for measuring sea surface disturbances, a high-resolution radiometer for temperature recording and the MOMS optical sensor. An idea that the satellite would be serviceable by the Shuttle has also been abandoned. It is hoped that Radarsat will have a working life of about five years and will fill the gap between ERS-1/JERS-1 and the Space Station polar platform.

Space station, Columbus and the future

The next major development in remote sensing from space will be the establishment of an international space station. This was originally proposed for construction between 1993 and 1995, but the programme has been severely delayed by the postponement of Shuttle launches. The plan was initiated by the USA, with backing from Europe, Canada and Japan.

The central part of the space station concept is a manned element in a circular orbit at an altitude of approximately 500 km and an inclination of 28.5°. However, global remote sensing is not served by such an orbit, which only covers tropical regions, and thus two polar-orbiting platforms have been proposed, one to be funded by the USA and the other to be part of ESA's Columbus programme. The preferred orbits for the polar platforms are sun-synchronous at an altitude of 950 km, with the ESA satellite crossing the equator at 10 a.m. and the NASA satellite at 2 p.m. Each satellite will have a payload weight limit of about 2,000 kg and will be serviced every 2 or 3 years. The list of candidate instruments for these platforms is already large, and studies are currently underway to specify the instruments to meet the needs of users in different disciplines and the operational, experimental and demonstration requirements of the platforms.

In the USA, one view of the space station has been proposed by a NASA team working on a study to examine the broad issues facing the earth sciences and how best they can be analyzed. The Earth Observing System (EOS) is envisioned as a total comprehensive earth science information system, rather than a series of single experiments or discipline-dedicated scientific systems, and as such must represent the optimum way forward.[35]

References

Note The National Remote Sensing Centre at the Royal Aerospace Establishment, Farnborough, Hants, has prepared a number of fact sheets on remote sensing, including a series on satellites and sensors. These fact sheets are available to any interested organizations or individual.

1. Curran, P.J. *Principles of Remote Sensing* Longman, Harlow, 1985, p.260.
2. Harris, R. *Satellite Remote Sensing – An Introduction*, Routledge & Kegan Paul, London, 1987, p.220.
3. Hord, R.M. *Remote Sensing Methods and Applications*, Wiley, New York, 1986, p.362.
4. Jensen, J.J. *Introductory Digital Image Processing: A Remote Sensing Perspective*, Prentice-Hall, Englewood Cliffs, NJ, 1986, p.368.
5. Lillesand, T.M. and Kiefer, R.W. *Remote Sensing and Image Interpretation*, Wiley, New York, 2nd edn, 1986, p.721.
6. Lo, C.P. *Applied Remote Sensing*, Longman, Harlow, 1986, p.393.
7. Mather, P.M. *Computer Processing of Remotely Sensed Images: An Introduction*, Wiley, Chichester, 1987, p.352.
8. Richards, J.A. *Remote Sensing Digital Image Analysis: An Introduction*, Springer-Verlag, Berlin, 1986, p.281.
9. Sabins, F.F. *Remote Sensing: Principles and Interpretation*, W.H. Freeman, New York, 2nd edn, 1986, p.449.
10. Townshend, J.R.G. (ed.) *Terrain Analysis and Remote Sensing*, George Allen & Unwin, London, 1981, p.232.
11. Greaves, J.K. and Shenk, W.E. The development of the geosynchronous weather satellite system. In A. Schnapf (ed.), *Monitoring Earth's Ocean, Land and Atmosphere from Space – Sensors, Systems and Applications*, American Institute of Aeronautics and Astronautics, New York, 1985, pp.150–81.
12. National Oceanic and Atmospheric Administration, *Satellite Programs, Briefing*, NOAA, Washington, DC, 1985, p.264.
13. Honvault, C. The operational Meteosat program. In A. Schnapf (ed.), *Monitoring Earth's Ocean, Land and Atmosphere from Space – Sensors, Systems and Applications*, American Institute of Aeronautics and Astronautics, New York, 1985, pp.48–92.
14. European Space Agency, Current earth observation programmes – a worldwide overview. In *Earth Observation Quarterly*, No. 18, ESA Publications Division, Noordwijk, June 1987.
15. Homma, M. and Minowa, M. Geostationary meteorological satellite system in Japan. In A. Schnapf (ed.), *Monitoring Earth's Ocean, Land and Atmosphere from Space – Sensors, Systems and Applications*, American Institute of Aeronautics and Astronautics, New York, pp.570–88.
16. Rajan, Y.S. Remote sensing activities in India – past, present and future. In A. Schnapf (ed.), *Monitoring Earth's Ocean, Land and Atmosphere from Space – Sensors, Systems and Applications*, American Institute of Aeronautics and Astronautics, New York, 1985, pp.621–38.

Satellite systems

17 Schnapf, A. The TIROS meteorological satellites – twenty five years: 1960–1985. In A. Schnapf (ed.), *Monitoring Earth's Ocean, Land and Atmosphere from Space – Sensors, Systems and Applications*, American Institute of Aeronautics and Astronautics, New York, 1985, p.51–70.
18 Haas, I.S. and Shapiro, R. The Nimbus satellite system R & D platform of the 1970's. In A. Schnapf (ed.), *Monitoring Earth's Ocean, Land and Atmosphere from Space – Sensors Systems and Applications*, American Institute of Aeronautics and Astronautics, New York, 1985, pp.71–95.
19 US Geological Survey, *Landsat Data Users' Handbook*, US Geological Survey, Arlington, VA, revised edn, 1979, p.292.
20 National Remote Sensing Centre, *Data Users' Guide*, National Remote Sensing Centre, Farnborough, 1987, p.350.
21 McCandles, S.W. Jr. Seasat – a retrospective. In A. Schnapf (ed.), *Monitoring Earth's Ocean, Land and Atmosphere from Space – Sensors, Systems and Applications*, American Institute of Aeronautics and Astronautics, New York, 1985, pp.399–418.
22 National Aeronautical and Space Administration, *Users' Guide for Direct Readout Applications – Heat Capacity Mapping Mission (HCMM)*, NASA, Greenbelt, MD, 1976, p.113.
23 Kasturirangan, K. The evolution of satellite based remote sensing capabilities in India. In A. Cracknell and L. Hayes (eds), *Remote Sensing Yearbook*, Taylor and Francis, London, 1986, pp.73–90.
24 Elachi, C., Cimino, J. and Granger, J. Remote sensing of the Earth with spaceborne imaging radars. In A. Schnapf (ed.), *Monitoring Earth's Ocean Land and Atmosphere from Space – Sensors, Systems and Applications*, American Institute of Aeronautics and Astronautics, New York, 1985, pp.639–83.
25 Schardt, B.B. and Mollberg, B.H. The orbiter camera payload system's Large Format Camera and attitude reference system. In A. Schnapf (ed.), *Monitoring Earth's Ocean, Land and Atmosphere from Space – Sensors, Systems and Applications*, American Institute of Aeronautics and Astronautics, New York, 1985, pp.685–709.
26 Bodechtel, J. and Haydn, R. MOMS-01, mission and results. In A. Schnapf (ed.), *Monitoring Earth's Ocean, Land and Atmosphere from Space – Sensors, Systems and Applications* American Institute of Aeronautics and Astronautics, New York, 1985, pp.524–35.
27 Guyenne, T.D. and Hunt, J.J. *Metric Camera Workshop*, ESA Publications Division, Noordwijk, 1985, p.210.
28 US Geological Survey, *Landsat 4 Data Users' Handbook*, US Geological Survey, Arlington, VA, 1979, p.243.
29 National Remote Sensing Centre, *SPOT Users' Guide*, National Remote Sensing Centre, Farnborough, 1987, p.52.
30 Kusanagi, M. and Ishizawa, Y. Marine observation satellite MOS-1. In A. Schnapf (ed.), *Monitoring Earth's Ocean, Land and Atmosphere from Space – Sensors, Systems and Applications*, American Institute of Aeronautics and Astronautics, New York, 1985, pp.589–605.
31 European Space Agency, *European Dissemination of Marine Observation Satellite (MOS-1) Data*, ESA Publications Division, Noordwijk, 1987, p.6.

32 EOSAT, *Landsat 6 and Sea Wide Field Sensor*, Landsat Technical Notes 2 and 3, 1987.
33 UK ERS Data Centre, *ERS-1 Fact Sheet Set*, ERS Data Centre, Farnborough, 1987.
34 Horikawa, Y. Studies on Japanese Earth Resources Satellite 1. In A. Schnapf (ed.), *Monitoring Earth's Ocean, Land and Atmosphere from Space – Sensors, Systems and Applications*, American Institute of Aeronautics and Astronautics, New York, 1985, pp.606–20.
35 Broome, D.R. Jr. The earth observing system. In A. Schnapf (ed.), *Monitoring Earth's Ocean, Land and Atmosphere from Space – Sensors, Systems and Applications*, American Institute of Aeronautics and Astronautics, New York, 1985, pp.797–822.

Chapter three

Telecommunications satellites

G. Groom

Introduction to the Intelsat Organization

The world's global satellite communications revolution began in 1945, when Arthur C. Clarke published in *Wireless World* a description of how a network of three geosynchronous communications satellites could be launched and a global system operated. No one took the concept very seriously, including Clarke himself. He envisaged that such a satellite system would require manned space stations and concluded that a maintenance crew would be needed to maintain and operate the system. He simply did not believe that such a system would be operational within his lifetime. Only a few years later, a dramatic breakthrough occurred at the Bell Laboratories when transistors were developed which became the enabling technology that produced, among other achievements, the age of satellites.

In the late 1950s both the USA and the USSR began to develop satellites and the necessary launch vehicles to place them in orbit. In 1957 Sputnik, the world's first artificial satellite, was launched and was followed by the United States Explorer in January 1958. In December 1958 Score, the world first active communications satellite, was launched; active satellites amplify signals from the earth and retransmit them. The Echo satellites that followed in the early 1960s were passive; they merely reflected signals back to the earth. The active medium altitude satellites Telstar and Relay were launched in 1962. The rockets available in the early 1960s could only place satellites into orbits no higher than 10,000 km above the earth, i.e. at a medium altitude. The challenge was to increase the orbital height to approximately 36,000 km above the earth's Equator in a circular equatorial orbit; the orbital period would then be 1 day and the orbit would be geosynchronous, i.e. its position in space would appear fixed relative to the ground stations. The first geosynchronous satellite was Syncom 11, which was launched in 1963 and had the obvious advantage of simplifying the ground-station's antenna tracking system. As early in 1959 the potential use of satellites

Telecommunications satellites

for international communications was recognized and it was agreed at the World Administrative Radio Conference (WARC) held in that year that there should be an Extraordinary Administrative Radio Conference in 1963 to allocate frequencies for this purpose. Subsequent to the adoption of this resolution, the Communications Satellite Act of 1962 was passed into law in the USA. This law created the Communications Satellite Corporation (COMSAT) and established a US legislative mandate to set up a global communications satellite system. On 20 January 1964 the Interim Agreement establishing the International Telecommunications Satellite Organisation (INTELSAT) was signed by eleven founder members. COMSAT provided the USA's representation on the Interim Communications Satellite Committee (ICSC) which governed the consortium. This predominance gave concern to other countries. However, the Interim Agreement provided a practical solution in that there was an obligation to negotiate a definitive set of agreements in the future which, among other things, were to reflect the expected technologies in the rest of the world. In February 1973 the definitive Intelsat arrangements came into force and now Intelsat has 114 member countries.

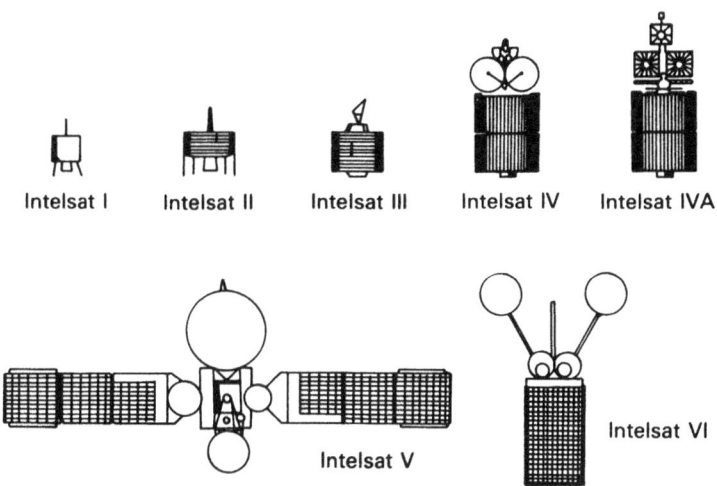

Figure 3.1 Growth of Intelsat satellites

Satellite systems

The Intelsat Satellites

There was concern regarding the effects of the time delay associated with the greater than 70,000 km total transmission path of a one-way channel. Furthermore, there were those who believed that a series of small low-cost communications satellites, launched several at a time into a lower earth orbit, could be a more cost-effective approach. In the years from 1965 to 1975, the Intelsat network grew from sixty telephone circuits to approximately 10,000 circuits and the number is expected to exceed 40,000 by 1990 (Figure 3.1).

Intelsat I – Early Bird

In April 1965 Intelsat launched Intelsat I and it not only demonstrated that geosynchronous operation was feasible but it also stimulated new telephone, telegraph and television services. Although the satellite with an in-orbit mass of only 40 kg represented a rather primitive technology by today's standards, it was an important and significant beginning.

In 1965, in addition to the earth stations in the UK and France, two more had been built in Europe, one at Raisting in the FRG and the other at Fucino in Italy. However, the characteristics of Intelsat I were such that only two earth stations could access the satellite simultaneously, and therefore it was possible only to establish point-to-point trunk traffic between Europe and the USA. To enable all the European earth stations to participate in this venture, a three week rota was established between the German, French and UK earth stations. On this basis, operations grew over the next two years from sixty circuits to 240 circuits. In addition, a second earth station in North America became operational at Mill Village, Nova Scotia, Canada, and shared operations with the Andover earth stations in the USA. As an alternative to the telephony service, television transmission could be provided. Intelsat I was initially expected to have a lifetime of 18 months but it was still operational, although not in use, five years after its launch.

Intelsat II

Intelsat II was designed with a life of 3 years and was at the same height as Intelsat I but twice the diameter. Because of its multiple access capability, it was possible to provide a simultaneous television transmission by reducing the telephony capacity by 50 per cent.

The first Intelsat II was positioned over the Pacific Ocean in January 1967. Initially it provided a service between the Brewster Flats earth station near Washington on the west coast of the USA and an earth station at Paumalu on the island of Oahu in the Hawaiian group. Because of its 120 MHz transponder bandwidth it was able to support traffic between the two earth stations in the USA and Japan and Australia. In April 1967 the second Intelsat II satellite was launched and positioned over the Atlantic Ocean. It enabled all seven of the existing earth stations in the region to operate continuously, rather than on a rota basis. In November 1967 the third Intelsat II satellite for service in the Pacific Ocean region was launched and in 1968 both regions had a two-satellite complement.

Intelsat III

By July 1969, some six months after the first Intelsat III went into service in the Atlantic Ocean region, a truly global system had been established with Intelsat III satellites in the Atlantic Ocean, Pacific Ocean and Indian Ocean regions. These were spin-stabilized satellites 1.4 m in diameter and 1.0 m high, and they weighed 300 kg at launch. They utilized the two 500 MHz bands allocated to the fixed-service satellite system in the 4GHz and 6 GHz frequency bands with two transponders, each of bandwidth 225 MHz. Each satellite received signals in the 3,707–4,193 MHz band through an antenna system that provided global earth coverage, i.e. coverage over the whole of the earth's surface as visible from the satellite. The capacity of an Intelsat III satellite was approximately 1,200 circuits plus one television channel.

By the end of 1970, just over two years from the start of the launching of the Intelsat III satellites, there were twenty stations operating in the Atlantic region, fourteen in the Pacific region and twelve in the Indian Ocean region. The Intelsat III satellite programme was no an unqualified success. Of the eight attempted launches, three were abortive, and out of the five successful launches, two had serious antenna de-spin problems and received an early retirement from service. Two others had serious communications equipment problems, which resulted in their traffic capacity being considerably reduced. Another later developed the same antenna de-spin problem and was prematurely retired from service. Although the satellites were intended to have a life of 5 years, the time from the launch of the first one to the replacement in service of the last one was barely 3.5 years.

Despite these difficulties, the Intelsat III satellites will always have an honourable place in the history of satellite communications as the satellites which provided the first truly global international satellite communications system.

Satellite systems

Intelsat IV

Eight Intelsat IV satellites were launched between January 1971 and May 1975, and Flight 7 was the only one which failed to achieve operational status. They were 2.4 m in diameter and 5.3 m high with a mass of 1,385 mg (mass in transfer orbit) and their design life was 7 years. The prime power supply was developed from solar cells, developing 480 W at end of life; also included were two 15 A h batteries to ensure continuity of service during the eclipse periods when the satellite is in the shadow of the earth. The Intelsat IV satellite had a theoretical maximum traffic capacity of approximately 9,000 circuits, but when configured to meet the actual traffic requirements the capacity was of the order of 4,000 circuits plus television. A circuit is a two-way connection and consists of two satellite channels. The increase in capacity, compared with an Intelsat III, was due to the increase in the power from the solar cells (134–480W) and the inclusion of spot beam antennas which increased the effective power in the downpath. The effective downpath power is known as the effective isotropic radiated power (EIRP) of the satellite and is quoted in dBW.

The Intelsat IV satellites used the same 500 MHz bands for transmit (4 GHz) and receive (6 GHz) as the Intelsat III. However, the spectrum was divided into bands of 36 MHz by using twelve separate transponders (Figure 3.2). Significant features of the Intelsat IV satellite included:

- single polarization sense in the receive antenna (left-hand circular);
- four independent pre-amplifier/drive chains;
- single-frequency conversion from receive to transmit frequencies;
- a twelve-channel input multiplexer;
- channelized group delay equalization and gain adjustment;
- redundant travelling-wave tube (TWT) amplifiers for each of the twelve channels;
- single polarization sense in the transmit antennas (right-hand circular).

The first eight channels could be individually connected to either global or spot-beam transmit antennas; the remaining four channels were permanently connected to the global transmit antenna (Figure 3.3). Channels 1, 3, 5 and 7 were connected to either the global beam antenna or to the west spot-beam antenna. Channels 2, 4, 6 and 8 were connected to either the global beam antenna or to the east spot-beam antenna.

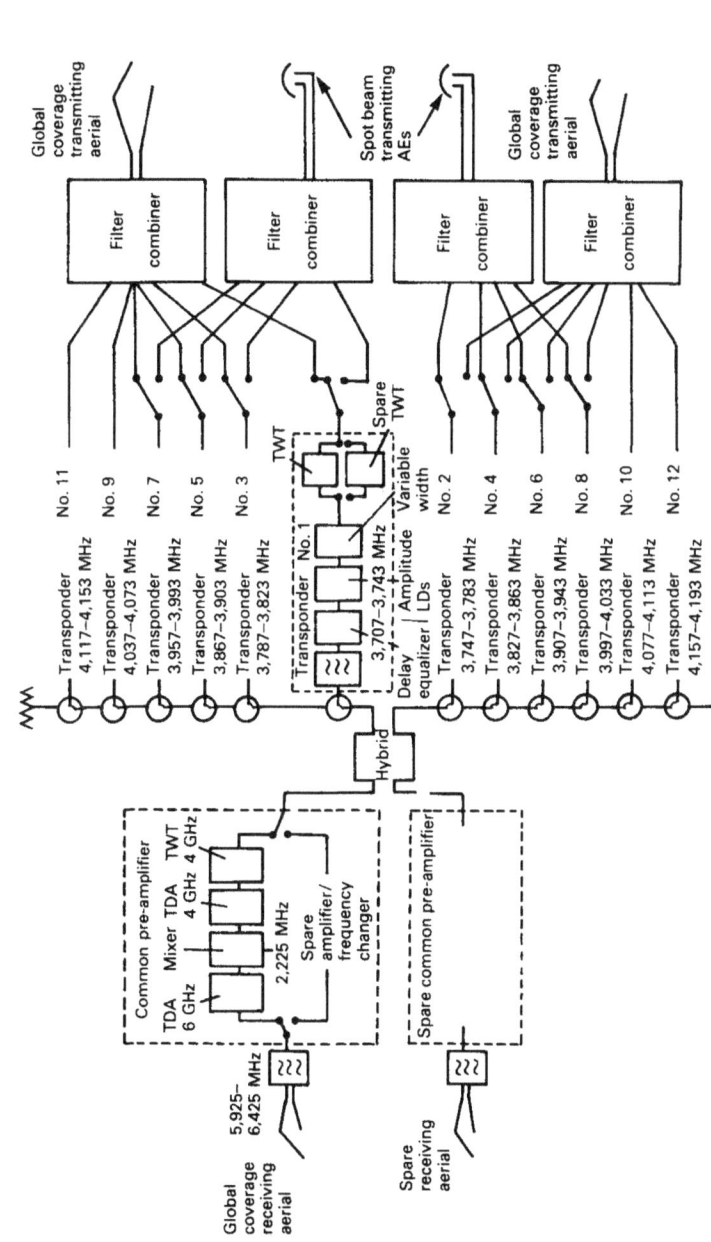

Figure 3.2 Schematic diagram of Intelsat IV

Satellite systems

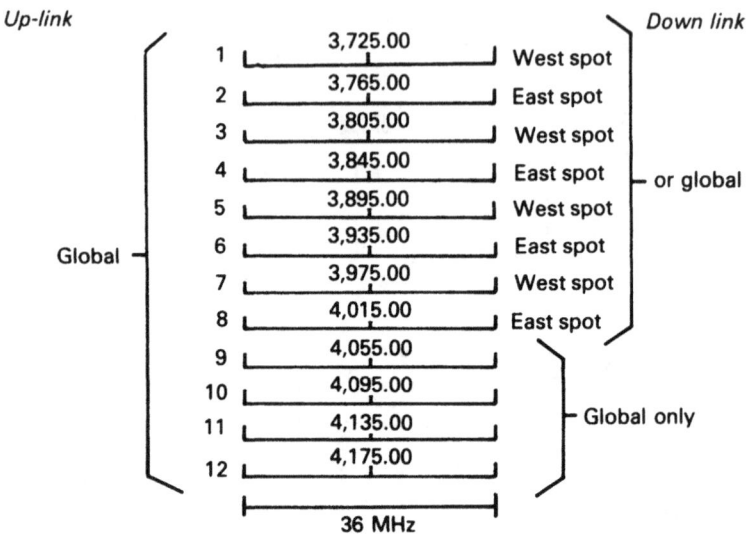

Figure 3.3 Transponder frequency plan and beam switching

Intelsat IVA

The first Intelsat IVA was launched in 1975 in response to the ever-increasing demand for international communications. Six were launched, although Flight 4 was a launch failure. The satellite, which was an enhanced version of Intelsat IV, introduced a new concept of frequency re-use by spatial beam separation. Although 500 MHz of bandwidth was allocated, the satellite utilized isolation of eastern and western continental beams to achieve an almost twofold increase in the available bandwidth. This frequency re-use technique increased the capacity of 6,000 circuits without a significant increase in the mass of the satellite.

The frequency and polarization plan was the same as in the case of Intelsat IV, with the frequency band divided into twelve channels, each 36 kHz wide and spaced at 40 MHz intervals. Channels 6, 8, 10 and 12 were used for global coverage communications, while the other eight channels were available for frequency re-use. Therefore there was an effective twenty-channel capability. If required, the number of global channels could be increased to six by ground command, with a corresponding decrease in the number of shaped-beam (spot-beam) channels.

This facility is of particular importance in the Indian Ocean region, where increased global capacity is required. Some of the channels used identical frequency bands, e.g. transponder (or channel) 1A used the same frequency band as transponder 1B but was connected to a different beam; therefore earth stations in the eastern hemisphere could transmit on identical frequencies to those in the western hemisphere.

Intelsat V

Nine Intelsat V satellites were launched from December 1980 to June 1984 with Flight 9 being an Atlas Centaur launch failure. Flights 5–9 included a maritime communications subsystem module (MCS). With the launch of this satellite three major technical advancements were introduced into the Intelsat system:

1 three-axis body stabilization of the spacecraft by using momentum wheels;
2 frequency re-use at 6/4 GHz by polarization discrimination as well as by spatial separation to give a fourfold use of the frequency band;
3 use of the 14/11 GHz bands with orthogonal linear polarization for the two directions of transmission.

The capacity of an Intelsat V satellite is approximately 12,000 simultaneous circuits and two TV channels, depending upon how the traffic is configured. If a satellite is accessed by frequency division multiplexing (FDMA) by a large number of small carriers, then the capacity will be less than accessing it by fewer larger carriers. Four different types of beam can be transmitted and received by the satellite; global, west/east hemispheric, west/east zone and west/east spot.

The global and hemispheric coverages in the 6/4 GHz band are overlaid by two coverages in the same frequency band but of reverse polarization. Additionally, there are two spot-beam coverages in the 14/11 GHz band and these are reverse polarized with respect to each other. It is possible to interconnect various receive coverages to various transmit coverages within the satellite. To achieve the required signal paths, transmission channels are established by connecting a receiver which is accessible from one of the reception coverages in either the 6 or 14 GHz frequency bands to transmitters associated with the same and/or any of the other transmission coverages in either the 4 or 11 GHz frequency bands, with each connection established over a segment of each frequency band.

There are two separate feed arrays and reflectors associated with the 4 and 6 GHz cross-polarized hemispheric and zone coverage 'footprints'. The 14/11 GHz spot-beams are provided by two separate

Satellite systems

antenna systems, and global coverage is provided by the 6/4 GHz horns. The transponders are configured with fifteen receivers, seven input multiplexers, a matrix-switching arrangement and up-converters for ten channels to 11 GHz, followed by forty-three TWT amplifiers in a redundant configuration. There are twenty-seven independent channels with bandwidths ranging from 34 to 241 MHz. Flexibility, by means of interconnections through the output multiplexer, results in 534 combinations of global, hemispheric, zone and spot coverages. A total bandwidth of 2,241 MHz is realized in a RF spectrum of 912 MHz.

In summary, an Intelsat V satellite has a launch mass of 1869 kg, generates 1200 W of d.c. power from 20 m^2 of solar cells with a 'wing span' of over 15 m and has a lifetime of 7 years.

Intelsat VA

Three Intelsat VA satellites were launched between March 1985 and September 1985. In terms of its communications capabilities, Intelsat VA is basically an Intelsat V without an MCS package but including:

1 three additional global beam transponders operating in the opposite sense of polarization from the Intelsat V global beam transponders;
2 two additional zone coverage transponders which are switchable to the global beam;
3 a set of two cross-polarized steerable spot-beams operating in the 4 GHz band for the provision of domestic services.

Intelsat VB

Three Intelsat VBs, alternatively known as Intelsat VA (IBS), have been built, but unfortunately the first was an Ariane launch failure. Their communications capabilities for conventional international services are basically the same as Intelsat VA with additional capabilities for the provision of high-powered business communications services:

1 a switchable K band capability will enable the operation of the K band transponders at either 14/11 GHz or 14/12 GHz;
2 an expanded west spot beam equal in size to the elliptical east spot beam, but with a different orientation, will be used in order to provide K band coverage to a larger number of business centres in North America.

Intelsat operational satellites

Currently the Intelsat operational satellites are:

- two Intelsat IVAs;
- four Intelsat Vs;
- four Intelsat Vs with maritime communications subsystems, which are leased to Inmarsat;
- three Intelsat VAs;
- two Intelsat VBs are to be launched.

Intelsat VI – 1990

In 1981 Intelsat completed the specification for Intelsat VI and, after competitive bidding, five satellites were ordered from the Hughes Aircraft Company in 1982. Approximately 17 per cent of the work was placed with non-US companies. The first launch is scheduled for 1989 and others are scheduled for 1990 and 1991. The launch vehicle will be either the two-stage Titan III with an additional perigee stage so that the satellite will achieve the required transfer orbit, or the three-stage Ariane 4.

Intelsat VI is a spin-stabilized satellite 11.8 m high when the solar drum is lowered and the antennas deployed. It maintains compatibility with Intelsat V with some additional features:

1. an operational life of 10–14 years;
2. improved frequency re-use by using the 6/4 GHz bands six times and the 14/11 GHz bands twice;
3. additional zone beam transponders;
4. two additional 72 MHz hemispheric beam transponders in the band 3.6–3.7 GHz;
5. additional Ku band transponders;
6. increased EIRP (global beam, 26.5 dBW; east/west hemispheric, 31 dBW; east/west zone, 31 dBW; east/west spot, 41.7–47.7 dBW);
7. satellite-switched time-division multiple access (SS-TDMA).

An interconnection matrix is able to switch rapidly so that the TDMA bursts can be dynamically routed from various uplinks to specific downlinks. The pattern of switching can be reconfigured by ground command and can be bypassed by static switches if the satellite is being used in a role where TDMA is not operational. This represents a major advance in efficiency over the present static uplink–downlink transponder assignments.

It is expected that three Intelsat VIs will be deployed in the Atlantic Ocean Region (AOR) and two in the Indian Ocean Region (IOR).

Satellite systems

Intelsat VII – 1993

The current procurement plans are flexible with an initial buy of three to four spacecraft with an option for further purchase. These satellites are designed primarily for the Pacific Ocean Region (POR), and in their technical complexity will be between Intelsat V and Intelsat VI. They will be used in a less demanding role in the AOR. An exciting feature of these satellites is the possibility of using xenon ion thrusters for North–South station keeping and this could lead to the satellite's having a 20 year lifetime.

Future prospects for the Intelsat system

In view of the declining telephony trunking over satellites because of the competition from optical fibre submarine cables, Intelsat has already adopted two methods for the re-alignment of its services.

1 Reducing the specification of the ground-stations necessary to access the satellites, which will have the effect of reducing the cost of the earth stations but decreasing their channel capacity.
2 Introducing new services.
 (a) Planned Domestic Services (PDS) will give the opportunity for the members of Intelsat to purchase transponders on a planned non-pre-emptible basis for voice, data and television distribution.
 (b) The VISTA service provides domestic and international voice and low-rate data over leased transponders using 10 m or 5 m ground-station antennas.
 (c) The Intelsat Business System (IBS) is used for voice, high-speed data, fax, electronic document distribution, funds transfer and video conferencing.
 (d) Mobile Satellite Services (MSS): existing maritime services are to be joined by aeronautical and land-mobile systems.
 (e) Intelnet is a digital data distribution system for light traffic streams on a full or occasional use basis. It uses antennas down to 0.6 m in diameter and is used by financial and news organizations. For example, Reuters is using the system for communicating with Latin America using 1.4 m antennas.
 (f) Very small aperture terminals (VSATs) provide a receive-only or transmit–receive service for point-to-point traffic or as part of a private network. VSATs have proved popular in the USA and Intelsat have been promoting the implementation of VSAT networks through the Intelnet services.
 (g) TV distribution: in 1986 the figure for occasional use over the Intelsat satellites increased by 20% over 1985 to over 60,000 channel hours.

Telecommunications satellites

The European Satellite Communications Organization (Eutelsat)

Eutelsat was established in 1977, as an interim organization, by seventeen PTTs within the European Conference of Postal and Telecommunications Authorities (CEPT). The definitive status of Eutelsat was adopted in 1985 with twenty-six signatories. When it was formed its prime objectives were to provide the space segment for a public telecommunications service in Europe and to enable the European Broadcasting Union (EBU) to extend its Eurovision network. Originally the European Space Agency (ESA) agreement with Eutelsat called for a two-satellite in-orbit configuration, one operational and one in-orbit spare. The configuration is now three in-orbit, one 'main mission' satellite and two satellites carrying leased television services.

Types of service

There are three main categories of Eutelsat services.

Public telecommunications

The routing of telephone circuits including telex, facsimile, low-speed data etc. is by pulse code modulation (PCM) of the channels, TDM and four-phase quadrature phase-shift keying (QPSK) with absolute encoding and coherent demodulation at a bit rate of 120 Mbit s^{-1}. Multiple access to the satellite uses TDMA technology. Digital speech interpolation (DSI) effectively doubles the number of simultaneous calls that can be established.

Television

Two leased transponders of the Eutelsat 1-F2 satellite are used, within the framework of Eurovision, for the transmission of high-quality television programmes between broadcasting authorities that are members of the EBU. The transmission uses an analogue technique with wideband frequency modulation and sound-in-sync for the associated sound. Full digital techniques are planned to be introduced at a later date. Transponder leasing on a long-term basis (3 year average) for domestic reception and distribution to cable television networks has been a rapidly expanding area of activity, and because of the unsatisfied demand the system had to be developed from a two-satellite system to three operational satellites.

Satellite multiservices – 12 GHz downlink

Satellite multiservices include a variety of digital integrated services covering the transmission of data, speech, text and image. They are aimed at the business community whose telecommunication needs

Satellite systems

cannot be satisfied by the existing European public network. Therefore Eutelsat has established its Satellite Multiservices System (SMS) for business applications in Europe. It is designed to operate with small dish terminals which can be installed on the business premises, thus avoiding the need for long terrestrial extensions. The 12 GHz frequency band is not allocated to the terrestrial microwave system and this enables satellite terminals to be located anywhere in the system coverage area without regard to the problems of mutual interference. The system offers user bit rates between 2.4 kbit s^{-1} and 2 mbit s^{-1} and the channels are allocated on a full-time or part-time basis with a standard quality of 10E-6 BER for 99 per cent of the year or an optional higher quality of 10E-10 BER for 99 per cent of the year. Access to the satellite is by single channel per carrier (SCPC) Eutelsat SMS was designed to operate as an open network in which all transmissions fully comply with specified characteristics. However, individual customers requirements can be met by operating in a closed network with transmission parameters and earth station characteristics departing from the specified SMS system.

The Eutelsat satellites

The Eutelsat I satellites were constructed as the result of a European Communications Satellite (ECS) programme undertaken by the ESA in the early 1970s. Five satellites were produced, including Flight 3 which was a launch failure in 1985. There are now three in operation, one 'main services' and two carrying leased TV services: Eutelsat 1, F1 at 13°E (1983); Eutelsat 1, F2 at 7°E (1984); Eutelsat 1, F4 at 10°E (1987); Eutelsat 1, F5 will be launched in 1989 (Table 3.1).

Eutelsat will start replacing the first-generation satellites by the Eutelsat II series in 1990. For the Eutelsat II series, control will be moved from the ESA Satellite Operations Centre in Darmstadt, FRG, to Paris, with back-up/reference stations in Rambouillet, France, and Sintra, Portugal. The main control centre in Paris, with manual, automatic and scheduled control options, will be linked to the other two via a private packet switched network.

European television broadcasting by satellite

The existing satellites Eutelsat I and Intelsat V with an EIRP of 45 dBW are primarily intended for cable television (CATV). The medium-powered satellites Eutelsat II (1990) and Astra (1988) of the Société Européene des Satellites (SES), Luxembourg, with an EIRP of 52 dBW, will be able to be received using an antenna 60 cm in diameter (Table 3.2).

Table 3.1 Summary of the Eutelsat satellites

	Eutelsat 1-F1	Eutelsat 1-F2-F5	Eutelsat II
Date launched and position	10/86 13°E	F2 8/84 7°E F3 9/85 failed F4 10/87 10°E F5 1989	1990-1
Frequency bands (frequency re-use by orthogonal linear polarization)	Up-path 14–14.5 GHz Downpath 10.95–11.2 GHz 11.45–11.7 GHz	AS F1 + 12.5–12.583 GHz (SMS)	As Eutelsat 1 with 12 GHz band extended to 12.75 GHz
Number of transponders	12, with 10 in simultaneous use and 6 in eclipse	12 x 14/11 GHz 2 x 14/12 GHz 10 in simultaneous use and in eclipse	16
Transponder bandwith	72 MHz		80 MHz and 40 MHz
TWT amplifier output power	20 W		50 W
Transmit beams	Spot Atlantic Spot East Spot West Euro beam	AS F1 + SMS	Widebeam coverage High gain coverage
ERIPs	Spot beams Euro beams	45.5–46 dBW 41dBW at beam edge 41dBW at beam centre 37dBW at beam edge	Widebeam 44 dBW High gain 50 dBW

The high-powered satellites, which can be classified as direct broadcasting satellites (DBSs) with an EIRP of greater than 60 dBW, will require antennas of 30–40 cm in diameter in order to receive acceptable quality television signals. The high-powered European satellites include the following. The British Satellite Broadcasting (BSB) won a franchise from the Independent Broadcasting Authority (IBA) and was operational in 1990 offering a three-channel service for the UK only. It will be a two-satellite system. The FRG's Deutsche Bundespost has a commitment to a two-satellite system (TV-SAT). However, the first satellite, after a successful launch, was unable to operate after one solar panel failed to open. Telediffusion de France (TDF-1) is to be launched in late 1988. TV-SAT and TDF-1 are a joint Franco-German venture and will have four channels which will be extended to five channels. The receiver band is 17.3–18.1 GHz and the

Satellite systems

transmit band is 11.7–12.5 GHz. In addition, the Deutsche Bundespost's system, the Deutsche Fernmeldesatelliten-System (DFS) Kopernikus programme, represents a major national communications system. The first satellite was launched in November 1988 and the space segment will consist of two operational satellites with one back-up. Television distribution is fundamental to the Kopernikus programme and two out of seven transponders of the first launch will be dedicated to business services using TDMA with demand assignment (DA).

Table 3.2 Technical criteria of the Astra satellites

Manufacturer/type	RCA 4000
Launch vehicle	Ariane 4
Orbital longitudes	19°E and 1° E
Stabilization	Three-axis
Design life	10 years
Channel capacity	16 transponders, fully eclipse protected and 6 spare
Transponder bandwidth	2426 MHz
Polarization	Dual linear
EIRP	50–51 dBW minimum
TWT amplifier power output	47 W
Mass on station	1,020 kg
Electrical power	2,850 W at end of life
Frequency bands	Receive 14.2–14.5 GHz
	Transmit 11.2–11.45 GHz
Telemetry beacons	11.2030 and 11.4465 GHz

Part II
Satellites and the teaching and learning of subjects

Chapter four

Geography and environmental science

Keith Hilton

Introduction

When the first weather satellite was launched in 1960, geography was awaiting its conceptual revolution and school geography was dominated by the regional paradigm. Almost thirty years later people-environment, ecosystem, spatial analysis and humanistic paradigms compete. Concerns stressing the process of learning, enquiry learning and values clarification confront vocational–utilitarian philosophies. Issues of relevance have also been debated – the relevance of the content of geographical and environmental education to the pupils and students, and the relevance of the disciplines themselves to society. Finally, of course, there are the professional issues like examination developments and changes in school organization which have also absorbed teachers' energies. Describing the achievement of satellite remote sensing in geography and environmental education therefore has to be undertaken with a realistic awareness of such a background.

This section explores satellite remote sensing in geography and environmental education through a brief review of aims and objectives in general, and then overviews the history of provision in this curriculum area. It then looks at two products which illustrate the exploitation of satellite remote sensing in geography and the kinds of classroom work which can be undertaken.

Aims, objectives and satellite remote sensing

Geography has traditionally been eclectic. It has borrowed concepts, skills and data from a range of cognate disciplines. In the recent past it has adopted curriculum change readily, the Schools Council's projects being a case in point. It has also absorbed new technology and has been one of the humanities' pacesetters in Computer-assisted learning (CAL). In this kind of spirit it has 'borrowed' satellite remote sensing. The geographer's prime interest has lain, not in how the images have been obtained and processed, but much more in what environmental information they contain and what sort of cognitive and affective stimulus they can offer. Geographers have also been restricted in the range of satellites that they have been interested in. Their attention has been focused largely on earth resources satellites like Landsat and SPOT and to a lesser extent on the meteorological satellites.

During the period of satellite remote-sensing development, partly as a consequence of the aspects mentioned earlier, geographical education has become more explicit and sophisticated in its consideration of aims and objectives. These are now frequently based on an interplay between considerations of general educational aims and discipline-derived aims. The latter dimension involves considering how geography can satisfy general educational needs.

A school geography course related only to the environments which the pupils and students can experience at first hand would be very limiting. Geography teachers have thus always been faced with the need to provide substitutes for first-hand experience. They have done this by means of the words, pictures and data in books and by slides, film, video and of course maps. Each of these substitutes for direct environmental stimulus and data have involved their own range of demands on teachers and pupils. For example, learning the language of maps, the distortions of low-level oblique aerial photography, and the bias of photographs and text have been practical issues of concern to geography teachers at all levels, as is revealed in the attention given to them in the Geographical Association's handbook[1] and the UNESCO handbook.[2]

Traditionally the training and education of geography teachers has involved them in exposure to 'classroom escape mechanisms' – the slides, videos, texts and maps mentioned above – in both their own geographical academic training and their professional training. In the case of satellite remote sensing the situation is more complex. The speed of development of satellite remote sensing has meant that only about a third of geography teachers have been exposed to it and a much smaller proportion explicitly trained in it.[3] This lack of remote-sensing expertise was also commented on by the House of Lords Select Committee on Science and Technology in their investigation of remote sensing and digital mapping.[4] It has also been frequently cited as a problem in the diffusion of educational remote sensing.[5]

Although teachers' knowledge has been a limiting factor in the development of educational remote sensing, its positive attributes have long been identified and promoted. In 1976 NASA produced *Mission to Earth*, a superb collection of Landsat images, and in the *Educator's Guide* it was stated that Landsat Imagery holds promise of being important in helping students become more aware of the world in which they live. If this awareness can be considered a basic objective of

Geography and environmental science

education at all levels it is necessary that educators find realistic and efficient approaches to meet this objective.[6] Milne[7] made a number of claims about the potential of Landsat in teaching about the environment, and Smith[8] claimed that pupils using Landsat made more statements with greater accuracy and more interest. In 1986 the HMI report *Geography from 5 to 16* stated that 'in recent years remote sensing from satellites has improved our knowledge of weather systems, contributed to resource exploration and to land use mapping, and aided systematic monitoring of natural disasters and of the environmental impact of human activities. The study of geography should help make sense of the information which can be obtained from such sources.'[9] The task has therefore been to match this promise with the real knowledge and abilities of geography teachers and pupils. How this task has been met can best be seen by examining the history of satellite remote-sensing educational products.

The history of provision

Satellite remote sensing is a classic example of a product-led educational innovation.[10] The results of a new technology have, with varying degrees of success, been laid before geography and environmental educators who have then been faced with the tasks of learning about it and assessing its educational utility. Only in 1988 in the Spaceview UK package[11] have classroom teachers been able to influence the remote-sensing provision. (More substantial details of provision and availability can be obtained from the *Sourcebook of Remote Sensing*[12] and from Carter's section in the *Handbook for Geography Teachers*.[1])

A basic characteristic of the history of provision is lag: between the start of meteorological satellite operations and the first appearance of a pupil hardcopy package (SATPAC); between the start of the Landsat series and the appearance of slide sets.

Another element has been the lack of continuing commercial inputs. Provision has been characterized by what can only be called a series of 'one offs'. The slide sets which appeared in 1981 using Landsat MSS false colour composites have not been followed by a similar Landsat thematic mapper (TM) product and the same is true of overhead projector transparency provision. This reflects the small market base and the relatively high cost of satellite remote-sensing products. Costs have certainly been cited as a problem by Curran and Wardley[5] and the same message came through from survey evidence.[3] The diversity of potential demand may also contribute to the market size problem. Teachers often wish to have imagery of their local or field work areas, and when this is combined with a wish for large-scale images a commercially viable market can hardly be said to exist. Even large-scene

The teaching and learning of subjects

coverage is difficult because in conceptually defined syllabuses schools can have considerable choice in the exact geographic location of their examples.

Meteorological provision has been rather mixed. Specific meteorological courses are very small in number and most UK pupils experience it within their geography courses. The subject is perceived by geography pupils and many teachers as being 'difficult'. When options exist it has tended to be avoided, and the largest Schools Council curriculum project, the Avery Hill project, had a human geography bias. For reasons of this type the use of satellite remote-sensing products in this area has been limited. This could change with more collaborative work by geographers with science departments, aided by the arrival of low-cost receiving equipment giving real-time images as a teaching resource for the first time.

Many of the products have had little educational research backing and have not provided products with the most useful scale, format or coverage. Many items have good technical detail included (on satellites and their sensors) and descriptions of the contents of the scenes. However, two products may be worthy of more detailed discussion as they illustrate the possibilities of linking satellite remote sensing to established teaching situations.

Incorporating remote sensing in geography teaching: two exemplars

The first example is the Australian *Landsat Images for the Classroom*.[13] These were promoted as 'a series of kits bringing the latest advances in space technology into your classroom'. They contained a Landsat MSS OHP and overlays, slides sets, coloured prints, maps and a teacher's handbook. Their coverage was based on city-centred areas in Australia.

The handbook claimed that Landsat MSS offered a new way of looking at regional geography; it suggested using the OHP and treating it as a map adding successive OHP overlays of place names, contours, water features and communications. An interesting part of the project was the way in which the authors used major geographical concepts from the Queensland Syllabus.[14] This identified four basic spatial concepts – location, distribution, association and movement. It also addressed concepts of scale, change through time and perception, and involved ideas of geographical contributions to planning and decision-making.

Table 4.1 outlines the approach of the kit (the example here is from the Brisbane, Queensland, materials) and the way in which it linked geographical concepts, derived from the syllabus, to the classroom use of the Landsat 1:1,000,000 MSS false colour composites, overlays and slides.

Geography and environmental science

Table 4.1 Examples of linking geographical concepts to pupil use of Landsat MSS: the Jacaranda kits

Concept aspects	Examples of pupil use of Landsat MSS
Location distance	How far is it from Brisbane to Toowoomba? Why would it take longer to travel from Brisbane to Boonah than Brisbane to the Gold Coast, although the distances are similar?
Direction	What is the direction of (list of Queensland towns) from Brisbane?
Site	What factors would have influenced the decision to found the earliest penal settlement at Radcliffe in 1824 rather than Brisbane? Why is the Wivenhoe dam being constructed on the Brisbane River?
Situation (relative location)	Where is Brisbane located with respect to (list towns)? Suggest why Brisbane is the major urban centre in the region. Indicate some problems in building a main road west from Brisbane

The handbook also suggested that the four aspects of location could be integrated by asking pupils to identify the water storage areas, identify the largest and comment on its site; methods suggested involved tracing overlaps on the hard copy with work as individuals or groups

Distribution	Density	Using a grid calculate the density of land use...?
The arrangement of one phenomenon on the earth's surface	Dispersion	Activities involving measuring aerial extent
Distributions produce aerial association	Centralization	Trace and locate Brisbane and *x* other towns; insert main roads, railways and describe the pattern and how it relates to physical features
	Patterns of distribution	Describe the facilities of the Port of Brisbane and suggest why new facilities are situated on the estuary mouth. Describe the distribution of irrigated farmland and explain why a dam is important to this pattern
The degree to which one distribution is similar or different to another; raises the question of casual relations	Association	Trace upland areas and dense vegetation. Suggest how upland distribution influences the distribution of dense vegetation

83

The handbook also commented on the concept of the region and how Landsat MSS could contribute to the classification of single-feature and multiple-feature regions. It also included some points about hypothesizing, together with examples from physical and economic geography. Finally there was a short comment on Landsat images and the development of aesthetic appreciation.

Each of the slides in the set contained a paragraph on 'content' and a paragraph on 'suggested use'. For example one slide contained bands 4, 5, 6 and 7 of the Brisbane area. The content section explained these, and the teacher use section suggested a classroom discussion of what is 'visible' which would lead into a discussion of the infrared bands 6 and 7. Some slides were false colour composites, some had annotation and scale grids, and there were a number of subscene enlargements.

Given the date of its production this series was an excellent product exploiting the aerial coverage of Landsat MSS and working within the limits of its resolution. In retrospect, the attempt to link the material to an actual geography curriculum was its major contribution.

The second product described, Spaceview UK,[11] is rather different. Since it was published a decade after the last example, an obvious difference is in the basic source of satellite data. Unlike the Jacaranda kit, which used early Landsat MSS data, Spaceview UK used TM imagery with its 30 m resolution. Second it is an example of a non-commercial collaborative effort to produce sets of low-cost hard copy (i.e. 30 cm x 30 cm 1:100,000 scale colour prints). The collaboration was between the National Remote Sensing Centre (NRSC), the Field Studies Council, the Remote Sensing Society and the Geographical Association's Satellite Remote Sensing Working Group, each of whom committed resources and/or manpower to the project. Third, of course, Spaceview UK has been produced in the context of a different educational system. Finally, and the reason for describing it here, it tried to incorporate the results of experience and research.

The limited amount of educational enquiry undertaken in the field of satellite remote sensing in the UK has been largely completed by practising teachers undertaking personal unfunded research for higher-degree work. Their sample sixes, their range of topic coverage and so on has inevitably been small. Only one survey of use, teacher opinion and the policy of providers (publishers and the remote-sensing institutions), has been undertaken[3] and this was restricted to southeast England. Experience, research and survey have, however, thrown up three problems: costs, teachers' knowledge and the need to interpret. These will now be considered in turn, although in reality they interrelate.

High cost has been a frequently voiced criticism of educational satellite remote sensing. The cost factor hardly applied to some of the products. Slide sets are a case in point. Those provided by the NRSC

Geography and environmental science

(*Introduction to Remote Sensing, Coastal Processes* and *Applications in Geology*) and the sets produced by Focal Pint in 1981, for example, had similar prices to those of other educational sets. Posters, because of their larger print runs, are inevitably a relatively low-cost hard-copy provision. The NRSC currently has five: *Britain and Ireland*, a mosaic in simulated natural colour, *The Third Planet*, a Meteosat view, *The Isle of Lewis*, false colour, and *Europe*, a NOAA AVHRR simulated natural colour mosaic. Whilst suitable for wall decoration and general stimulus the temporal/seasonal span in such mosaics causes problems. The cost of colour photographic prints, however, has always been high and this has undoubtedly been perceived as a real barrier.

There is some evidence that sets of hard copy generate more pupil talk, thinking and responses.[15,16] They are also more flexible in school use than slide sets of videos, which require viewing facilities which are not present in the majority of classrooms. Slides also tend to be used in the illustration mode and are difficult for pupils to use in enquiry and group work. For reasons of this type it was decided to produce prints for a limited number of areas in the Spaceview package. With this limitation a viable print run could be achieved for each area and the per print cost reduced to less than 40p.

Teacher knowledge, or rather lack of it, has been frequently mentioned as a limiting factor in geographers' uptake of satellite remote sensing. There are now a number of texts specifically aimed at undergraduate and postgraduates which are accessible to teachers.

The NRSC has also responded to the problem with its Factsheets series (which have been available free) and its new series of professionally produced videos (e.g. *Introduction to Remote Sensing, Towards a Greener Planet*, which looks at environmental management, and *Image Processing*). The free Department of Trade and Industry/British National Space Centre (DTI/BNSC) introductory booklet *The Earth Below* has also been aimed at teachers. The NRSC mobile exhibition unit *The Earth from Space* went on an extensive national tour, ending in the autumn of 1987. It typically spent a week in a town around which schools and colleges had been mailed so that school parties accounted for a substantial amount of its demonstration use. The Science Museum's Exploration of Space gallery, which opened in October 1986, has a section on remote sensing including the Globetrotter interactive audio-visual display.

The teacher knowledge factor has therefore improved recently through initiatives of this kind. However, there has been little expansion in formal teacher education either at the initial level or through Inservice Education and Training (INSET). The scale of INSET required may be quite modest. Kirman[17] in reviewing teacher training needs, suggested 5 workshop hours with time in between for reflection. The experience of

The teaching and learning of subjects

the Geographical Association's Working Group is similar: a limited technical and educational briefing soon has teachers asking where they can obtain imagery so that they can experiment with using it themselves!

The third limiting factor is the need to interpret remote-sensing imagery. Whilst scale and lack of annotation (feature names) have been critical areas, a central problem in interpretation has been colour. Learning the 'language of false colour' is a real perceptual problem facing teachers and their pupils. The range of colour possibilities depending on sensors, bands, image processing, ground area character and season can easily bewilder the novice. Yet it is the existence of colour which gives environmental information, provokes thought and stimulates emotions – educationally worthwhile outcomes.

This has been a fundamental dilemma. A geography teacher is primarily interested in the information in a Landsat or SPOT scene; he/she feels unwilling to 'start with the electromagnetic spectrum and offer a course in remote sensing before commencing the geography'. This unwillingness may reflect a lack of scientific confidence and of course an awareness of the demands of a crowded syllabus. The need for cross-subject discussion is obvious – achieving it is a key task for the next decade.

For the geography teacher the problem lies in the well-expressed pupil question: 'What do the colours mean?' A number of solutions have ben attempted.

1 The provision of a colour key: this is obviously possible with a single image for a specific date (i.e. it is less easy with mosaics). This approach was common in the early years of Landsat MSS false colour composites when tables of colours with typical interpretation points and comments on seasonal differences applicable to a range of images were produced. Whilst helpful, this approach can give a feeling of false confidence. The arrival of Landsat TM products has rendered this kind of blanket approach impossible, and so Spaceview UK did not provide such a table.

2 Text comments and explanations: this is a solution dating back some time. Depending on the anticipated readership the detail has varied from simple 'colour x is item y on this October scene' to more complex attempts to explain why the colours appear as they do. Spaceview UK, because of the seasonal and environmental range of its nine images, adopted this approach. Attempts were made in its teachers' handbook to give concise colour keys for all images, but the reasons for the differences were expanded in a number of cases. However, a part of its strategy was restriction. The pack uses only Landsat TM bands 3, 4 and 5 assigned to blue, red and green

respectively. The thrust of the text is thus on only one satellite system and one processing option so that the environmental and seasonal effects can be explored without undue distraction.

3   Natural colour: Landsat MSS composites were most frequently represented as false colour composites. However, various attempts have been made to create a 'green mode' when vegetation is green rather than the reds of false colour. As Mueller-Wille[18] wrote, 'normal colour makes it easier to recognise familiar landscapes' which justified their use in atlas and map products like *Images of the World*. The bands of Landsat TM are more amenable to producing natural colour effects. Natural colour's advantages lie in its familiarity and in the fact that the human visual system is most sensitive to greens and yellows. The other side to the argument might mention that false colours usually have greater contrast, and contrasts vital in differentiating features on an image. False colour (i.e. data from the near infrared) also contains far more environmental information. Experience with pupils using both conventions has been mixed. Homewood[15] carried out some experiments comparing false colour (FC) and near natural colour (NNC) for the same image/area/date. She found the usual relationship between IQ and performance; Whiteman[19] had found that ability in using Landsat products increased with age of secondary school pupils. Homewood's results showed no overall significant difference between the groups using FC and those using NNC, but she concluded that NNC might be better for lower ability when the pupils had limited experience of remote sensing. However, her detailed results led her to conclude that FC produced higher scores for tasks related to urban, port, vegetation (except woodland) and physical features. She also found that FC was better for tasks which involved detecting smaller items. As a result of considering findings of this type, Spaceview UK was produced using only false colours, albeit with only one convention. In this it contrasts with the earlier Jacaranda kit which had used a range of colour conventions including false colour and 'green mode'.

4   Starting from the familiar: a fourth strategy lies in starting pupils with images of their local areas, or images of areas with which they are familiar from their normal teaching and its related resources (text, maps and slides), or areas in which they have undertaken field work. Such a strategy of starting with an area which is already known, often with basic skills, had been shown to be productive.[16,20,21] Not only can the issue of false colour be attacked directly by the pupils, but also issues like image scale, resolution and so on can be explored on familiar territory. Other forms of environmental information such as Ordnance Survey and Land Use

The teaching and learning of subjects

Maps, planning department documentation and personal knowledge of local environmental issues are normally at hand.

Before leaving Spaceview UK two areas need to be mentioned for completeness – image and pupil activities. 1:100,000 images were produced. This scale was selected as a compromise. 1:50,000 would have enabled immediate comparison with Ordnance Survey maps but the individual pixels would have been visible. For desk-top use print size is a consideration, and anything much larger than A4 becomes unwieldly, easily worn and difficult to store. The selection of a 1:100,000 print scale thus allows substantial detail to be detectable for a reasonably sized area and the addition of a margin grid eases pupil uses. The areas finally selected were very much influenced by potential market. Strategy 4 was a consideration, and field work areas, particularly those studied by 14–16 year olds and areas where well-documented environmental issues (like the Broads and National Parks) were also relevant. The inclusion of urban areas, Merseyside and Northeast London, rounded out the aerial and topic coverage.

Many of the small-scale studies of educational remote sensing have shown that pupils like remote sensing, but once the novelty factor wears away the utility of it in secondary schools needs to be on a firmer base. Steele's survey[3] has shown that A-level was the largest group with which remote sensing was used. Evidence from Homewood[15], Ritchie[16] and Whiteman[19] in the UK, and Kirman's work in Alberta,[20] had suggested that younger pupils could use Landsat. Spaceview UK therefore followed on from the suggestions made earlier by the Geographical Association's Satellite Remote Sensing Working Group in their article *Teaching Geography* in January 1987 and included exercises for the whole 11–19 age range.

Conclusion

In the space of a chapter it has been necessary to be selective. The descriptive detail has related to only two products but it is hoped that this detail has illustrated some general achievements and problems.

There are probably three main achievements. First, experience over the last decade has shown that it is possible to relate remote sensing to established teaching situations. In other words it can be used to illustrate or, at the other end of the spectrum, as a basis for action learning. In the latter context the major use has been of Landsat imagery as a modern and up-to-date land use map where skills and concepts traditionally learned on the new dated *Land Utilisation Maps* can be reinvigorated. Second, remote sensing can be used to acquire and practise skills. Third, satellite data can facilitate conceptual understanding.

Geography and environmental science

The basis for successful development during the 1990s has thus been laid in geography and environmental education. Three needs remain: more imagery (of different dates and seasons, for different areas and to illustrate global environmental issues), more teacher education and more collaborative with other subject areas.

References

1. Boardman, D. (ed.) *Handbook for Geography Teachers*, Geographical Association, Sheffield, 1986.
2. Graves, N.J. (ed.) *UNESCO Sourcebook for Geography Teaching*, Longmans, Harlow, 1982.
3. Graves, N.J. *Geography in Education*, Heinemann, London, 1984.
4. Steele, J. Remote sensing in secondary school education, M.Sc. Thesis, University of London, 1986.
5. House of Lords, Select Committee on Science and Technology, *Remote Sensing and Digital Mapping*, HMSO, London, 1984.
6. Curran, P. and Wardley, N. Remote sensing in secondary school geography: the place of Landsat MSS, *Geography*, 70, 237-47, 1985.
7. Tindal, M.A. *Educator's Guide for Mission to Earth: Landsat Views the World*, NASA, Washington, DC, 1978.
8. Milne, A.K. Landsat imagery and teaching about the environment, *Geographical Education*, 3 (3), 319-30, 1979.
9. Smith, R.M. Landsat photography as a resource in secondary school geography, M.A. Thesis, University of London Institute of Education, 1978.
10. Homewood, T. *Geography from 5 to 6*, HMSO, London, 1986.
11. Hilton, K. Landsat imagery and curriculum considerations in geography: an innovation at a turning point. In W. Kent (ed.), *Recent University Work in Geography and its Relation to Schools*, University of London Institute of Education, London, 1981.
12. Hilton, K., Stewart, N. and McMorrow, J. (eds) *Spaceview UK*, Remote Sensing Society, Nottingham, 1988.
13. Carter, D. *The Remote Sensing Sourcebook*, McCarta/Kogan Page, London, 1986.
14. Falconer, A. and Gerber, R. *Landsat Satellite Images for the Classroom*, Jacaranda, Melbourne, 1978.
15. Board of Secondary School Studies Queensland, *Introduction to Syllabus in Geography Years 11-12*, 1977.
16. Homewood, T. An evaluation of the use of near natural colour and false colour Landsat imagery as a means of communication in the geography curriculum of secondary schools, M.A. Dissertation, University of London Institute of Education, 1987.
17. Ritchie, A. An investigation into the use of false colour Landsat images of land use as a means of teaching selected geographical skills and concepts, M.A. Dissertation, University of London Institute of Education, 1987.

The teaching and learning of subjects

18 Kirman, J. Landsat map teacher training, *Aviation Space*, 8(6), 14–15, 1984.
19 Mueller-Wille, C. *Images of the World*, Collins Longman, London, 1984.
20 Whiteman, P. The relative influence of false colour and Landsat imagery in classroom geography, M.A. Dissertation, University of London Institute of Education, 1982.
21 Kirman, J. The use of infra red false colour satellite images by grades 3, 4 and 5 pupils and teachers, *Alberta Journal of Educational Research*, 23, 52–64, 1977.
22 Whiteford, G.T. Tomorrow's perspective today: satellite geography, *Journal of Environmental Education*, 15(3), 21–8, 1985.

Chapter five

Satellites and language teaching

Brian Hill

The fundamental changes that have swept through the language teaching world have both excited and frustrated. Few would now challenge the new framework of theoretical objectives. We should be producing communicators: people who are confident and able to speak the language; people equally at home in the streets of Paris, Padua or Portsmouth. Our students should be equipped with the practical skills to function effectively in foreign countries and to understand the cultural, economic, social and political backgrounds to their cultures. Teachers and pupils are set free to make the language learning experience varied, interesting, relevant and enjoyable. Imagination, creativity and the development of personal skills can flourish. And yet, where are the tools to carry out the job? Teachers need little convincing of what they should be doing, but they certainly need support to achieve their communicative goals. This is where the judicious application of educational technology is vital.

The benefits of using satellites

The possibility of beaming programmes from foreign networks into language teaching classrooms is one way of stimulating that excitement, realizing communicative ambitions and informing students of what is going on. The integration of authentic television into curricula, which is made so much easier by satellite technology, brings several key benefits:

1   the motivation achieved by basing lessons on attractive informative core material;
2   the exposure to a varied range of authentic speech, with different registers, accents, intonation, rhythms and stresses;
3   language is used in the context of real situations, which add relevance and interest to the learning process;
4   satellite television enables teachers to capitalize on topicality – there

The teaching and learning of subjects

     is a unique fascination in participating, albeit vicariously, in events as they actually happen;
5   regular exposure to satellite television helps construct a picture of the country whose language is being studied, providing learners with insights and experience of how its people live;
6   there is a rich seam of topics and programme styles with something to suit a variety of interests and needs;
7   satellite television is capable of flexible exploitation in the classroom – the same programme can be used with learners of different levels to support different language skills in different ways;
8   it provides an easy and palatable answer for teachers to the problem of keeping in touch with what is going on and keeping their language 'on the boil'.

Some problems

There are, of course, problems associated with exploiting satellite television which have to be confronted, but which can be overcome. Teachers are spoilt for choice and the selection of material can be time consuming and frustrating. The medium is, by its nature ephemeral and ways have to be found of arresting the flow of language and focusing on 'how' something is been said rather than 'what' is being said. Some learners need persuading that television is a serious tool, and not just a purveyor of soporific entertainment. From the point of view of the language learner 'good' television can be 'bad' teaching material. Visuals and presentation gimmicks can all too easily distract from the sound, which must remain the principal concern of the language learner. Information and publicity about programmes is hard to come by in some cases and is often insufficiently explicit to enable a selection to be made. The copyright position is complex, and official permission to edit and exploit is difficult to obtain.

All these are real problems which have to be recognized, but none are insuperable and they certainly do not outweigh the benefits.

Sources of material

At the time of writing (1988) there are some nineteen foreign language channels available in Europe. By 1990 there could be thirty-five channels beaming programmes into our homes and classrooms. For English learners there are currently twelve channels with a further ten likely to come on stream within the next two years. The scene is fast moving and impossible to predict with any certainty. Just what changes the launch of new satellites such as Olympus, Astra and Eutelsat II will bring is uncertain. It would therefore be of little use to speculate on the content and usability of every channel. However, it is interesting to select a few examples of established channels, to give a flavour of what they offer. These channels are broadcasting now and are likely to continue even if they switch frequencies and satellites in future.

For French learners there are some newcomers such as La Cinq and TV3, but the most popular and most frequently viewed is TV5. A typical evening's programming provides a topical magazine, *Aujourd' hui en France*, news, a sports event, a taste of cuisine in *Bonjour Bon Appétit*, a film and a cultural documentary.

Two German channels, SAT 1 and 3 SAT compete for viewers in Europe. Although some light programmes such as *Tele-Zoo* are transmitted, 3 SAT tends to be more serious with an authoritative news report, *Heute*, a *Kulturjournal* and a documentary such as *Bilder aus der Schweiz* making up the evening schedules. SAT 1 has a news magazine that is easily exploited in the language classroom (*Blick*) but much of the air-time is taken up with programmes such as *Airwolf* or *T.J. Hooker*, American series dubbed in German. SAT 1 is expanding: breakfast-time television often has interesting snippets and the mid-day *Tele-Borse* provides plenty of language practice and information for those wanting Business German.

RA1 Uno broadcasts in Italian all day long and carries the same programmes as seen by viewers in Italy. There is a wide selection each day from news programmes such as *Telegiornale*, popular quizzes, films and cartoons.

For Russian specialists satellite television is particularly important. As with RA1 Uno it is the national programme received throughout the USSR and it offers fascinating insights into the complex political and social background of the country. Nowhere is *glasnost* more visible, and the daily mix of news (*Vremya*), sport, culture, film and documentaries gives Russian teachers, otherwise starved of materials, a wealth of possibilities from which to choose.

The staple diet of most English satellite companies is film and disco music, but Super Channel, broadcasting for most of the day and night, has some of the most popular series from BBC and ITV networks, together with news, weather and coverage of sporting events. Teachers of English as a foreign language (EFL), for whom the availability of other materials is no problem, are likely to want to make use of satellites more to exploit their topical potential and to provide a general boost to morale than to generate core learning activities.

Other languages such as Spanish, Swedish and Arabic are also available, and it will not be long before satellite links are established to give us Japanese, Urdu, Indonesian or Chinese.

The teaching and learning of subjects

Organizing the use of satellite television

The main problem for language teachers is not the existence of authentic material but is much more a question of how to select, process and integrate television into existing curricula. Many educational institutions do not currently attempt much more than simply to make programmes available on an *ad hoc* self-service basis. Students are able to come and view when they wish and what they wish, sometimes live and sometimes viewing recordings of satellite programmes stored in the mediatheque.

The value of encouraging informal viewing should not be underestimated. Regular exposure of this kind raises interest in learning, informs and entertains, and certainly develops crucial aspects of successful learning such as aurdal acuity. Vocabulary is reinforced and the subconscious learning patterns identified by Krashen and his followers are stimulated.

However, the potential of satellite television for involvement in the language learning process is much greater. It can play a far more active role as the starting point for a whole range of more 'structured' activities. However, the key of this mode of use is team-work. It is extremely difficult for a teacher working alone to find the time necessary to view, select, edit, build up learning strategies and develop ancillary materials.

Some efforts have been made to bring teachers together at a national level. A consortium based at Newcastle Polytechnic produces follow-up materials for nominated programmes from TV-5 with members of the consortium taking turns to write worksheets and notes for circulation to others. The Association of Teachers of German working with the Goethe Institut in London is attempting to develop a scheme for teachers of German based on selected excerpts from SAT 1, but such national initiatives, whilst obviously of interest, are unlikely to replace the need for specialists in schools to get together and to organize their use of satellites.

Some of the most effective uses within schools and colleges are where a dual policy has been developed. On the one hand satellite programmes are made readily available in the library or the mediatheque for *ad hoc* individual viewing, while on the other the staff decide on the programmes that are likely to prove most useful, record them and nominate one of their number to develop exploitation materials which can then be used by other members of the team.

Exploiting satellite broadcasts

A recent survey undertaken at Brighton Polytechnic into the current use of foreign language programmes in the UK suggests that authentic television in one form or another is used in just over a third of schools. A convincing 98 per cent of teachers, whether users or non-users, recognize the value of such broadcasts and feel that they are an important addition to existing resources. An overwhelming majority are in favour of installing satellite systems in schools, although many express reservations about the time involved in making the most of the material and about the difficulty of overcoming barriers such as the speed of delivery, the level of vocabulary and tight examination schedules. Over 90 per cent of existing users of authentic material would like to use it more than they do at present.

It is clear that teachers perceive a wide range of uses for authentic television. The most frequently found is developing gist comprehension, closely followed by stimulating oral work, the extension of vocabulary and the provision of background information about the country. Few see specifically written activities as being appropriate for work based on satellite broadcasts. News programmes are most commonly used in UK schools, although with children up to General Certificate of Secondary Education (GCSE) level advertisements are, perhaps obviously, also popular. Other types of programme considered useful by teachers are documentaries, drama, sport and humour. It is clear, then, that in the area of foreign language teaching, authentic television is recognized as valuable, that most teachers would like to increase their use of it and that those who have access to satellites have found television useful in developing seminal communicative skills based on a range of different types of programme.

So far in this chapter the term 'authentic television' has been used in a general way, but if the teaching and learning potential of satellite material is to be realized, it is necessary to examine some of the constituent parts in rather more detail. The notion that the effective exploitation of satellite television can be considered *in toto* is no less acceptable than the suggestion that all print-based materials have the same characteristics which are equally amenable to standard techniques of exploitation. It is clear that the text of a Shakespeare play will most probably generate different activities than the Jobs Vacant column of a newspaper. If we are to make the most of the opportunities presented by this new technology, it is pertinent to examine the characteristics of some of the different types of television. Having achieved an understanding of these characteristics we can better understand the implications for introducing satellite television into teaching and learning schema. This will be approached by looking at some of the advantages and disadvantages of each of the programme types most commonly used and by suggesting activities which eminate from this understanding. The interpretations below are not intended as finite statements; rather, they should be seen in the light of suggestions or criteria for selection.

The teaching and learning of subjects

News broadcasts

Some of the advantages of news broadcasts are as follows:

- they are readily available (most satellite channels carry several bulletins per day);
- they divide up into short modules, facilitating exploitation;
- they are by nature topical, thus providing motivation and enabling easy comparisons with national news bulletins;
- any news is likely to provide exemplars of a variety of language situations;
- since they are largely studio based, the spoken sound is usually clear and there are close-up shots of presenters to facilitate the interpretation of lip movements.

However, news broadcasts have certain disadvantages:

- they quickly date and lose their topical appeal;
- the news is often depressing, and a diet of murder, tragedy and atrocities is inappropriate over a period of time;
- the stories covered, often culled from the macropolitical scene, are far removed from the everyday experience of most learners;
- there is little transactional language and spoken text can be unnatural register, often tempting the presenter to speak faster than normal.

With considerations such as this in mind there are a number of activities which suggest themselves for classroom use. A listening grid can be constructed – who? what? where? when? etc. – which can serve as a standard worksheet, thus saving the teacher valuable preparation time. Bulletins can be compared and contrasted with newspaper reports, and notes can be taken or summaries written. Informal discussion can be provoked or debates initiated.

At a lower level or for more structural work students can be asked to rearrange an out-of-sequence text, to match the split parts of sentences together, to give the context in which keywords are spoken or to develop associagrams.

Advertisements

Although some satellite channels are paid for by licences or the sale of decoders, the main stations used by foreign language (FL) or EFL teachers are financed by advertisements. The main advantages of television advertisements for language teaching are as follows:

- they are attractive and popular with students;
- they can be presented in very short segments and are therefore easy to handle;

- the detailed preparation which goes into them produces close links between sound and vision with the function of every word or phrase to be included having been carefully discussed;
- the language is compact with plenty of catalysts for the discussion of idiom;
- discussions of who an advertisement is intended for produce interesting linguistic and cultural insights.

Certain disadvantages also need to be signposted:

- they are artificial and distort 'real' life;
- they are frequently difficult to understand, as they rely on obscure linguistic or cultural associations to make their point;
- problems of speed and clarity are often evident, particularly since the adage 'if you've nothing to say, sing it' all too frequently applies.

In view of the number of advertisements available, it is relatively easy to select for exploitation those containing more of the positive characteristics. A standard worksheet, where students are asked to note down such information as the brand name, the product, the target buyer and the target user and to define information about the product and the seller, is again a useful tool.

For oral work advertisements can be stopped after a few seconds with an invitation to guess what they are going to be about and why. Students can be asked to translate or to give synonyms for selected phrases or to describe a freeze-frame. Many students also enjoy the challenge of scripting and possibly performing their own advertisement.

Drama

Drama comes in many forms on satellite television, but on most evenings some slots are filled by films, crime series, adaptations of Molière and the like. Too often use is made of sound-tracks dubbed onto old English or American films, but sufficient original material does exist to make analysis of the advantages and disadvantages relevant. Drama as a genre has certain clear advantages in the language teaching context:

- good productions can hold a class's attention and make a forceful impact;
- there is usually plenty of transactional languages and the sound quality is good;
- professional actors and actresses provide clear exemplars of accents, intonation and rhythm;
- many dramatic productions are filmed on location and background studies markers abound.

The teaching and learning of subjects

With drama, confusion between the characteristics of 'medium' and 'message' is all too easy but two particular disadvantages need to be taken into account:

- most examples are too long to condense into standard classroom timetables;
- themes are occasionally inappropriate, as they distort and over-dramatize reality.

Many teachers will want to encourage their students to see the whole production through as though they were watching in their native language, and this is where the mediatheque is of particular use. However, it is possible to develop a number of linguistically based activities in the classroom. These include predictive speech, where the video is paused and the class is asked to say what will happen next, and information gap strategies with some students seeing one part of a film and some another before sharing experiences. Students can also be asked for summaries or reports on different aspects of the film, and sequences from the plot can be used as the basis for role play. Keyword context analysis, matching statements, synonym work and the practice of stress and intonation can all be introduced if appropriate model sequences can be identified.

The discussion of the characteristics of each type of television and the resulting implications for language teachers could equally be applied to other areas, particularly documentaries, sports programmes, children's programmes and humour. Such consideration is helpful in coming to terms with the new technology, but is not, perhaps, appropriate in any greater detail here. The three examples discussed above give some idea of the sort of criteria that need to be applied in selecting from the ever-increasing range of material on offer and of the sort of activities that can be initiated in the classroom.

The role of the teacher

If the potential of authentic television is to be tapped, much more consideration needs to be given to helping the teacher cope with innovation and change. Many colleagues feel under assault, assailed from all sides by new examinations, new organizational structures and new methodologies.

The management of innovation in schools and even in higher-education institutions is given all too little prominence. A coordinated national trust is needed to give direction and impetus. Teachers need first of all to be exposed to satellite television themselves: to enjoy the experience of watching the evening news as it goes out, of seeing a lavish production by the Comédie Française or a gripping Maigret. Then they need time and support to consider how the richness of material can be adapted and integrated into the pattern of teaching in their own schools. They need encouragement to work in teams and they need the equipment to allow the excitement of what could be done to be translated into practice.

Satellite television is at one and the same time the herald and the vehicle of change. The barriers to communication are being dismantled throughout Europe. Those of us concerned with language teaching must not remain studiously aloof if we are to exploit the technology adequately and, perhaps more important, to match the increasing expectations of our students.

The Olympus Project

The discussion so far has centred on the use of existing programmes which are downloaded and exploited. Preparations are now well advanced for a European educational channel based on the Olympus satellite and sponsored by the European Space Agency. For the first two years of the project air-time is free to bona fide educational organizations, and forty 'pioneers' have been selected. These range from large established broadcasters such as the Open University through specialist bodies such as medical practitioners and the churches to smaller units such as individual polytechnics or universities. A wealth of existing ideas have been put forward and the basis for a genuinely international broadcasting channel now exists. Some problems of infrastructure and, inevitably, funding still need to be addressed, but the strength of enthusiasm for the idea is evident.

There are obvious opportunities here for modern linguists and several of the slots have been allocated to projects in this area. There are basically three types of interfaces which are under consideration: view and receive only; satellite receive and phone in after the programme; satellite receive and live audio conferencing.

1 Satellite receive: this mode is accepted as being of particular relevance where the programmes are for reception by the general public. Possibilities here include programmes which can be defined as of minority interest on a national scale but which when given a pan-European dimension achieve viability. In direct contrast, there are general possibilities for the straight transmission of language courses and, in particular, for the re-transmission of authentic material shaped for foreign language teaching, along the lines, perhaps, of the successful BBC series *Telejournal*.
2 Satellite receive and phone in after the programme: in this mode it is expected that there will still be a large 'viewing only' audience, but

that possibilities will exist for feedback or for questioning and clarification. A series is planned by Brighton Polytechnic, for instance, which focuses on management training. A number of themes will be explored with a European angle – the management of innovations, instituting organizational change, the response of trade unions and the challenge of information technology. The programme structure will be such that reactions to one programme will be able to be built into the next, achieving a sort of European dialogue although slightly distanced in time.
3   Satellite receive and live audio-conferencing: this is particularly appropriate for putting like-minded groups in direct contact with each other. It could be used, for instance, to support town-twinning, class-links or language teaching, with groups from different countries discussing and reacting to topics. It could also be used in a more conventional format with a panel of 'experts' contributing directly to the programme as it is being broadcast.

The ideas for exploiting Olympus in the teaching of languages and allied fields are certainly there. It may be that some proposals will founder this time around, but the potential for developing language awareness strategies for fostering cooperation and stimulating interactive exchanges is real and will surely become a feature of the European learning community once the uplink facilities are further expanded and a properly resourced infrastructure is in place.

The future

The future for language teachers has rarely looked brighter than at present. So much is happening on the political front to promote links between countries. Engineering and technological developments are set to bring European communities closer together. Companies are increasingly operating at a multi-national level – 1992 will give considerable impetus to the thrust to internationalize trading patterns, and more and more people will be spending part of their working lives in other countries. Pivotal to the success of this international thrust is the acquisition of more languages by more people. Pivotal to the acquisition of languages is the effective implementation of educational technology, an important element of which is the wide-scale exploitation of satellites.

At the beginning of this chapter the reasons why we should be using satellites in language teaching were set out. It is surely not too fanciful to foresee a situation in a decade or so where each language classroom can receive satellite programmes. Pan-European language courses will become more common, just as the EFL world has for some time come to terms with the fact that many of the groups in which English is taught will be from multilingual backgrounds. The initial challenge, therefore, is to have the technology in place and functioning efficiently. Then teachers must become familiar with it and integrate it effectively. At the same time, developers of software will have to widen their horizons and begin to think and produce for an international audience – a change which will have profound implications for traditional mononational course designs. The increased flexibility created by advanced technology will also enable the targeting and resourcing of more much specialist areas which are nationally uneconomic, but which when viewed internationally achieve viability. French, German, Spanish etc. for minority interests will become a reality when distributed by satellite.

Teachers in the next decade will also have access to an increasing range of interactive possibilities. Uplink stations will multiply as will the feedback and interchange facilities. This will have the effect of putting groups of learners in touch with each other, fostering the development of communicative activities, whilst at the same time promoting more personalized individually sensitive learning strategies. The next decade will provide major developments in satellite technology. We in language teaching must have the foresight, the imagination and the commitment to exploit the possibilities we are offered, so that the experience of learning (and holding on to a language) becomes more relevant, more attractive, more interesting, more effective and more enjoyable.

Foreign language broadcasts via satellite

Some useful addresses are given below.

TV5 (French)
Satellimages
21 Rue Jean Goujon
75008 Paris
France
Tel: (1) 42994125; Telex: 643517

SAT1 (German)
Satellitenfernsehen GmgH
Hegelstrasse 61
6500 Mainz
Federal Republic of Germany
Tel: (6131) 38640; Telex: 17131959

The teaching and learning of subjects

RA1 (Italian)
Radiotelevisione Italiana
Viale Mazzini 14
00194 Rome
Italy
Tel: (6) 3878; Telex: 614432

TELECLUB (Swiss German)
Teleclub AG
Fluelastrasse 7
Postfach, CH 8048 Zurich
Switzerland
Tel: (1) 492 4445; Telex: 823516 TCAG

RTL-Plus (German)
11 Bvd de la Foire
Postfach 1005
L1528 Luxembourg
Tel: 449041; Telex: 2959 TRLPLU

3 SAT (German)
ZDF
Postfach 4040
D6500 Mainz 1
Federal Republic of Germany
Tel: (6131) 70–1; Telex: 4187661

Satellite Europe (Monthly magazine giving programme schedule for all major broadcasts)
21st Century Publishing
531–533 Kings Road
London SW10 0TZ
Tel: (071) 351 3612

Chapter six

Science

Craig Underwood

Introduction

The existence and use of earth-orbiting satellites is now a common part of our everyday lives. We have rapidly grown used to the idea of global telephone communications, television broadcasts and weather pictures provided directly to our homes. Information gleaned by satellite is used in planning our cities and roads, monitoring our agriculture and providing safe navigation across the world. However, although we accept the facilities granted by these satellites, very few of us outside the space technical community have any knowledge of the science and technology that makes them possible.

Few would dispute the importance of making young people aware of the rapidly advancing technologies of telecommunications and data handling which are in the process of transforming our lives, and it would seem that the direct reception and use of satellite data provides a natural vehicle for this kind of scientific and technical education because it involves young people directly. This has a number of advantages including:

1 introducing students to contemporary technology, which is important within the context of the 'entitlement curriculum';[1]
2 providing a mechanism for process and skill-based learning, which is a major factor in the concepts of modern science teaching methodology;[2]
3 introducing a science- and technology-based activity into education which has relevance to areas outside the conventional science curriculum, thus providing a medium to exploit cross-curriculum and inter-curriculum links.[3]

For many young people, 'space' and 'satellites' are still emotionally exciting topics, stirring their imagination in a way that is difficult to emulate in other disciplines. Until recently their involvement with satellites has been, of necessity, largely a second-hand experience

The teaching and learning of subjects

owing to the cost and complexity of setting up suitable ground-station facilities. When these facilities are available, young people *do* respond with interest and enthusiasm.[4] However, mere accessibility to satellite data and ground-station equipment is not enough for satellites really to become an integral part of the school, college or university curriculum. For this to happen, and for the role of satellites in education to be seen as anything other than a 'novelty', a number of other criteria must be met.

Criteria for the successful introduction of satellites into the curriculum

First, students should have the chance to have direct access to space technologies to be able to experience, for themselves, the advantages and limitations they offer. This obviously implies that there must be spacecraft available, with dedicated educational payloads, providing data in a way that is easily and cheaply accessible to educational establishments. The role of the UoSAT and radio amateur satellites has been crucial in this respect, and these projects are examined in detail in Chapter 1.

Second, the proper support structures must be in place before any new initiative can be taken up. This implies that curriculum support must be available in the form of hardware, software and texts so that teachers can have ready access to relevant materials. Equally important, teachers must have access to relevant in-service and pre-service training so that they are able to incorporate these materials into their day-to-day teaching. Again, these issues are discussed more fully in Chapter 8.

Third, the benefits of satellite education must be made clear to the ordinary teacher, and the role that satellites can play in the curriculum must be properly researched. There are many 'new' technologies and curriculum developments that are vying for the attention of the educational community, and satellites will not be taken up unless they can clearly be shown to be of relevance to current educational practice and, preferably, shown to be a cost-effective way of meeting educational goals. It is this criterion that is addressed in this chapter, with particular reference to science education.

Satellites in the school science curriculum

The major emphasis of this chapter is on the use of satellites in secondary school science (11–18 age range), not because they are irrelevant to other educational sectors but rather because this represents one of the largest growth areas for satellite education in the near future. In particular, it is students within this age range that need to be influenced if we are to encourage young people to enter careers directly related to

Science

science and engineering. Such encouragement may come from channelling a student's enthusiasm for a particular area of science and technology, such as satellites, into a more broadly based scientific interest. There is certainly much evidence for the need to do so, as it is clear that we are currently unable to meet the demand for scientists and engineers required by our industrial and academic institutions.[5]

Developments in the science curriculum

There have been many exciting educational initiatives over the last few years, and a great deal of attention has been directed towards the curriculum, the examination system, and the role of the school in society, in particular its relationship with industry. Many of these initiatives place particular emphasis on changing the way that science and technology are taught in schools. Curriculum innovation and development are extremely complex processes, working at many different levels in the educational system ranging from centralized national initiatives to local classroom-based projects. The complex nature of these tasks makes changing the curriculum a very difficult process.

In this chapter we shall focus on the three aspects of 'applied and relevant knowledge', 'science across the curriculum' and 'science processes and skills' by examining illustrative uses of satellites within these contexts.

Satellites and scientific knowledge

Although much emphasis of late has been placed on the teaching of scientific skills and processes, it must be realized that there is a significant body of scientific knowledge and concepts that need to be acquired by students before they can be considered competent in the field. Many of the concepts of science involve abstract ideas that can prove difficult for students to grasp, and any material that can help get these ideas across, whilst also introducing students to a contemporary use of technology, is to be welcomed. This is illustrated by considering how remote-sensing satellites can help in teaching about the electromagnetic spectrum – an abstract concept that forms part of every conventional school science curriculum.

Remote-sensing satellites

Remote sensing from space, which is discussed in Chapter 2, began in 1960 with the launch of the TIROS-1 meteorological satellite. Educational programmes on remote sensing have spread widely through the tertiary education sector, drawing together specialists and specialized

The teaching and learning of subjects

information from many aspects of what can broadly be defined as environmental science. However, only now are we beginning to see remote sensing enter the secondary education sector, and much work needs to be done to encourage and support this move.

To date, the major inroads into the secondary sector have been made through the humanities, particularly geography (see Chapter 4). However, the principles and technology involved in remote sensing have a direct impact upon some aspects of the school science curriculum, and it is proposed that the introduction of materials based upon satellite remote sensing will be of benefit to existing science curricula, as well as providing opportunities for curriculum change and development.

The use of satellite remote-sensing in science can be broken down into the following major areas:[6]

1 atmosphere physics including meteorology and climatology;
2 ocean and polar ice physics;
3 land applications including geology, hydrology, agriculture, land use planning and civil engineering;
4 solid earth physics including geodesy and geodynamics.

Under each of these four major areas, a host of measurements can be made, with many potential applications: mineral exploration, earth dynamics, crop production, environmental monitoring, soil survey, agriculture, civil engineering, land use, water resources management, climate studies, topographic mapping, fisheries, off-shore operations, weather forecasting, radiative balance etc.

There have recently been a number of curriculum innovations aimed at changing the way science and technology is taught in schools – in particular making the students more aware of the world of industry. For example the Technical and Vocational Education Initiative (TVEI) has gone some way to encourage a more practical and less 'academic' approach, and has been an associated in-service training (INSET) programme (TVEI-related in-service training (TRIST)) to help teachers cope with the changes. For the less academically motivated student, a new examination scheme has been created: the Certificate of Pre-Vocational Education (CPVE), with a great deal of emphasis on the world of work. Indeed, the entire examination system at 16+ has been changed dramatically with the introduction of the General Certificate of Secondary Education (GCSE), replacing the older Certificate of Secondary Education (CSE) and the General Certificate of Education at Ordinary Level (GCE O level).

GCSE is not just a mixture of the older examination systems; it is a complete rethink of the way that subjects are taught – their content, objectives and assessment. The framework for GCSE is made clear in

Science

the National Criteria. For example, the National Criteria for Science state the following aims:[7]

to provide through well designed studies of experimental and practical science a worthwhile educational experience for all pupils whether or not they go on to study science beyond this level and, in particular, to enable them to acquire sufficient understanding and knowledge to:

(i) become confident citizens in a technological world, able to take or develop an informed interest in matters of scientific import;
(ii) recognise the usefulness, and limitations, of scientific method and appreciate its applicability in other disciplines and in everyday life;
(iii) to be suitably prepared for studies beyond the GCSE level in pure sciences, in applied sciences or in science-dependent courses...

Reviewing the above, the major themes are as follows:

1 increasing students' awareness of the applications of the knowledge and skills they are acquiring;
2 making that knowledge and those skills relevant to their everyday lives;
3 introducing 'science for all' across the whole school curriculum – not just within the narrow context of single-subject physics, chemistry or biology;
4 improving the links between industry and academic establishments.

Satellites can play an important role in each of these areas, and, with particular reference to (iv), schools have used the theme of satellites to establish contact with local and national aerospace and technology-based industries[8] – to the mutual benefit of both the industry and the school. The sensors involved include active microwave instruments (wave heights/directions), microwave sounders (atmospheric temperature), radiometers (temperatures, spectral colours for crop/mineral differentiation), ocean colour monitor, infrared sounders (temperatures), synthetic aperture radar (topography) etc.

Remote-sensing satellites and school science

At both GCSE and General Certificate Education at Advanced Level (GCE A level) standard, science students are expected to have a grasp of the electromagnetic radiation spectrum, from the ultrashort wavelength gamma rays through to very long wavelength radio waves.

The teaching and learning of subjects

Different aspects of this range are often demonstrated using the students' everyday experience as a baseline. The colours of the 'rainbow' are a fairly obvious demonstration of the range of visible wavelengths, and placing a black-bulb thermometer just off the end of the red can indicate the presence of infrared radiation by a small temperature rise. Also, infrared radiation can be demonstrated as the 'heat' felt coming off an electric fire. Similarly, the presence of radio waves can be demonstrated by using a transistor radio; ultraviolet radiation can be detected using fluorescent paper and most students will be aware of X-rays, and their detection by photographic means, from their medical usage.

However, although each broad band within the spectrum can be demonstrated, and a suitable detector shown, this does not necessarily emphasize that these are all manifestations of the same physical phenomenon and that the electromagnetic spectrum forms a continuum. For example, it is quite hard for some students to appreciate that ordinary objects at room temperature emit infrared radiation – after all, they do not necessarily feel warm.

One application of remote sensing could be to play a major unifying role in the investigation of the electromagnetic spectrum. It could be used to emphasize the continuous nature of the spectrum, showing that ordinary 'cold' objects do indeed show up in the infrared and microwave parts of the spectrum, and that by 'looking' in these unaccustomed parts of the spectrum, new information (e.g. the presence of minerals in rocks, disease in vegetation etc.) can be obtained.

The principles on which some of the imaging instruments work can be used to back up work in optics. The scanning radiometers flown on the TIROS-NOAA or Landsat spacecraft contain all the physics that could be desired on the topics of refractive optics (for the telescope), the laws of reflection (for the scanning mirrors) and the splitting of the visible spectrum via prisms or diffraction gratings. In fact a study of the technology of this single instrument would cover most of the optics required for present-day GCSE or A level physics courses. The applications of such an instrument cover work in the biological, chemical, geological and environmental sciences – with the extra benefit that these applications are both contemporary and relevant to the lives of young people, unlike the usual study of the optical instruments of the last century.

Heat is another major topic in school science. The ability to have access to infrared and microwave data for the earth could enliven this essentially dry subject area. In fact, the whole concept of energy and the finite resources of the earth would be helped considerably by the ability to look at satellite imagery of hydroelectric schemes etc.

Moving away from imagery, the ability to receive from spacecraft other remotely sensed data, such as radiation and magnetic field measurements, can provide insight into some aspects of radioactivity and the behaviour of charged particles. For example, the radiation data from the UoSAT spacecraft, which can easily be received and decoded in schools, show the interaction between electrons and the geomagnetic field very clearly. These kinds of investigation are no longer just the province of university departments.

In chemistry, a study of the technology used by spacecraft to detect chemical species in the atmosphere would enable students to become aware of many modern concepts about molecules, bonding and the interaction between matter and electromagnetic radiation (particularly with respect to infrared and microwave spectroscopy). The use of remote sensing for agriculture, fisheries and environmental monitoring would also have a direct input to school biology, and of topical importance here would be the discovery, by spacecraft, of the 'hole' in the protective ozone layer over the polar regions with its implications for life on the planet.

The examples given show how an exploration of the technology associated with satellites, and the ability to receive a variety of data directly from space, can lead to interesting ways of presenting scientific concepts and applied scientific knowledge to students in a way that is both contemporary and relevant to their lives. The concepts and knowledge are not new; they are already a well-established part of the conventional science curriculum. What is new is the way that these ideas are presented.

Satellite remote sensing could become a very useful 'tool' in the science teacher's repertoire, particularly as it conveys the use and benefits to society of the applications of science in general, rather than compartmentalizing science into the often perceived 'mutually exclusive' subjects of physics, chemistry and biology. Hopefully, this will 'open the doors' of science education to a much wider audience – fitting in well with the idea of 'science for all'. It may also help in redressing the balance of the sexes between the perceived 'hard' and 'soft' sciences.

Satellites and science in the broader curriculum

Satellites are not, and should not become, perceived as the province of a single school subject. As already shown, the technology and applications of satellites provide interesting case studies in all three conventional sciences, whilst naturally opening up 'new' scientific fields such as environmental science. Work based on the remote-sensing satellites fits in well with the teaching of the humanities, and the use of communications satellites in modern language teaching and media studies provides a scientific input to students who might otherwise not receive

The teaching and learning of subjects

one (see Chapter 5). Thus, by studying satellites, students following a course structure that is biased towards sciences should become more aware of some of the applications and social impact of their work. Similarly, students following courses biased away from the sciences might at least have the opportunity to examine part of the impact that science has on their discipline and understand some of the scientific principles involved.

Using satellites to teach science within a broader context

So far we have looked at the impact of satellites on a school curriculum within conventional subject boundaries. There is no reason why we should not pull together ideas, skills and knowledge from a number of disciplines, and put them together in a special course based around satellites. This could have a general scientific theme, but include material that would normally be covered elsewhere.[9]

A proposed syllabus for such a course is given below.

1 Communications:
 (a) detection of signals from satellites;
 (b) antenna systems – simple dipoles, interference;
 (c) receivers – LCR tuned circuits;
 (d) electromagnetic radiation – c, polarization, Doppler shift.

 This might include recording actual signals on magnetic tape, transmitting via satellites (if licensed),[10] designing and constructing antennas, receivers, automatic tracking systems etc.[11] involving electronics, control technology and programming.

2 Information theory:
 (a) modulation – AM, FM, PM, PCM, AFSK:
 (b) coding – digital (binary/hex), analogue, Morse;
 (c) conversion – analogue-to-digital, pictures from numbers;
 (d) bandwidth – information content, speed, fidelity;
 (e) redundancy – voice versus bits;
 (f) signal processing – noise, filters, picture enhancement.

 This might include recording and analysing satellite transmissions, comparing the effectiveness of Digitalker transmissions to digital telemetry (on UoSAT),[12] building electronic filters, amplifiers etc., producing pictures from NOAA satellites, grey-scale modification, picture sharpening etc., remote sensing, collection and transmission of data.

3 Orbits:

(a) mechanics/physics of orbits;
(b) geometry – map projections;
(c) modelling – computer, numerical, physical;
(d) general mathematics – geometry, statistics, graphs;

This might include constructing models of satellite orbits, both physically and in computer-based mathematics, using an OSCARLOCATOR,[13] tracking software, calculation from basic orbital data and direct observation – satellite sleuthing, experimental determination of the earth's radius, confirmation of the inverse square law for gravity, height and speed of the satellite,[14] lower school mathematics[15] including work on angles, geometry etc., construction of simple computer programs based upon this work, mathematical manipulation of telemetry data, graphing, averaging, correlations etc.

4 Space science:

(a) radiation – particle physics;
(b) magnetism – the geomagnetic field;
(c) geodesy – gravity.

This might include analysing the results from the experiments on board UoSAT,[16,17] presenting these data in an easily understood format, designing automatic data-capture systems so that the spacecraft can be monitored during the night.

5 The humanities:

(a) interpretation of weather pictures;
(b) looking at infrared photographs to determine temperature;
(c) studies of land use (Landsat data);
(d) history of space flight – political implications;
(e) history of communications – the 'global village';
(f) social impact/implications of communications satellites;
(g) Third World development – earth resources.

This might include receiving and interpreting pictures from the polar-orbiting and geostationary weather satellites.[18] Although Landsat images are not directly receivable by schools, there are many published pictures which show land use, mineral resources and man's impact on the environment in a very striking way.[19-21] Seasat carried out similar work for the oceans, and this is being continued with the Shuttle Imaging Radar, Radarsat etc.

The teaching and learning of subjects

The syllabus outlined above gives an indication of the type of course that could be put together, based around the theme of satellites, teaching many aspects of science and scientific skills within a broad framework. The advantages of choosing satellites are ready to access to live data, obvious application across a wide range of disciplines and an example of modern technology put to socially useful purposes.

Satellites and scientific processes

Skill-based learning in science

In recent years there has been a steady move away from a 'knowledge'-led science curriculum, to one with emphasis on scientific 'processes' and the development of perceived scientific skills. According to the Department of Education and Science:[2]

Priorities within Science Education:

The essential characteristic of education in science is that it introduces pupils to the methods of science so that scientific competence can be developed to the full. The courses provided should therefore give pupils at all stages appropriate opportunities to:

- make observations
- select observations relevant to their investigations for further study
- seek and identify patterns and relate these to patterns perceived earlier
- design and carry out experiments, including appropriate forms of measurements, to test suggested explanations for the patterns of observations
- communicate (verbally, mathematically and graphically) and interpret written and other material
- handle equipment safely and effectively use their knowledge in conducting investigations
- bring their knowledge to bear in attempting to solve technical problems.

The important scientific processes might be identified as those which are engaged when researchers take part in a scientific investigation: observing, inferring, classifying, predicting, controlling variables and hypothesizing.[22] Scientific investigation based around data received directly from satellites can play a pivotal role in developing such processes, and in this respect the UoSAT spacecraft are of particular value.

Science

Development of scientific skills and processes using the UoSAT spacecraft

The UoSAT scientific and educational satellites, which are designed, built and operated from the UoSAT Spacecraft Engineering Research Unit, based at the University of Surrey, Guildford, are discussed in Chapter 1. Although the UoSAT Unit is primarily concerned with research into cost-effective spacecraft technologies, through the design, construction and orbital operation of its own satellites, it also has a strong interest in space education.[23] It has supported this both through the inclusion of educational provision on its spacecraft and by providing a 'home' for the UK Resource Centre for Satellites in Education. This unique relationship between a spacecraft engineering unit and an educational resource centre provides for a very strong liaison between the respective communities.

Traditionally, the role of satellites in education has been that of a communications medium for the dissemination of educational material. Whilst UoSAT-OSCAR-11 (UoSAT-2) can easily play this role using its Digital Communication Experiment[24] payload and Bulletin Service, the UoSAT spacecraft have gone further, providing the first dedicated schools' experiments stimulating a growing interest in space technology via direct and active participation by educational groups. UoSAT-OSCAR-9 (UoSAT-1) launched on 6 October 1981 was the UK's first low-cost satellite focusing on cost-effective spacecraft engineering and space education. One of its mission objectives is 'to stimulate and promote a greater awareness of, and interest in, space engineering and science in schools, colleges and universities by direct, active participation in the satellite experimental programme...'[25] The satellite engineering and experiment data are transmitted in such a manner that they are readily received by simple low-cost amateur ground-terminals. UoSAT-OSCAR-11 (UoSAT-2), launched on 1 March 1984, has joined UoSAT-1 to continue with these mission objectives. Both UoSAT spacecraft are in near-polar low-earth orbit, taking a little over 90 min to orbit the earth. During the course of a day, they come within range of any location in the world, and so their transmissions can be received by any school world-wide each and every day. A school at middle latitudes might expect to 'see' each satellite six times a day, whilst more northerly or more southerly schools would receive the satellite more often. A typical pass lasts for around 10–15 min.

The UoSAT programme offers schools, colleges and universities a unique opportunity to take a direct part in space research, with the minimum of cost and complexity. The data provided by the two UoSAT satellites are of such a quality and quantity that they are having a significant impact on science teaching in the UK and elsewhere – fitting

The teaching and learning of subjects

in very well with the criteria laid down for the GCSE outlined above. A typical UoSAT system for use in schools[25,26] consists of a crossed-yagi antenna, a pre-amplifier, a receiver tuned to 145.825 MHz (within the VHF amateur band), a demodulator and a microcomputer. All the 1,200 baud ASCII encoded data transmitted by the satellites can be displayed and processed by the computer including telemetry, whole-orbit data, bulletin, on-board computer status messages, digital communication experiment titles and newsflashes. The typical cost of such a system purchased from established educational equipment manufacturers is around £250,000 sterling (not including the microcomputer) (1988 prices).

Using Digitalker in the classroom

In order to support the minimum possible ground-station, each satellite also carries an electronically synthesized voice (Digitalker) that can speak simple messages and relay telemetry and other data. The reception of Digitalker requires nothing more than a simple hand-held VHF FM amateur radio.

An example of the educational use of this system was being demonstrated, in April 1988, as part of the activities centred around a joint Soviet–Canadian ski expedition. The eleven-man team, made up of Soviet and Canadian citizens, was attempting to ski across the North Pole from the coast of the USSR to the coast of Canada on a 2,000 km journey that was expected to last between 90 and 100 days. They carried all the necessary equipment for the journey in their rucksacks, including provisions, a tent, sleeping bags, pneumatic dinghy boats, a radio station, navigational equipment, instruments and devices for carrying out scientific experiments and observations in the fields of medicine and geophysics.

The team set off from Cape Arktichesky on the Severnaya Zemlya archipelago in March 1988 and were due to arrive at the Cape of Columbia on Ellesmere Island sometime in May 1988. The main obstacles *en route* were open water, thin ice, pressure ridges and the extremely low temperatures (–40 to –50°C) at the start and 0 to –10°C at the finish). During the expedition, six air-drops were planned to replenish supplies. The aircraft would not land except in the case of an emergency. Food, fuel for heaters, and electrical and scientific equipment would be dropped by parachute, and the team would be able to set up a base for 1–2 days. It would be during these 'rest' periods that the bulk of the research programme would be fulfilled; however, a number of scientific observations would also be made on a daily basis during the trek. Apart from these air-drops, the team would act completely autonomously.

In order to provide for the safety needs of the expedition, and also to

Science

provide navigational data, the team had two emergency location beacons (ELBs). Radio signals from these ELBs were received by the international series of COSPAS/SARSAT (search and rescue) satellites, which relayed positional information to centres in Canada and the USSR. The skiers' location was then calculated and relayed, via amateur radio, to the University of Surrey Mission Control Centre at Guildford. From here, the information was coded and sent to the UoSAT-2 satellite so that it could be 'spoken' by Digitalker. As the satellite passed over the Arctic (every 90 min), the skiers were able to pick up the 'voice' transmissions from UoSAT-2 on simple hand-held radios and thus be 'told' their location.

The message format included a message number, a priority level and the skiers' location at a specific time, e.g.

...NUMBER 01
PRIORITY 000

DATE 23RD OF MARCH
TIME 02 HOURS AND 23 MINUTES GMT
YOU ARE AT 88.02 DEGREES N AND 132.22
DEGREES W
73's...
(Note '73's' is the radio amateur short hand for 'Best Wishes'.)

Many hundreds of schools world-wide followed the progress of the expedition by tuning in to the 'voice' transmission from UoSAT, providing a novel introduction to technology, whilst also supporting general work in geography and biology assisted with the study of the Arctic. Receiving the Digitalker transmissions from UoSAT is so simple that even the youngest children can actively participate in receiving 'data from space'.

Using UoSAT data in the classroom

The use of telemetry data taken 'live' from the UoSAT satellites provides a number of exciting educational opportunities, in terms of both pupil project work and investigative science.

To begin with, the work associated with setting up an inexpensive satellite receiving station within a school and the procedures involved in obtaining data from the spacecraft on a regular basis have a tremendous educational potential. There is a great scope for pupil project work involving scientific, mathematical, design and organizational skills, which have a wide impact on the school curriculum. This kind of project work, involving the basic 'technology' of satellite reception, is of direct relevance to craft, design and technology courses, particularly within

The teaching and learning of subjects

the scope of the new GCSE examination with its emphasis on practical work as the solution to 'real' problems. Once a ground-station has been constructed, the data obtained from the satellite become a valuable educational resource in themselves.

Data from the UoSAT spacecraft are of particular relevance to the teaching of science because of the quality and quantity of data transmitted:

1 practical work based on UoSAT data provides an ideal basis for problem-solving activities, and the devising and testing of hypotheses, reflecting the approach indicated in the GCSE National Criteria;
2 the use of UoSAT data provides a closer match to 'real' scientific experiment, such as that carried out in industry and higher education, than that associated with more traditional school science.

A single UoSAT pass may produce many thousands of data items. This means that the selection of data, the identification of 'good' and 'bad' data (and the criteria for making this distinction), and the handling of this data using numerical, graphical and computational techniques become real issues (as indeed they are in a real research context), in a way that is not possible when using the small quantities of data associated with more conventional school science experiments. Thus, UoSAT data provide a vehicle for the development of the skills of judgement and discrimination that are vital to those pursuing an interest in a scientific or technological discipline. In particular, the sheer quantity of data available for analysis provides an excellent opportunity to use a school microcomputer performing a task which mirrors closely the use of its 'real-world' counterpart – that of an information handling tool, enabling the user to concentrate on the higher-order problems of analysis and interpretation. Obviously, this also has relevance to information technology courses, and a comparison of the means by which UoSAT – an all-digital spacecraft – transmits its data with the analogue methods used by the NOAA satellites' Automatic Picture Transmission (APT) system can prove instructive.

Analysis of UoSAT-2 data

Every 4.84 s, the UoSAT-2 telemetry subsystem compiles a telemetry 'frame' (Figure 6.1) which is transmitted to the ground, having been modulated onto the 145.825 MHz RF carrier. This signal is detected by the antenna and radio receiver at the ground-station, and the data are demodulated for input into a microcomputer.

It has become a common procedure in schools to record the raw data

```
|UOSAT-2            8510270104133
00505001478A02673003349D04052305039F06025107052008047B09037D
10295F11332212000313063714129F15440416181F175157184863195397
20443121184E226600230001240006250007260 97A27556328512C295248
30513431040632286D33579B340007352657363170 37430338476E39504B
40766341120642642643063244166145000146000247494A48506F494779
50563551102752676053682A5465315500005600035749965849 4459507E
60826A615BE7621F4E6333056444026517056647ED67700668000E69000F
```

Figure 6.1 A typical UoSAT-2 telemetry frame

on audio-tape with the computer switched off in order to minimize RF interference. After the satellite pass, the computer is switched on and the audio-tape is played back into the computer, usually via a hardware demodulator. The computer is then used to decode and process raw data by means of software. To date, the BBC Microcomputer[27,28] is one of the best-supported machines for this purpose, although similar packages also exist for the Sinclair Spectrum.[29] The raw data can be displayed on any microcomputer which has a serial interface port and can run a terminal-emulation program. The software described below is widely available and provides a BBC Microcomputer-based menu-driven data-handling package that allows data to be stored, processed and analysed.[30]

The main program takes the raw data stored on disc and processes and validates it. Each sensor in the spacecraft produces a block of digits corresponding to its identification number and sensor reading. Each block has a transmission error-check digit associated with it. This can detect simple bit-errors in transmission, but it cannot correct such errors. Individual digits, whole blocks or indeed major parts of the telemetry frames may become corrupted in the transmission-receiving stage, and one of the functions of the program is to discriminate between corrupted and acceptable data. The procedures used are similar to those that would be employed by a person who was given the same task, and they provide useful examples for exercises in devising algorithms for pattern-seeking and discrimination. This process – the extraction of a signal from the associated noise – is very common in scientific work, and it is well worthwhile introducing such concepts at secondary school level.

Eventually, the data are ready for display in graphical form. The experimenter can 'roam at will' over a menu of all the sensors, and plot or tabulate their outputs against time. Analysis of these graphs can give a detailed picture of the behaviour of the satellite under a variety of operating conditions.

The teaching and learning of subjects

The role of the student

One model for the use of these data in schools is to present students with some information as a 'seed' for discussion. Students can then be asked to put forward suggestions as to the meaning of the data and, in the process, their understanding of scientific principles can be drawn out and (hopefully) enhanced.

The process of giving student some 'seed' information, so that they form hypotheses and then develop tests and experiments to confirm or deny them, is extremely useful in developing the kinds of skills demanded by science and engineering. The amount of graphical and numerical work involved gives ample opportunity for data interpretation and presentational skills to be developed. The role of the microcomputer becomes one of serving a real need, rather than one with just cosmetic value, and many exercises in small-group learning could be developed around this.

For example, UoSAT's attitude is controlled passively by the gravity-gradient boom (see Chapter 1). The forces involved in this system are very small and insufficient to maintain stability for any length of time. For this reason, and to achieve initial gravity lock, an active attitude control system is implemented using magnetorquers – electromagnet coils wrapped around the edges of the solar panels. When currents are passed through these, a magnetic field is generated, which interacts with the earth's own field to create a small torque on the satellite. However, under normal conditions, the boom maintains the satellite in a 'gravity-locked' mode, so that the 'bottom' of the satellite ($-z$ axis) remains pointing to the centre of the earth. With this initial information in mind, students can be presented with data from the navigation magnetometers – instruments that measure the earth's magnetic field as seen by the spacecraft.

Examination of typical data (Figure 6.2) shows an interesting sinusoidal variation in both the x and y magnetometers, but only a slight variation in the z magnetometer. What is happening? Could it be that the satellite is spinning? If so, what further evidence could we look for? Perhaps the spin might show itself in other sensor reading – the 'solar-array currents' for example (the satellite is basically a box shape with four solar panels facing the $+x$, $+y$, $-x$ and $-y$ directions of a Cartesian coordinate system). Examination of the panels (Figure 6.3) does indeed show the expected response. This leads to the conclusion that there is a spin, and the period of the spin is consistent with variations in the solar array currents. Also, the non-periodic response of the z-axis instrument is further indication that the satellite is spinning around this particular axis.

(a)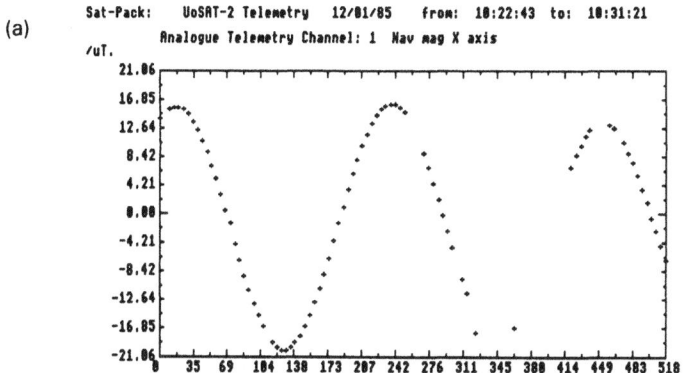

(b)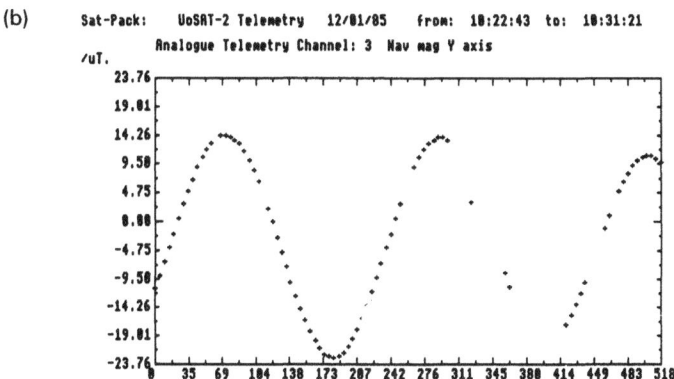

(c)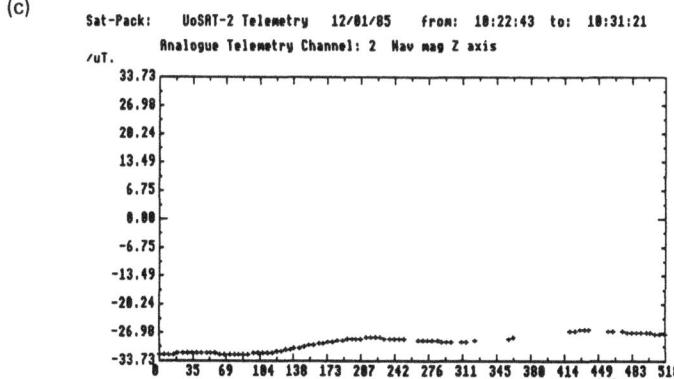

Figure 6.2 UoSAT-2 navigation magnetometer telemetry

The teaching and learning of subjects

(a)
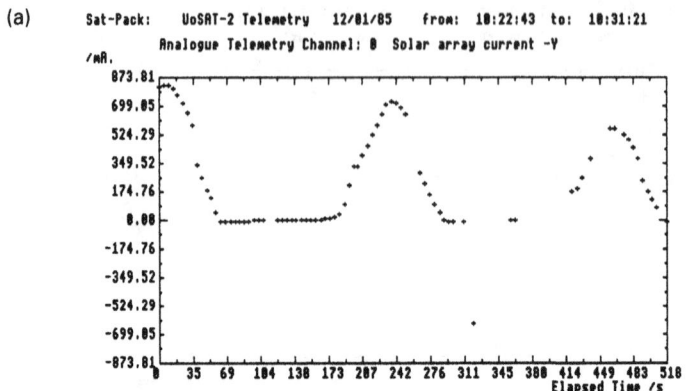

(b)
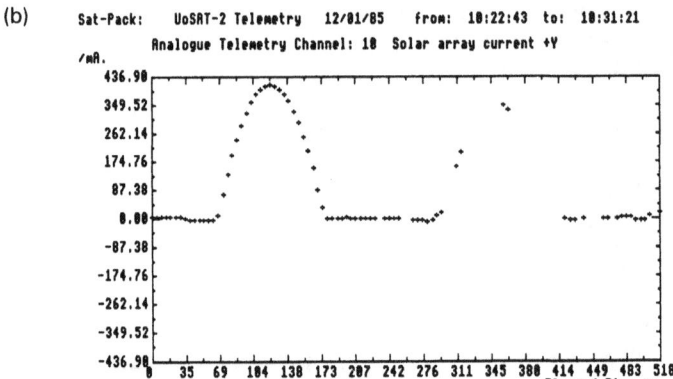

(c)
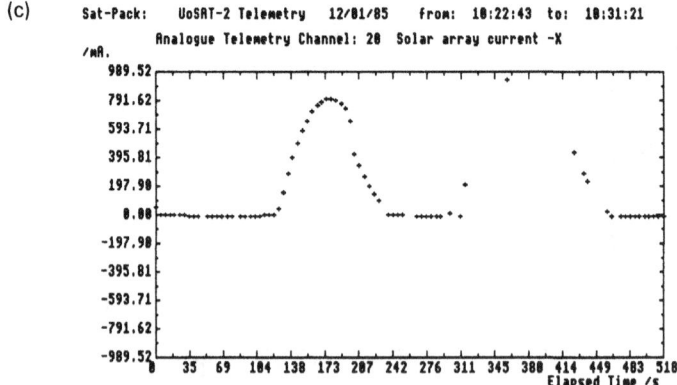

Figure 6.3 UoSAT-2 solar-array current

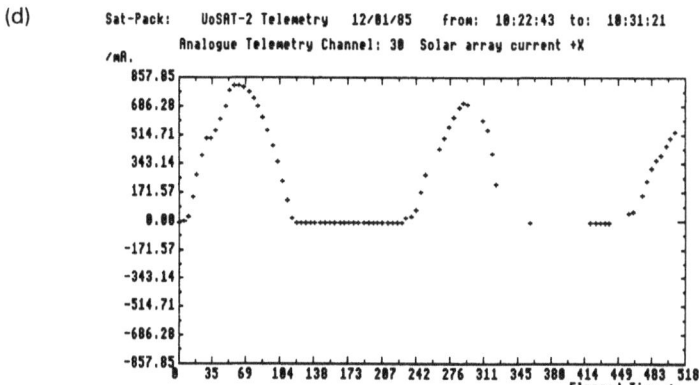

Figure 6.3 (continued) UoSAT-2 solar-array current

Telemetry

Closer examination reveals a small 'ripple' (the satellite is wobbling) and the magnitude of the field strength is slowly decreasing. Why? What might be the effect of the satellite's motion along its orbit during this time? The answers to these questions can be found by examining data taken over one or more orbit. Over the period of a single pass (typically 10 min), slow variations are difficult to discern; however, the satellite also transmits 'whole-orbit data', which can reveal the longer-term behaviour of the spacecraft subsystems (Figure 6.4).

The navigation magnetometers on the UoSAT spacecraft represents only a small part of the total number of telemetered sensors; there are also temperature, current, voltage, power and radiation monitors. These provide ample opportunity to investigate aspects of spacecraft dynamics and orbital operation and to examine the near-earth environment.

For example, the temperature sensors on both UoSAT spacecraft show the effect of the sun and the earth on the satellite. These sensors are of scientific interest because they clearly show the effect of heat transmission via radiation and conduction – in the vacuum of space there are none of the convection mechanisms that play a major role in the temperature control of objects in air. As the spacecraft comes out of earth eclipse, the sun rapidly warms the exterior of the satellite, and the spin shows up clearly as a sinusoidal modulation on the general increase in temperature. Students may not necessarily appreciate that the sun shines in space (which they probably associate with a black 'night-time' sky), and that outside the protection of the atmosphere the sun's radiation is extremely intense (up to 1400 W m^{-2}). As the satellite moves further into the 'day' side of its orbit, it continues to heat up, but then,

The teaching and learning of subjects

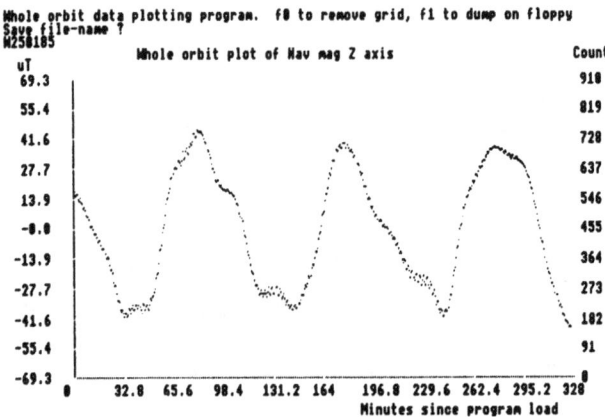

Figure 6.4 UoSAT-OSCAR II: whole-orbit data plot for the z-axis navigational magnetometer

paradoxically, as the satellite approaches the sun's location in the sky, the side (x and y) panels begin to cool! Why is this? A moment's thought will give the answer: the gravity-gradient-locked nature of the satellite means that under these conditions the sun is shining more directly on the top (+z) facet of the satellite, and so less heat falls on the side (x and y) facets. This can be confirmed by noting the temperature increase of the top (+z) facet. When the satellite enters the earth's shadow, it cools down rapidly, but the rate of cooling decreases over time. Students at a more advanced level will understand that the only heat-loss mechanism available to the spacecraft is thermal radiation to space and that this is dependent upon the fourth power of the spacecraft's temperature, and so naturally there is a decrease in cooling as the temperature drops (Figure 6.5). The bottom (−z) facet of the spacecraft is noticeably warmer than the top (+z) facet during this period. This is due to thermal radiation from the earth (at around 250 K) heating the spacecraft.

The near-earth radiation environment can also be investigated using UoSAT's sensors. Both UoSAT spacecraft orbit underneath the main Van Allen radiation belts but catch populations of particles (mainly electrons and protons) trapped in the geomagnetic field over the polar regions (these same particles shower down into the upper atmosphere to cause the aurorae). The Geiger–Muller tubes on UoSAT-1 provide a simple measure of the radiation intensity of the spacecraft's

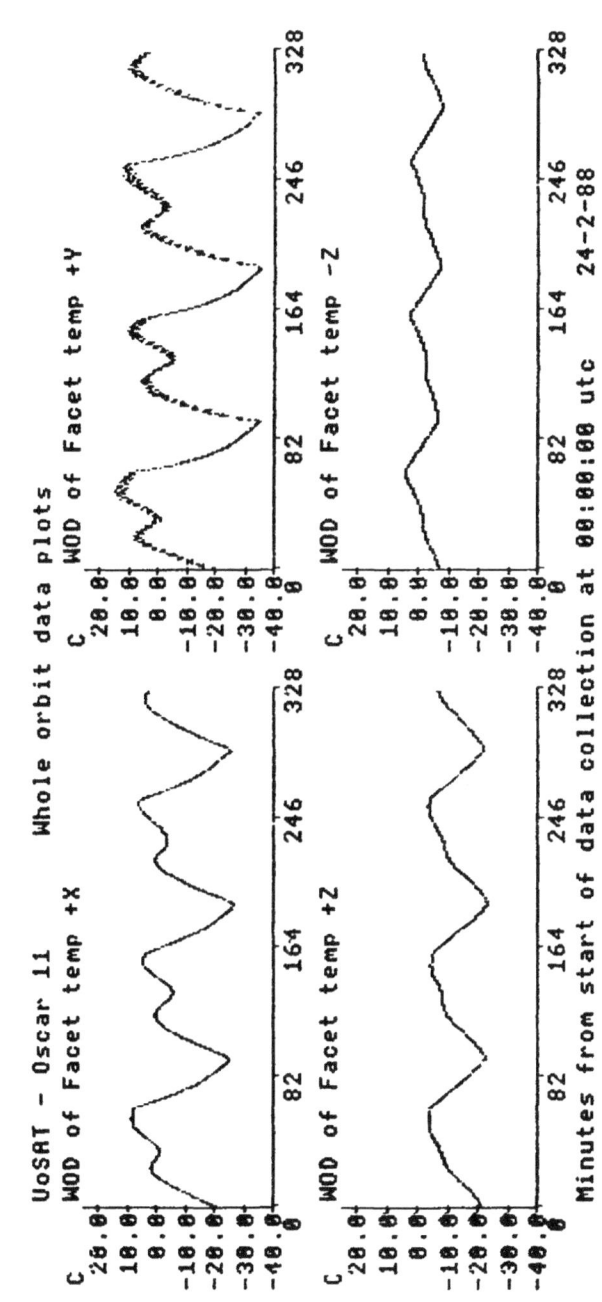

Figure 6.5 UoSAT-OSCAR II: whole-orbit data plots

The teaching and learning of subjects

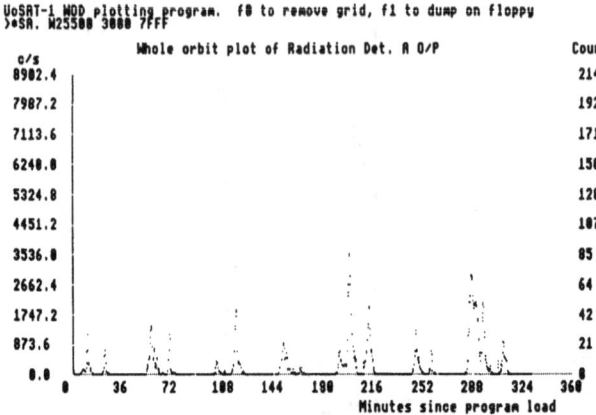

Figure 6.6 Whole-orbit data plot of radiation intensity

environment, and clearly show a double-peak as the satellite traverses these doughnut-shaped regions of particles (Figure 6.6). Examination of these results, taken together with data from any orbital prediction package, show the spatial distribution of these particles, and this can be correlated with the geomagnetic field to show the interaction between charged particles and magnetic fields. If many results are taken over a long period of time, fluctuations in the radiation intensity of these regions become apparent. It is possible to correlate these with solar events – in particular, the 27 day cycle associated with the rotation of the sun.

Summary of the use of UoSAT in the classroom

The examples outlined above begin to indicate the tremendous potential of UoSAT data in science education. The satellites can be considered to be orbiting experiment packages which are directly accessible to schools, colleges and universities, allowing investigations into the phenomena associated with both the behaviour of spacecraft and the nature of the near-earth environment. Many of these data are of direct relevance to the core science curriculum, e.g. radioactivity, dynamics, behaviour of charged particles, magnetic fields etc.

Conclusions

It is fair to say that, in general, the response of schools to satellites has developed more slowly than initially expected; obviously the provision of educational satellites alone is not enough and other kinds of support are also needed, such as texts, worksheets, easily assembled receiving

Science

equipment, software, advice and teacher training. However, it is expected that the use of satellites in education generally, and in science education in particular, will grow considerably over the next few years.

We have seen that work based around satellites and their data fits in very well with current thinking on the development of science curricula – in particular within the following major themes:

1. increasing students' awareness of the applications of the knowledge and skills that they are acquiring;
2. making that knowledge and those skills relevant to their everyday lives;
3. introducing 'science for all' across the whole school curriculum, not just within the context of single-subject physics, chemistry or biology;
4. improving the links between industry and academic establishments.

We have seen how satellites can be used in the context of conventional science syllabuses, and how new multidiscipline courses could be established, bringing science and scientific ideas to those groups which may otherwise miss out. Remote sensing satellites have their uses in science, but we have seen how the UoSAT scientific and educational spacecraft have played a pioneering and particularly valuable role in science education world-wide. The easily available satellite data provided offer a unique opportunity to participate directly in space research in a way that is educationally effective, and also stimulates interest in science, engineering and technology as careers. However, the major strength of UoSAT is the opportunity it affords in developing the skills and processes that are a vital part of science education. Satellites have a great potential for use in science education. To date, we have really just seen the 'tip of the iceberg'. Much needs to be done before satellites become an accepted part of every school's science curriculum, but several pioneering schools have shown the way.

Acknowledgements

My special thanks go to the many people who have contributed to this field. In particular I would like to thank Mr Eric Twose of Scarborough Sixth-Form College, Dr Robin Millar of the University of York and Mr David Duff of Unilab for their tremendous contribution to this work. Thanks are due to the Manpower Services Commission for supporting the 'National Resource Centre for Satellites in Education' and making possible the teacher-training activities that have taken place. Finally, thanks are due to Dr John Gilbert and Dr Martin Sweeting of the University of Surrey for their support of the Satellites in Education Programme.

References

1. DES, *Better Schools*, Department of Education and Science, London, 1985.
2. DES, *Science 5-16: A Statement of Policy*, Department of Education and Science and the Welsh Office, London, 1985.
3. Underwood, C.I. *Satellites in the Curriculum: A Project Report for C.S.C.S.*, Centre for the Study of Comprehensive Schools, University of York, 1986.
4. Duff, D.A. The use of satellites by schools and colleges (Part 1), *Physics Education*, 16, 352–6, 1981; The use of satellites by schools and colleges (Part 2), *Physics Education*, 17, 19–24, 1982.
5. Finniston, H.M. *Engineering: Our Future*, HMSO, London, 1980.
6. Kriegl, W.A. Remote sensing missions for the next decade, *Journal of the British Interplanetary Society*, 37(2), 75–80, 1984.
7. DES, *GCSE: The National Criteria*, Department of Education and Science, London, 1986.
8. Planterose, C. Industry backs college satellite project, *Spacecraft*, 29, 85–6, 1987.
9. Underwood, C.I. *Satellites in Education – A Guide for Teachers*, UK Co-ordinating Committee for Satellites in Education, University of Surrey, Guildford, 1985.
10. Department of Trade Industry, *How to Become a Radio Amateur*, Home Office, Radio Regulatory Division, Licensing Branch (Amateur), London.
11. Davidoff, M.R. *The Satellite Experimenter's Handbook*, American Radio-Relay League, Newington, CT, 1985.
12. UoSAT, *UoSAT Databook*, UoSAT Spacecraft Engineering Research Unit, University of Surrey, Guildford, 1987.
13. Gee, A.C. Satellites for the beginner, *OSCAR News*, No. 69, 8–15, 1988.
14. ARRL, *Space Science Involvement*, American Radio-Relay League, Newington, CT, 1974.
15. Spencer, S.J. *The Sheffield Project: Satellites*, AMSAT-UK, London, 1985.
16. UoSAT, *Radio and Electronic Engineering Special Issue on UoSAT – The University of Surrey's Satellite*, 52 (8/9), 1982.
17. UoSAT, *Journal of the Institute of Electronic and Radio Engineers Supplement on UoSAT-2*, 57(5), 1987.
18. Young, V. School's satellite weather watch, *Space Education*, 1(12), 530–4, 1986.
19. Sheffield, C. *Earth Watch – A Survey of the World from Space*, Sidgwick and Jackson, London, 1981.
20. Sheffield, C. *Man on Earth – The Marks of Man: A Survey from Space*, Sidgwick and Jackson, London, 1983.
21. Bullard, R.K. and Dixon-Gough, R.W. *Britain from Space – An Atlas of Landsat Images* Taylor and Francis, London, 1985.
22. WPSP, *An Introduction to Process Science (Trial Version)*, Warwick Process Science Project, University of Warwick, 1984.

23 UoSAT, *UoSAT – The University of Surrey Satellite Project, A Guide to its Capabilities, Operation and Usage*, Department of Electronic and Electrical Engineering, University of Surrey, Guildford.
24 Ward, J.W. and Price, H.E. The UoSAT-2 digital communications experiment, *Journal of the Institute of Electronic Radio Engineers Supplement on UoSAT-2*, 57(5), 163–73, 1987.
25 UNILAB, Schools Satellite Project (Promotional Leaflet), UNILAB Ltd, Blackburn, 1987.
26 SRW Communications, ASTRID + (Promotional Leaflet), SRW Communications Ltd, Malton, 1987.
27 Underwood, C.I. and Twose, E.R. SAT-PACK – Software for the BBC Microcomputer Series, UNILAB, Blackburn, and AMSAT-UK, London, 1984.
28 Underwood, C.I., Bean, N.P. and M.L.J. Meerman, University of Surrey UoSAT Software, Surrey Satellite Technology Ltd/National Resource Centre for Satellites in Education, University of Surrey, Guildford, 1987.
29 Taylor, N.B.P. SPIX and SUDD software for the 48K Spectrum Microcomputer, N.P. Taylor, Faringdon, 1987.
30 Underwood, C.I., Twose, E.R. and Millar, R.H. Satellites in schools, *Physics Education*, 22(1), 44–9, 1987.

Chapter seven

Information technology and satellites

John Gilbert and Annette Temple

Information technology

Information technology (IT) is, like wisdom, relatively easy to perceive if you are paying attention, but equally hard to define. Some definitions focus on the physical equipment involved: '... the various technologies centred around developments in computing and telecommunications'.[1] Others go further, and emphasize the use of physical equipment for the purposeful display of specific intellectual skills: 'IT involves techniques of handling data and information and using these to solve problems. The techniques include problem analysis, designing, collecting, interpreting, processing, recording, and communicating, by using systems, particularly those involving microtechnology and computers.'[2] The broadest view, and one which we particularly value because it is not necessarily associated with the use of computing hardware, is 'IT is the application of the principles, practices and technologies which are involved in the collection, storage, manipulation, transmission and presentation of information in its many forms'.[3]

It is worth remembering that, in the absence of pocket programmable calculators or physically very small microcomputers, much data are collected by searching in books, or other factual compendia, summarized in tables, and displayed in charts and graphs. This intermediate technology approach to IT seems likely to persist for some time; indeed the skills involved are used in electronically based IT. The primary drive behind the growing awareness of IT is undoubtedly economic, for it is often stated that an ability to compete in world markets will depend on IT and on its application to industry. Education and training systems are increasingly seen to have a key role in facilitating this economic revolution, both as a way of providing skills on a widespread basis and as a way of promoting an appropriate outlook: '... education has to provide the climate of opinions and attitudes of mind which will allow technological progress to flourish'.[4]

Information technology education

How, then, does the school system, which provides compulsory education for all citizens and therefore may be expected to make a major contribution to these aspirations, approach the provision of IT education? Basically it adopts three approaches: first, as a separate subject, on a par with other subjects, leading to public examinations, e.g. the General Certificate of Secondary Education (GCSE); second, as a set of skills which can be taught through, an which can hence contribute to an understanding of, existing school subjects; third, as enshrined within particular pieces of hardware, e.g. microcomputers and video discs, which can promote both more interactive and less teacher-dependent approaches to learning.

IT as a separate subject can be illustrated using the Northern Examining Associated GCSE 'Information Technology: Syllabus A'. This scheme consists of a Foundation Module (requiring 8 h tuition), three Core Modules (Control Systems, Communications, Data Handling Systems) (each requiring 18 h), two Extension Modules (a restricted choice from six: Programming, Computer-based Control, Electronic Office, Media Communications, IT in Society, and Graphics and Design) (each of 18 h) and a Unifying Module (of 22 h). A flavour of the core is conveyed by its aims:[5]

1. to develop an appreciation of the implications of Information Technology for society including the beneficial and detrimental aspects of introducing various Information Technology systems;
2. to promote an awareness of the effects of the rapid pace of development of methods, materials and systems in Information Technology;
3. to engender in each candidate a practical awareness and understanding of what characterises information, its processing, transmission and interpretation;
4. to develop the concepts of Information Technology and the ability of each candidate to generate, process, communicate effectively and interpret data and information through a variety of methods;
5. to encourage the development of individual and group skills in order to achieve solutions to practical problems;
6. to encourage the development of individual and group skills in the critical analysis of the suitability of solutions to practical problems;
7. to develop and promote the use of transferable skills which would be applicable to other areas relevant to the candidate and to develop the confidence to apply the new skills;

The teaching and learning of subjects

8. to stimulate and encourage all candidates regardless of sex or ethnic background to develop a wide range of personal and social skills through an interest in Information Technology.

Although many Examining Groups offer Computing Studies at GCSE, which inevitably take the more restricted view of IT, some interesting hybrid courses are emerging, e.g. the Southern Examining Group's 'Business and Information Studies'. However, it seems unlikely that IT as a subject will find a place in the mainstream curriculum in most schools to GCSE level.[6] Some schools, e.g. the City Technology Colleges, may persist with this approach, which has enabled a core of specialist teaching and learning skills to be built. In many schools, after a specific introduction to IT for the younger students, it will be integrated into the traditional subjects.

The place of IT in traditional subjects has been explored by the relevant professional associations, often in association with the Microelectronics Education Programme. The IT perspective has been explored in respect of history,[7] geography,[2] English,[8] mathematics[9] and science.[10,11]

In respect of history, IT is conceived of as a ways of exploiting the computer in the classroom. The computer is seen to be capable of:

1 stimulating student motivation to learn history: this is thought to arise from the interactive features in computer-run simulations of historical events and decisions;
2 developing historical understanding and ideation: this arises through the development of historical empathy associated with role play exercises, the understanding of cause – effect relationships, activities on the nature and handling of evidence, and especially through the use of data bases where the main advantages are as follows:

   (a) they are very fast so that calculations and visual display can be made in a matter of seconds;
   (b) pupils can work individually at their own pace or in groups;
   (c) computers will always respond to questions keyed into them;
   (d) they remove the tedium of manual searching and create interest;
   (e) the results of searches can be printed immediately;
   (f) they encourage extensive pupil participation;
   (g) they assist in developing computer literacy;
   (h) if the results can be displayed in graphical form – pie charts, histograms etc. – then they will also contribute to an understanding of graphical communication;

Information technology and satellites

3 developing decision-making and reporting skills: this is promoted by requiring the students to make decisional choices and to compare them with the actual outcome in history, by exploring generalized and typical situations in history, and by encouraging students to achieve an outcome which is counter-factual to that which historically took place;
4 promoting presentational and communication skills, e.g. through the use of a word-processor, or regarding the computer monitor as an electronic blackboard.

Again with emphasis being placed on the use of computers, IT can be used in the teaching of geography:[2]

1 to promote a familiarity with the vocabulary of geography;
2 to offer a particular context for reading and writing;
3 to help develop numerical and graphical skills in a geographical context;
4 develop informative processing skills;
5 provide opportunities for decision-taking, including those provided through simulations;
6 support project work.

English teachers see the 'new technology', yet again computers rather than IT, as providing opportunities to promote:[8]

1 literacy: the impermanence of the outcomes of composition is seen to be attractive in promoting the development of compositional skills, as are the opportunities for variation in styles of presentation;
2 language development: word-processing is seen as especially valuable here;
3 information handling.

Teachers of mathematics are enjoined[9] to exploit the particular attributes of computer in order to:

1 promote high-order skills, e.g. problem solving, cooperative working, communicating effectively;
2 extract meaning from complex arrays of numerical data;
3 promote an exploratory approach to mathematics which, it is hoped, will support students' interest and enjoyment;
4 develop mathematical concepts through using, adapting and developing programs.

Many of the categories of activity pursued by the science education community are very similar in purpose to those explored above, but inevitably make use of different examples.[11]

1 Word-processing: the need to promote the associated skills has been widely recognized, for example: 'courses . . . should therefore give

The teaching and learning of subjects

   pupils, at all stages, appropriate opportunities to . . . communicate (verbally, mathematically and geographically) and interpret written and other material'.[12]
2 Computer assisted learning (CAL): this can take a variety of forms, for example drill and practice to promote accuracy in concept and skill use, simulation programs through which normally inaccessible situations (for reasons of danger, inappropriate timed or physical distanced) can be 'experienced', game programs which resemble simulations but require some element of strategy and competition, and tutorial programs which can manipulate large quantities of information.
   Modelling: this may involve either building up programs as models of events, e.g. of biological evolution or, alternatively, using specific models to derive relations between parameters contained within them. For example, Osborne[12] has reviewed the use of computer-managed 'microworlds' in order to help students grasp the counter-intuitive concepts of Newtonian mechanics.
   Interfacing: this involves the use of probes, or sensors, to detect changes taking place within an experimental situation (usually in a laboratory) and monitoring those changes by transforming them into computer-compatible data forms, i.e. electrical signals. In the UK the Micro-electronics Support Unit, through its 'datalogging project', is developing an interface unit to enable data to be collected from a variety of probe types, and subsequently processed and displayed by a microcomputer.[13] Interestingly, Wellington[14] has observed that the use of such interfaces conflicts directly with the GCSE requirement that students directly make observations, record data, make tables and draw graphs – a case of where the 'new IT' is apparently in conflict with the 'old IT'.

The Association for Science Education[11] conducted a postal survey of members on the uses to which microcomputers were put in school science. Responses were sorted into those for 'within science up to age 16' and 'within A level physics'. With some rearrangement to provide common categories, the outcomes were as shown in Table 7.1. The increased emphasis at A level of understanding complex situations and of collecting and analysing data is shown in the table, although the reduced use of data bases and word processors is somewhat surprising.

The view of IT which sees it as embodied within a technique made possible by high-technology hardware is exemplified well by the use of Electronic Mail Services (E Mail),[15] by means of which students and teachers can communicate directly, either personally or as a group. Within the UK, the availability to schools of modems from the Department of Trade and Industry, and the development of networking systems

Information technology and satellites

such as The Times Network for Schools (TTNS) and Prestel Education have done much to bring this idea closer to fruition. An allied development has been that of the National Educational Resource Information Service (NERIS) which is a data base consisting of summaries of educational resources available to teachers and students. This set of approaches implies a shift of emphasis in the management of learning.

Table 7.1 Uses of microcomputers in school science

	(N = 190) Percentage of 'science to 16'	(N = 97) Percentage of A level physics
Simulations	60	67
Word processing	48	32
Interfacing	32	62
Data analysis	35	51
Data bases	21	10
Decision-making	9	7
Learning exercises	29	7

The value attached to IT within the 'new pedagogy' is considerable. This was given impetus by the extensively financed Technical and Vocational Education Initiative (TVEI) which sought to[16]

... explore and test ways of organising and managing the education of 14 to 18 year olds across the ability range so that:

(i) more of them are attracted to seek the qualifications/skills which will be of direct value to them at work and more of them achieve these qualifications and skills;
(ii) they are better equipped to enter the world of employment which will await them;
(iii) they acquire a more direct appreciation of the practical application of the qualifications for which they are working;
(iv) they become accustomed to using their skills and knowledge to solve the real-world problems they will meet at work;
(v) more emphasis in placed on developing initiative, motivation and enterprise as well as problem-solving skills and other aspects of personal development.
(vi) the construction of the bridge from education to work is begun earlier by giving these young people the opportunity to have direct contract and training/planned work experience with a number of local employers in the relevant specialisms;

The teaching and learning of subjects

> (vii) there is close collaboration between local education authorities and industry/commerce/public services etc., so that the curriculum has industry's confidence.

These broad aims have become associated with a diversity of educational developments which includes:[17]

1. reform of the education curriculum, e.g. modular organization, shifts towards integration, 'balanced science for all';
2. greater coordination between subjects in the curriculum;
3. the expansion of experiential learning, especially that involving off-site activities and experience in the community;
4. pedagogic shifts away from didactic exposition towards participative techniques, and from solo learning to group work;
5. reform of assessment, e.g. criterion-referencing, profiling, credit accumulation;
6. more emphasis on vocationalism, whether meaning preparation for the world of work or viewing industry as an opportunity for study and experience;
7. broader parental, pupil and societal participation in the organization of opportunity and the negotiation of choice;
8. an increased emphasis on problem-solving skills, whether by teachers in transforming centralized decisions into classroom realities, or by pupils in developing and deploying concepts.

Wellington[18] saw the implications of such trends for IT to be reflected in the following guidelines for school education:

> 1. The emphasis in school education should be on the use of information technology across the curriculum at all levels from primary upwards. This may involve computer assisted learning (CAL) as one of its facets but its broader aim should be to develop an awareness of a familiarity with I.T., as well as general skills in information handling.
> 2. A narrow, skills-based approach to I.T. education will have little vocational or educational value. The overall context in employment is one of constant change and gradual updating. In such a context the best strategy for I.T. education is to provide basic, general skills in the handling of information rather than specific skills. This will involve the traditional aims of education – literacy, numeracy, communication and personal development – as the general framework.

The implications of these guidelines for IT in education are revolutionary. Educators at all levels are currently attempting to come to terms with the role change which the technology enforces upon them.

Teachers used to be regarded as the prime source of information for their students. The students' learning path could be rigidly controlled by the teacher who would release to them such information as was felt to be relevant to the particular learning situation. Under these circumstances the teacher has almost complete control over the students' learning experience, and indeed the experience is often comfortable and secure for both students and teacher. The student has confidence in the teacher because questions which have been triggered during the learning situation have apparently been confidently and adequately answered. The teacher's view of the lesson is one of success, and indeed his views are continually reinforced by both the attitude and progress of the student. In this situation each answer given or piece of information introduced by the teacher reinforces previous parts of the lesson; he can answer every question asked of him by the students to both his own or the student's satisfaction. The relationship between teacher and student is therefore viewed by all concerned (teacher, student, parent, senior staff) as at the very least satisfactory. It is therefore easy to see that the advent of modem IT systems has introduced a degree of risk into this previously well-defined and bounded relationship.

Anderson[19] has made the following suggestions.

(a) All students should receive an 'I.T. education' because, as future adults, they will be working in a world where I.T. skills will be used widely and where a critical awareness of I.T. is needed in the democratic process.

This scope for IT education emphasizes its more human aspects. The capacity to access up to date information easily and cheaply means that many more people are sufficiently informed and are able either directly or indirectly to influence events whether in the world or within their own professional or personal lives.

> Information is the key to understanding, and to understand is to have the power to influence. International communications via satellite have transformed our ability to keep in touch with world events. It is now possible for us all to experience the joys and the anguish of other nations and peoples within our own homes and daily lives. It is unlikely that public horror and grief at the plight of starving Ethiopian families would have been so intense had this situation only been exposed via the printed word or still photo- graphs. Indeed public opinion is now able to influence world political events to a large degree and politicians who act on the world stage are constantly aware that they are being scrutinised and pressured by a public who are better informed about and more aware of world events and their

The teaching and learning of subjects

implications. Moreover, the 'process skill development' approach supported by I.T. is especially educational valuable.
(b) Some students will need a higher order of I.T. education because those skills will be needed for the understanding of academic subjects, because it fosters individual creativity, and because they may become workers in an I.T. using business.
(c) A few students will need a relatively specialist I.T. education, because they will need the skills to study academic subjects at a high level, because they have talent in the field, and because they may wish to work in a technological industry.

Although the educational system is growing towards a coherent IT education policy, it does seem likely that 'IT education for all' will start very early, for example at age 5, and continue at a low level throughout school life, 'IT for some' may be undertaken within traditional subjects, and 'IT for the few' will be provided through specialist courses, perhaps post-16. In any event, as Brown and Danby[20] point out, there will be a real need to ensure continuity, progression and differentiation in the IT education provided for students.

IT is often referred to in an impersonal, almost cold, manner, but in reality it has the capacity to give students the freedom to participate actively in the learning process, to involve students in learning to cope with a changing world and to give the teacher a hitherto unknown capacity to bring subjects to life.

The contribution of satellites to information technology

It can be argued that the use of satellites provides a way of integrating IT throughout the curriculum – not for its own sake but as a significant enhancement to education within our technological society.

As Chapters 1–3 have shown, broadly speaking, satellites break down into two categories: those which are used for remote sensing (taking pictures, capturing scientific data etc.) and those which are used purely to relay information (telecommunications satellites). Since their applications within the school curriculum, and hence in IT education, are very different, each will be considered in turn.

Remote-sensing satellites

Remote-sensing satellites provide a unique opportunity for staff and pupils to obtain and manipulate the same data as professional meteorologists, scientists or space engineers. The advantages of this type of work are primarily that staff can easily insert such work into their teaching schemes without having to reorganize the whole course, students recognize IT as being relevant to them in their everyday lives and not as a separate event to be experienced in 'technology' lessons and girls, who often shy away from subjects such as 'technology', are nevertheless exposed to its benefits in a natural and relevant way.

This is not to say that such data should be used in isolation, but rather that they can be used together with more traditional sources of information (such as newspapers, weather reports, land use maps) to provide a valuable enhancement of traditional courses. For example, high-quality Landsat images can be used for land use surveys in geography. These can be used in conjunction with existing maps and charts in order to mount up-to-the-minute investigations. In fast-changing situations, such as the movement of river sediments, satellite images provide the only practical means by which pupils can study the phenomena. Such high- quality images cannot be achieved within the school but the National Remote Sensing Centre (NRSC) has made limited materials available for educational purposes.

Remote-sensing satellites download vast quantities of data which can be captured, manipulated and interpreted. Patterns and relationships must then be established in order that relevant information can be provided to the user. Weather satellite data are now quite commonly used within UK secondary schools. Since a vast quantity of data are required to produce one image, computer data-handling techniques must be employed to undertake this task. These are in marked contrast with the normal data-handling techniques. How much better, therefore, to let pupils experience the real world situation by allowing them access to the same data as the professional meteorologist or scientist. These techniques are then a necessity, and the success or failure of the data processing can be clearly seen by the quality of the final image produced. Under these circumstances it is soon obvious to all concerned that the more sophisticated the processing techniques the better is the quality of the final image. Furthermore, there are great benefits to allowing students access to raw data, with all the imperfections and drawbacks, for they must not be allowed to enter adult life believing that all activities and learning situations are tailored to their individual needs. This access to raw unstructured data is an important part of the IT experience.

Satellite data streams provide a ready inexhaustible supply of such data but, furthermore, the data themselves have been collected by the student for a specific purpose, such as weather forecasting, rather than as a contrived data-handling exercise. There are very few such ready sources of relevant raw data available to school teachers. Additionally,

The teaching and learning of subjects

data are received directly into the classroom, access to a telephone line is not required and there are no significant consumable costs to be borne by the department or school.

Once an image has been produced by capturing and manipulating the raw data, it must be interpreted, and at once the limitations of using one data source become obvious. Indeed, in order to interpret the image and provide the end-user with relevant information, i.e. a weather forecast, other data are required such as the nature of the prevailing winds, weather station data and previous or later images so that trends can be established.

The satellite is therefore viewed as one source of weather data to be used in conjunction with other data sources rather than a sole provider of information. The more different data sources we have the more sophisticated will be the resultant forecast. Therefore the need is to find patterns and relationships within and between the different data types in order to formulate a forecast. When such a forecast is drawn up there are many opportunities for language development since it must convey accurately but succinctly a complex situation and its implications for individual users. It is often helpful for students to prepare both a verbal and a written forecast which can be displayed in a readily accessible (to students) part of the establishment or replayed to large groups, e.g. in a school assembly. Additionally, in the use of polar-orbiting satellites computer-based models must be used in order to predict when data can be captured. Students can readily see the need for such a model in such a rapidly changing situation which is extremely difficult to handle manually.

Although all these opportunities for activity exist it must be realized that not all the above tasks are relevant in all curriculum areas. For example, handling raw satellite data is time consuming and not appropriate to be undertaken in situations where a large number of images are required in a short space of time. For this reason we would not expect image processing to be dealt with in geography each time an image was required; instead, in this situation, it is imperative that a system is employed which gives the geographer quick and easy access to images. These images ideally should come live into the geography classroom where they can be used, archived (on slides, disc or video) and sequenced. Such activity does not preclude a cross-curricular approach to the use of satellites; indeed, work carried out elsewhere in the curriculum with regard to weather data capture, data handling and data processing can only be complementary, provided that these activities culminate in a meaningful end-product, e.g. a weather forecast, and are not seen as separate activities to be undertaken without due regard to an end-use.

Likewise, scientific satellites download vast quantities of data which

Information technology and satellites

must be captured, handled, processed and displayed in a meaningful manner in order that patterns and relationships can be established. Suggestions of applications of the use of satellite data within science are included in Chapter 6. However, it would be wrong to conclude that data from scientific satellites are only useful in science lessons; similarly satellite weather data can be used meaningfully in many areas of the curriculum. Indeed, one of the great strengths of satellite data is their flexibility of use. The raw data streams manipulated and presented in different ways can be used for specific teaching purposes in a wide variety of traditional subjects including science, mathematics, geography, computer studies, CDT, technology and electronics.

Furthermore, true cross-curricular initiatives seldom emerge within the secondary school. However, satellite data are of interest to a wide range of specialists from physicists to geographers, each with their own purpose for the captured and processed data. Such an opportunity for cross-fertilization of ideas must not be missed, and ideally senior management should seize the opportunity to break down departmental barriers and establish cross-curricular teams.

Finally, it must be realized that data-collecting satellites interest students and teachers alike. Motivation is a key component of the learning process and highly motivated students will progress rapidly. Without doubt, using satellites motivates students and we should recognize this fact and use it in order to enhance their progress.

Communication satellites

In the world of telecommunications the satellite merely relays data or information. In the case of satellite television the need for specialist receiving equipment means that the user is very aware of the vital function of the satellite. However, the satellite itself is not generating any data, but merely downloading exactly what has been uplinked to it.

The development of satellite television makes many additional television channels available to those with suitable receiving equipment. It is possible to receive broadcasts in many foreign languages including French, German, Italian and Russian. The implications of this for foreign language teaching are only just starting to be explored (see Chapter 5), but early indications are that many practical constraints will have to be overcome before this medium can be used to best advantage within the classroom. The use of live satellite television broadcasts within media studies lessons allows pupils to study current events from many different view points, thus prompting an awareness of the diversity of world opinion and hence discussion about the social implications of the freedom of information between nations and peoples made possible by modern communication.

The teaching and learning of subjects

From an IT point of view, the key issue is editing: who will do it, how, and when? While the ideal must be to develop in students the capacity to isolate material, relevant to a particular issue, from a general stream, for example from a newscast, the realities of institutional timetables necessitate the pre-selection of clips or items for closer study. This aspect of IT, which bears some similarity to the manipulation of word-blocks by word-processors, is not widely exercised outside the broadcasting fraternity. The early identification of the skills involved, and their rapid dissemination, is called for.

Conclusion

IT, in its current computer-linked form, is a relative newcomer to the educational and training scene. As such, it seems particularly prone to windy rhetoric, exaggerated claims and unsubstantiated achievements. If it is not to achieve the ultimate fate of becoming a distinct subject, and the National Curriculum makes that unlikely, and is not to degenerate into sterile exercises which bore teachers and students alike, it must be developed in such a way that it becomes embedded throughout the curriculum and involves the management of large quantities of data which are of latent interest to students.

The diversity of satellite functions, and the flood of data that they generate or transmit, provides a rich source of potentially interesting cross-curricular themes and projects for IT work. The realization of that potential must be one of the most attractive challenges facing the field of satellites in education.

References

1 House of Lords, *Education and Training for New Technologies*, Vol. 1, HMSO, London, 1984. para. 1.6.
2 Fox, P. and Tapsfield, A. *The Role and Value of New Technology in Geography*. The Geographical Association, London, 1986, p.30.
3 Telford, J. Getting going with I.T., *Educational Computing*, 8(6), 25–9, 1987.
4 House of Lords, *Education and Training for New Technologies*, Vol. 1, HMSO, London, 1984. para. 5.12.
5 Northern Examining Association, *GCSE: Information Technology, Syllabus A*, Joint Matriculation Board, Manchester, 1986.
6 Department of Education and Science, *The National Curriculum: A Consultation Document*, HMSO, London, 1987.
7 Blow, F. and Dickinson, A. *New History and New Technology: Present into Future*, The Historical Association, London, 1986, p.76.
8 NATE, *English Teaching and the New Technology into the 1990's*, National Association for the Teaching of English, Sheffield, p.24.

9 AUCBE, *Will Mathematics Count? Computers in Mathematics Education*, AUCBE, 1987, p.56.
10 ASE, *Information Technology and Science Education*, Association for Science Education, Hatfield, 1986.
11 Hinton, T., Owen, M., Dicker, R. and Cross, J. *Microcomputing in Science Education: Modules B2 of the Diploma in the Practice of Science Education*, University of Surrey and Roehampton Institute, Guildford, 1985.
12 Osborne, J, New technology and Newt nian physics, *Physics Education*, 22, 360–4, 1987.
13 Betram, J. M.E.S.U. and science education, personal communication, 1988.
14 We lington, J.J. *Times Educational Supplement*, 1 January 1988, p.16.
15 Bryson, M. and Lewis, R. *Computer Based Communication in Education*, University of Lancaster, Lancaster, 1987.
16 Manpower Services Commission, *T.V.E.I. Operating Manual*, Manpower Services Commission, London, 1983.
17 Hannon, V. The new education: What's in it for girls? In B. Taylor and T. Brighouse (eds), *The Revolution in Education and Training*, Longmans, Harlow, 1986.
18 Wellington, J.J. *Skills for the future* HMSO, London, 1987.
19 Anderson, J. *Information Technology and the Curriculum*, Council for Educational Technology, London, 1985.
20 Brown, D. and Danby, M. *The Transition between Primary and Secondary Schools: An Information Technology Perspective*, Birmingham Educational Computing Centre, Birmingham, 1986.

Part III
Satellites and sectors of the educational systems

Chapter eight

Schools and teacher education

Annette Temple

Introduction

'My school would like to purchase some satellite equipment with a dish large enough to be seen from our adjoining catchment area. Please can you advise us what to buy?'

This is one of the more amusing requests received from schools. However, the questioner was at least being honest about his motives for wishing to purchase satellite equipment and obviously had thought through at least one aspect of his requirements from the system! Much more common is the request: 'I have been made responsible for satellites within my school; please can you help?' Generally, in response to further questioning, it becomes obvious quite quickly that the questioner has no clear idea of a distinct curriculum need which he wishes to satisfy by using satellite data. Such a person is virtually impossible to help until he has thought through his own situation and identified a need.

The use of satellite data in the curriculum

Where, then, has experience shown that it is valid to use satellite data within the curriculum?

It can be argued that the use of satellites provides a way of integrating technology throughout the curriculum – not for its own sake but as a significant enhancement to pupils' education within our technological society. Broadly speaking, satellites break down into two categories: those which are used for remote sensing (taking pictures, capturing scientific data etc.), and those which are used purely to relay information (telecommunications satellites). Since their applications within the school curriculum are very different, each will be considered in turn.

Remote-sensing satellites provide a unique opportunity for staff and pupils to obtain the same data as professional meteorologists, scientists or space engineers. Furthermore, these data are obtained directly within the classroom without having to rely on a third party to disseminate it. It is possible to identify many areas where the use of satellite data enhances the learning process within the established curriculum. Examples of this are: (1) the use of UoSAT scientific data to design investigations into phenomena such as the earth's geomagnetic field; (2) the use of live NOAA or Meteosat images to investigate weather and climate.

The advantages of this type of application are primarily that staff can easily insert such work into their teaching schemes without having to reorganize the whole course, pupils recognize technology as being relevant to them in their everyday lives and not as a separate event to be experienced in 'Technology' lessons, and girls, who often shy away from subjects such as 'Technology', are nevertheless exposed to its benefits in a natural and relevant way. That is not to say that satellite data should be used in isolation, but that, together with more traditional sources of information (for example, newspapers, weather reports, land use maps), they can be used to provide a valuable enhancement of traditional courses. For example, high-quality Landsat images can be used for land use surveys in geography. These can be used in conjunction with existing maps and charts in order to mount up-to-the-minute investigations. In fast-changing situations, e.g. the movement of river sediments, satellite images provide the only practical means by which pupils can study the phenomena. Such high-quality images cannot be received within the school but the National Remote Sensing Centre (NRSC) have made limited materials available to the Geographical Association.

Another way that satellite technology can be introduced into the curriculum is via a thematic approach. This is particularly valuable in subjects such as mathematics and information technology where data must be handled, processed, sorted and presented to provide relevant information. Instead of using contrived sets of data (often hair colour or height of the members of the class) live satellite data can be used and real problems can be solved.

Additionally, since satellites download such vast quantities of data, the need for computer data handling and processing can be clearly demonstrated to pupils. Of course, this also applies to all curriculum areas where this technology is employed; for example, UoSAT data in science must be handled using relevant software packages if meaningful investigations are to be carried out. This experience of 'real-world' scientific investigations contributes greatly to the preparation of students for Further Education and the world of work.

In the world of telecommunication the satellite merely relays data or information. In the case of satellite television the need for specialist receiving equipment means that the user is very aware of the vital function of the satellite; however, the satellite itself is not generating

Schools and teacher education

any data, merely downloading exactly what has been uplinked to it. The development of satellite television makes many additional television channels available to those with suitable receiving equipment. It is possible to receive broadcasts in many foreign languages including French, German, Italian and Russian. However, the implications of this for foreign language teaching are only just starting to be explored, but early indications are that many practical constraints will have to be overcome before this medium can be used to best advantage within the classroom.

At present two-way communication between schools via satellite is not an option; however, experiments in this area are starting to take place. More widespread experiment in this area has been facilitated with the advent of the European Space Agency's Olympus programme, but it will be many years before most schools are able to participate in this way.

Finally, in curricula terms, there is the study of the technology itself, encompassing such areas as telecommunications, orbital mechanics and spacecraft engineering. Even in the context of the 16–18 curriculum the latter is too specialist to play a part, but satellite communications is a small but relevant area of study in any systems electronics or modular technology course; in the same way orbital mechanics are studied in physics and, to a certain extent, mathematics courses.

However, once individual teachers are involved in using satellite data they will find other spin-offs from its classroom uses. For example, with special needs classes the concept of time is often difficult to teach in a motivating way. Polar-orbiting satellites have a regular period, and once children are interested in receiving weather pictures from such satellites, perhaps as part of a general weather theme, they will often be motivated to learn how to cope with such things as the addition of time, the 24 hour clock and GMT. Somehow, time encountered in this way is more easily digestible than dry exercises involving train and bus timetables which tend to be favourite topics to cover in order to impart life skills to these pupils. Being able to read timetables is indeed important, but if your mother takes you everywhere by car or you live in a rural area without such services, its immediate importance may not be striking. On the other hand, if you want to obtain your next weather picture in 102 min from now, unless you work out accurately when to turn your receiver on again, you will miss the pass and will not have an up-to-date image. The benefits of knowing how to handle time are therefore far more readily apparent in the latter case than in the former.

The possibilities for the inclusion of satellite-related courses within the broad curriculum are many and varied; however, experience has shown that the most successful initiatives have included a high level of in-service training (INSET) support for the staff involved.

Sectors of the educational systems

Remote-sensing satellites

Only a very few of the many hundreds of remote-sensing satellites orbiting the earth are at present being exploited for educational purposes. Those in most common use educationally are the NOAA series (polar-orbiting weather satellites), Meteosat (a geostationary weather satellite) and UoSAT (the University of Surrey polar-orbiting scientific satellite).

During the past two years there has been a dramatic change in the satellite receiving equipment which is commercially available and this is now beginning to have a major impact on the use of satellites within both the secondary and further education sectors. In the past, it was only the most motivated teachers who were also fortunate enough to possess the necessary constructional skills and who were sufficiently motivated to build a ground station from scratch (in the main radio amateurs) that were able to enter the field. There were of course a few exceptions to this, as some schools were able to obtain sponsorship from organizations such as the BP Educational Trust to install systems (usually Meteosat).

All the major educational suppliers now carry a range of satellite equipment in their catalogues and the great advantage of this is that teachers can buy a working system from one supplier instead of putting together a hybrid system consisting of many components obtained from a multitude of sources. In my experience, these hybrid systems often do not work, and manufacturers of each part blame one another's equipment for the fault. Indeed, in many instances the system itself is not viable and teachers are faced with either abandoning the equipment or making expensive modifications. The advantages of buying complete systems are considerable since such equipment will have been extensively tested prior to being marketed, and can be up and running quickly after receipt. Building up a satellite receiving–decoding system from scratch is a very arduous task, and therefore this is not a route to be embarked upon within a school unless very specialist skills are to hand.

In this new area of the curriculum it is important that teachers who start using satellites do not fail at this first hurdle since they may never venture into this area again. For this reason, the entry of the major educational suppliers is of great importance to the penetration of satellite related topics into the curriculum. However, before considering purchasing equipment, it is imperative that a curriculum need has been identified: buying a satellite system with only a vague idea as to its use is a recipe for disaster. Prices of commercial systems range from £200 upwards and therefore it is essential that purchasers buy the correct system for their needs. It is therefore essential that teachers work out carefully at which points in the curriculum they wish to introduce satellite work and buy appropriate equipment. For example, the satellite

Schools and teacher education

equipment required for cloud identification within a geography module is different from that required to demonstrate image processing within an electronics course. Indeed, it is not possible to buy one satellite system that will cope with all possible curriculum needs; therefore it is important to define your need carefully and then seek equipment which most closely fulfills this.

There are some commonsense questions which potential purchasers should ask when considering equipment purchase and these are included below.

Weather satellite equipment

The key questions to ask when buying a weather satellite system are discussed below.

1. (a) What processes need to be gone through before a final image is obtained?
   (b) Is this process practical for you to undertake within the classroom on a regular basis?

Decoding satellite images can be time consuming; if you only require the image itself you may not be prepared to spend a lot of time in this aspect. Some systems do everything for you, instantaneously decoding and displaying the receiver image; others are very interventionist. In information technology where access to a raw data stream is vital an interventionist system is essential, whereas in geography this is probably not the case.

2. Is the resolution of the image sufficient for your particular purpose?

Systems based upon the BBC computer have lower resolutions than stand-alone systems. For more advanced applications in geography eight-colour images such as these obtained on the BBC system will not be sufficient.

3. What facilities are there for the storage and/or reproduction of the processed image? Are these facilities standard or are they add-on options?

Some classroom applications will demand that pupils have access to images on an individual basis where print-outs are required; check that their quality is sufficient for your needs. Not all systems have facilities for dumping images to disc. If you are likely to need this facility, check this out before purchasing a system.

4. It is possible to upgrade some NOAA systems to allow the reception of Meteosat. Conversely, some Meteosat systems can be upgraded

to receive NOAA images as well. This may or may not be important to you but should at least be considered.

5 In the case of polar-orbiting satellites, does the software take account of ascending and descending passes?

When NOAA passes from north to south over your ground-station, the image received will be upside down and laterally inverted unless the accompanying software takes this into account. (You could decide not to receive and/or decode such passes, in which case you are simply reducing the number of images received per day.)

UoSAT

Receiving data from UoSAT within school, although perfectly possible, is far more problematic than weather satellite reception. The following points should be remembered: the University of Surrey uses UoSAT for investigations into various aspects of spacecraft engineering and experiments into high speed data transfer, and when this work is being undertaken the satellite does not download data in a form which is useful to schools; signals from UoSAT are weak in comparison with those downloaded from the various weather satellites and therefore equipment performance is more critical. Much material published about UoSAT recommends the use of simple receiving–decoding equipment. However, extensive school trials have shown this not to be the case.

The key questions to ask when buying a UoSAT system are discussed below.

1 What aerial design is being used in the system?

Simple systems consisting of an omnidirectional aerial rarely, if ever, give satisfactory results. Signals will undoubtedly be received using such a system but will not be of the desired quality. The use of a head amplifier will help, but, better still, a more directional aerial should be used. Since tracking a satellite is normally impractical on a daily basis, directional aerials should be placed in a fixed elevated position at an optimum angle so that high-quality signals are received during the middle section of each pass.

2 Does the system include a decoding interface?

Data can be decoded by passing them directly into the cassette port of a BBC computer. However, in practice this is not a satisfactory method and a decoding interface should be viewed as an essential part of the system.

Motivation for involvement

There are many factors which prompt an interest within a particular establishment in the use of satellite data within the curriculum. Some of these influences are external such as TVEI initiatives or interest from a particular Local Education Authority (LEA) advisor. Others are internal; perhaps the headteacher or member of staff has become aware of work being done in this area and wishes to see it implemented within his/her school, and indeed it is often undoubtedly a matter of prestige. However, the most successful initiatives are generally those which originate from within the teaching staff of the establishment concerned. That is not to say that such initiatives should be undertaken by individual staff in an isolated manner, merely that there must be a perceived curriculum need on the part of the classroom teacher if lasting innovation is to occur. Clearly the ideal would be for a group of interested staff to form a cross-curricular satellite development group which allows each individual to support his colleagues and in turn to be supported himself. Internally this group would require support from senior management within the school, and to a certain extent the amount of this support normally depends on the status within the school of the individuals who comprise the curriculum group. If such a group contains senior heads of department who control departmental policy and budgets, then quite obviously any initiatives proposed by the group stand a high chance of being successfully implemented.

However, what if, as often happens, the driving force for implementing the use of satellite data on the curriculum comes from a relatively junior member of staff? Unfortunately, experience shows that such an initiative is often doomed to failure because of lack of support from senior colleagues. Such initiatives can often be crushed for lack of funds, although the sums of money concerned are pitifully small. Very often such staff display great ingenuity in building equipment from scratch, using materials acquired at no cost to the school, only to fall at the last hurdle perhaps because they are unable to have access to a computer on a regular basis or because they do not have sufficient funds to buy computer discs or to pay to have worksheets photocopied. This clearly is a very unsatisfactory situation but it is surprisingly common. Sometimes the situation can be resolved if LEA advisory staff become aware of the situation and offer support, but often such initiatives wither and die because of lack of nurturing.

What, then, can be done to overcome this problem? The most difficult problem encountered by junior staff is lack of funding, and the existence of a small fund (say £200–£300+), allocated specifically for curriculum development initiatives which junior staff could bid for, would probably alleviate a high proportion of the problems presently

Sectors of the educational systems

encountered. Additionally, it should not be underestimated just how difficult it is for many classroom teachers to obtain access to even basic equipment such as overhead projectors, and therefore microcomputers are felt by many to be unattainable. It is not unusual for microcomputers to be regarded as the personal possession of a particular member of staff which can only be borrowed as a personal favour (usually not at the time when they are really needed). Therefore, in order to facilitate the use of satellites within schools it is imperative that a critical look be taken at the use of resources within each establishment.

Teaching styles

Satellite data have their greatest classroom impact when pupils are involved in live data capture. There really is a challenge for both teacher and pupil in dealing with data in this way, since there are no guarantees as to what information the decoded data will reveal once processed and analysed. For this reason dealing with live data is a high risk situation for the classroom teacher – will he/she be able to cope with the problems encountered *en route*? A whole series of such questions pose themselves in the minds of many staff and these often include a worry about not being able to give definite answers to every question raised by students. There is still a strong feeling among many teachers that it is unacceptable to admit to pupils that they do not know the answer to a question which is posed. Until their basic attitude is changed such staff will not place themselves in high-risk situations, a glaring example of which is the reception of live satellite data.

Additionally, if a teacher knows exactly the content of his/her lesson, he/she is able to control its course carefully and quite possibly predict the majority of student questions which arise. The lesson can thus be 'successfully' completed, and neat and tidy conclusions reached to a precise timetable. It is easy to see that using live data puts this whole process under threat. If this is the case, would it not then be better to rely on archived data which the teacher can review prior to its use within a particular lesson? This strictly controlled situation would then conform to that outlined above, and all the problems outlined would appear to have been resolved.

Without doubt there are a few occasions where archived data can be used to great effect in this way; however, in the main such carefully controlled access to data by students emasculates the power of its use. It *is* important that students encounter 'raw' situations, together with all the problems which ensue, that they question those around them and themselves about their approach, and the significance of the data which they are analysing, and indeed that they realize that not all situations are readily explainable or have cut and dried solutions. They must be taught

Schools and teacher education

how to research problems which they encounter, teacher and pupil working together to try to solve what is now a common problem. Under these circumstances it matters little, if at all, to the pupil that the teacher is unable to come up with a potted solution to the problem, because they are now receiving far more than this – skills which will enable them to research and solve problems in whatever sphere of life they are encountered. Indeed, these are life skills in the truest sense and are additional to the direct curricular benefits which have already been outlined earlier in this chapter and elsewhere in this book.

Undoubtedly, there are natural risk-takers amongst us who will readily take to heart the above approach, and probably most of those who have identified themselves to date as being interested in using satellite data fit into this category. However, we have now reached the stage in the development of the 'Satellites in Education' programme when LEAs are formally incorporating its use within nationally funded programmes such as the Technical and Vocational Education Initiative (TVEI) pilot programme and more recently the TVEI extension. The consequences of this are that individual staff can no longer decide for themselves whether to become involved in the area, since its use is being laid down in a corporate programme. It is easy to see that this could cause resentment, particularly if such an imposition is not accompanied by a coherent INSET programme.

In-service training

A most critical area is the provision of INSET support for teachers to enable them to use their equipment to the best effect. Often expensive systems are purchased and not used. They may be switched on, but the data and images produced are just admired and marvelled at, rather than being put to any direct use. This is clearly unsatisfactory, but it is quite common. The majority of teachers will require a high level of initial support in order to overcome this and, indeed, a sizeable number will not even venture into the area until they know that such support is available.

It must be remembered that most staff encountering this area for the first time have little or no background on which to base their teaching. It is important initially to fill this gap in a way which is not subject specific. Ideally, a short awareness-raising course should be run which is general in nature and which is attended by staff of several disciplines. Thus the cross-curricular nature of the area is apparent and the staff concerned are encouraged to look over a broader base than just within their own specialism. Subject-specific courses then follow naturally from such an approach and, hopefully, are built upon firmer foundations. It is certainly true that staff who have received training based on this approach generally feel more confident about using satellite data than those whose only experience is upon a strictly subject basis. It is also essential that staff are brought into contact with a range of satellite equipment very early on and that they receive guidance as to the strengths and weaknesses of each system, for only then are they in a position to decide for themselves which equipment meets their requirements.

However, the major problem facing those who wish to implement a corporate satellite programme is training those teachers who are not natural risk-takers to cope with the problems surrounding the use of live data within the classroom. This unwillingness to take risks manifests itself in many ways across the curriculum. for instance, geographers may restrict themselves to archived 'classic' weather situations, scientists may only use data of 'particular interest' and modern linguists may need to edit and transcribe 'live' foreign language television programmes before they are 'usable'.

The problem is not unique to satellites, but solving it is particularly critical in this instance. It is easy to see parallels with the way in which industry trains its staff to become more entrepreneurial, and there are lessons to be learnt here. It is essential that research is carried out on how to alter people's perception of and attitude to risks, and that this training is then incorporated into INSET programmes.

Pupil involvement

It is very quickly apparent to those involved that the vast quantity of data which can be captured daily is overwhelming to even the most enthusiastic participant. Therefore, is is tempting to restrict pupils' access to data to that which the teacher feels to be relevant. However, when this is done, pupils miss learning a vital skill – that of discrimination. If pupils are to cope with life they must be able to sort the chaff from the wheat, and very restricted access to data will not achieve this. Receiving equipment should be located within the establishment in such a way that pupils have ready access to it. The system should not be so lax that no controls are exercised over its use, but such access is important for pupils. How this is achieved will obviously vary from establishment to establishment, but arguments for locating equipment safely away from pupils should be vigorously opposed. Pupils who are actively involved in using satellite equipment do no damage it; in fact, they become more concerned with improving and upgrading the installation. In 5 years of using satellite equipment within Dyfed schools, not a single wilful act of damage to equipment by pupils has occurred, despite it being located in busy accessible (to pupils) places. Indeed, this is one area where pupils can make a great contribution by receiving, decoding and/or analysing data on the teachers' behalf, provided that they have access to sufficient tutor support.

Chapter nine

Higher and continuing education

B. Groombridge

The mood of the UK trade press over satellite communication oscillates: entrepreneurs swing from optimism – contemplating the rich rewards of direct broadcasting to mass markets living in footprint areas – to scepticism, more coolly appraising the daunting difficulties in their way. 'Change is in the Air' reads the headline over a recent article whose expert author is impressed by the ten million homes across Europe that receive additional satellite channels. 'Is this the year of the Satellite?' runs another, wondering whether 'we are really on the verge of a breakthrough'. In this atmosphere, anyone daring to contemplate the use of satellite communications for purposes as specialized as higher, adult and continuing education (HACE) needs to be circumspect.[1,2]

Pioneers

The conjunction is not preposterous, however. India has been using a satellite for education since 1975, and for higher education since 1981. Canada has considerable experience of using this technology for HACE, as have several other parts of the world. Europe lags behind as yet and UK caution is related to that. The European Space Agency (ESA), with its provocative inducement of free time on Olympus which was launched early in 1989, may have initiated a change in this continent. Experiments in India were a technical success and educationally they were encouraging enough, at school level, for the Indian University Grants Committee (UGC) to set up six centres to explore satellite broadcasting for higher education (HE) using Insat 1B. By 1987, 196 low-powered transmitters had been installed, with 1,000 direct reception sets and 20,000 community television receivers. The Indian UGC purchased colour sets for 1,400 colleges to add to their existing monochrome receivers. It has been estimated that there is a viewing audience for HE in India of about 570,000 (including retired people, housewives and members of the armed forces as well as college students, who have reacted favourably to the programmes). There is one hour of HE programming per day. The content is decided by the participating universities, and the programmes are made for them by media centres. The Indian UGC financed eleven of these production units (four large educational media research centres and seven smaller audiovisual research centres), adding two new ones each year. The larger centres have twenty-four staff, and the smaller ones fourteen. So far, the programmes have been mainly for enrichment and awareness, but the Indian Open University has started to prepare curricular programmes with more didactic aims. One leading participant, Dr I.V. Reddi of Osmania University, Hyderabad, has justly claimed: 'India has made an impressive start on bringing satellite ETV to the universities'.[3]

In Canada, convincing use is being made of the Anik-C satellite for HACE. Over thirty organizations make use of the satellite for education, six of them operating regular schedules. These include Nova Scotia's DUET (Distance University Education via Satellite), TV Ontario and Knowledge Network (British Columbia). DUET transmits 130 hours per month; the material is prepared by different institutions which share an uplink and transponder time on Anik C with commercial broadcasters; TV Ontario makes full-time use of an Anik C transponder and in October 1986 the station commissioned its own uplink which is now uses to distribute its new *chaîne française* as well as its long-established English language channel. Knowledge Network also makes full-time use of an Anik C transponder, serving some 190 communities and twenty-five educational institutions, for 100 hours a week, via cable systems and direct to homes.

As in other countries, many of these Canadian organizations use satellites to supply educational programming at different levels. TV Ontario, for example, divides its output into children and youth, part-time learning and adult education (the French equivalents make the distinctions clearer – *Enfants et jeunes, formation a distance, grand public*). In 1986–7, courses (using video and print) that were particularly well received by educators, media commentators and audiences included *Hooked on Reading* and *Fitness over forty*, courses in production included one on artificial intelligence and another called *R-2000: the Better-built House*. Courses wre being developed on archaeology, the sociology of the family, women and politics and, a co-production, *The Life Revolution*. The new French language productions for *formation à distance* comprised the 'more demanding' *telecours* or the 'less formal' *ateliers* on such topics as finding a job, free trade and medical science. The medical series (*Etape par étape*), produced in collaboration with the faculty of medicine at the University of Ottawa, was the first French language learning system from TV Ontario specially designed to suit the credit-granting criteria of post-secondary institutions. *Tele-ateliers* produced in 1986–7 were on such

Sectors of the educational systems

matters as money management, French language skills and health (the latter attractively entitled *La Santé Contagieuse*). [4,5]

Such activities and achievements have been matched in the USA, Japan, Australia, Indonesia and elsewhere. Since 1984, sixty undergraduate courses have been delivered in Indonesia (using the Palapa satellite) in statistics, research methods, forestry and other subjects. Sometimes the satellite provides the technological focus for a system, as in India; sometimes it supplements more conventional forms of distribution. Thus the University of the West Indies uses a terrestrial network linking a campuses and centres in Barbados, St Lucia, Antigua, Dominica and Trinidad. For the link between Trinidad and Jamaica it uses Intelsat.[5]

Professor Tony Bates of the Open University and others have identified five different 'communication configurations' for educational satellite use: 'one-way video/receive-only transmissions (e.g. INSAT), offering all the advantages and disadvantages of conventional broadcast TV, but at lower cost; one-way video and two-way audio (by telephone), as in Project SHARE – sometimes referred to as 'Interactive TV'; two-way audio only, as used by the University of the South Pacific, to connect different sites; narrow-band transmission for graphics (using CYCLOPS) and audio, as used by PALAPA, Indonesia; and two-way video (videoconferencing) – rare in education, because of its expense.'[6]

Europe and other interested parties

In his authoritative survey of educational broadcasting in the United States, *To Serve the Public Interest*, published in 1979, Robert J. Blakely reports that the Public Service Satellite Consortium, formed four years earlier 'to research and facilitate public service satellite utilisation', was then seeking out 'high'-probability satellite users in order to establish demonstration projects.[7] Those words are a precise description of what the ESA now intends with its Olympus Project, twelve or more years later. Dr Jim Stevenson, Secretary of the BBC Educational Support Services, believes that there are several reasons why Europe has not featured among the pioneers in this field: 'While Europe leads the world', he writes, and he has written something similar in Chapter 10 of this volume 'in the provision of general, entertainment-led, low power satellite services, it lags in the utilisation of this technology for educational purposes... the countries of Europe have, in the main, effective high penetration of telecommunications at all levels. The telephones work, the mail services are good and for information and entertainment the television and radio services are of relative excellence. Add to this the separate but highly developed educational systems and couple this with the language barriers and the

result is a reasonable recipe for educational satellite non-development.'[8]
In contrast, countries which have already explored the educational potential of satellite communications are on the whole those with isolated pockets of population in vast areas or territories where satellites may provide 'the only reasonable delivery system.'

In 'Educational Television', Units 25 and 26 in the innovatory interdisciplinary Open University course, Communication and Education, Professor Bates poses a key question to which an answer will be needed before Europe becomes significantly involved in satellites for education: 'Who is going to put up the investment to make educational programmes especially for cable or satellite TV? There is not likely to be a profit in it. The most probable educational producers will be polytechnics, universities (and possibly further education colleges) with their own production facilities.' He believes that 'there will no doubt be a profusion of *experimental* projects on both cable and satellite in the UK, but it is unlikely that there will be a sustained educational provision' through them. Hence he concludes: 'The main effect is likely to be on increased pan-European educational activities, and "closed" services for particular education user groups, such as inter-university communication.'[9]

The Olympus satellite was built mainly for just such demonstrations and experiments, at a cost of around £400 million. This cost was met from public funds by the governments of Austria, Belgium, Denmark, Italy, the Netherlands, Spain, the UK and, as it happens, Canada. It was built by an international team of some forty industrial contractors, headed by British Aerospace. The ESA is offering time on Olympus free for 2 years in the first instance for educational experiments designed to test learning systems and their marketability.[10]

So far, interest in mounting demonstration projects on Olympus has been strong in the UK. As a result, the UK has been allocated a third of the total time available for education. This is due largely to the keen interest shown in the project by the British National Space Centre (BNSC) and, in particular, to the enthusiasm of the BNSC's consultant, Mr Brian Champness (Director of Communication Studies and Planning Ltd). The French Government is also providing support for educational bodies wishing to use Olympus. It has set up an umbrella organization under the Ministries of Education and Foreign Affairs. Institutions from several other European countries have put in bids. In allocating time to more than fifty applicants from different parts of Europe, the ESA was advised by an independent international committee chaired by Dr Alan Hancock (of UNESCO, but in his private capacity). The UK's 'high'-probability satellite users include ten universities, two polytechnics, three umbrella organizations, such as the British Universities Film and Video Council, and other bodies, of which the Manpower Services

Sectors of the educational systems

Commission is probably the most unexpected. With the exception of the latter, these demonstration projects, though initiated in Britain, are intended to be European, taking advantage of the generous Olympus footprint, and many of the British contributors expect to be collaborating with their opposite numbers in other countries. Thus, for example, the bid in the name of the University of London Department of Extra-Mural Studies involved communication with Belgium, Denmark, Finland, France, Federal Republic of Germany, Ireland, The Netherlands, Norway and Sweden (countries taking part do not have to be co-founders of Olympus through the ESA).

The direct broadcasting satellite (DBS) payloads will enable educators to use broadband television linked with several sound channels and facilities for transmitting data. As explained earlier Olympus is a high-powered DBS. Earlier satellites were low powered and needed expensive ground-stations to receive their signals. DBS, being much more powerful, can be received by small dish antennae (between 45 and 90 cm in diameter) suitable for purchase by individual householders. Educators who wish to take advantage of Olympus or other satellites have the prospect of addressing people in their homes as well as in educational centres and workplaces.

Rationales and reasons

When considering the use of any communications technology for education, it is essential to have good educational reasons for doing so. This may sound too banal to be worth saying and yet, over the years, educators have had to remind themselves of it and to become wary of the blandishments of audiovisual enthusiasts. An international group meeting at Wye College (the University of London's agricultural outpost in Kent) in the summer of 1986 adopted a dialectical stance:[11]

> Whenever a new communications technology is developed there follows a phase when its promoters are looking for applications. This often leads to complaints from educators and others that the process is 'technology-led' or a 'solution in search of a problem'. The implication is that the process should be 'education-led' but in this case the relevance and usefulness of new technologies may not be envisaged at all since the problem will be defined in terms of the old technologies. What is needed is a dialogue between technologists and educators.

Such a dialogue seems to have informed the developments in British Columbia which have already been mentioned. Knowledge Network, now merged with the Open Learning Institute, justifies itself by a

Higher and continuing education

straightforward plea for equity. Dr Walter Hardwick, chair of Knowledge Network, has said that in a huge mountainous province, the satellite enables small firms, voluntary organizations and others who need access to training to enjoy 'equal opportunities' with British Telecom or Canadian Pacific for the first time. John Taylor, Director of Programmes at North Island College (part of the network at ground level), asserts that all communities in the province, no matter how isolated, should have the same right to academic support: 'If it can be made available to the wife of a lighthouse keeper, it can be used in a town of 30,000 but not the other way round.'[12]

Europe will need to find reasons as potent as that Canadian combination of geography and equality of opportunity. 'We must first clearly explore the unique characteristics of satellite delivery', advises Dr Jim Stevenson, to be confident that they 'extend educational possibilities beyond those systems which currently exist in the telephone, cable television, terrestrial radio and television and the postal services'.[8]

Participants in the seminar at Wye College considered that there were several reasons for taking ESA's invitation seriously. What they called the 'creeping expansion' of conventional public entertainment television through the day was reducing the time available for education and training; pressure on channel time was increasing at the very moment when Europe-wide interests required 'new communication initiatives'. Issues needing further discussion included the Europeanization of higher education and professional activity, the interests of ethnic, cultural and other minorities in maintaining contact and communities of interest between populations dispersed across frontiers, and the needs of the general and specialized publics to participate in the affairs of a Europe-wide learning society which might begin to embody in reality some of the rhetoric of a People's Europe.[11]

Particular educational enterprises will also need cogent reasons for using Olympus or other satellites. One of the best thought out schemes so far comes from Birkbeck College, London, where the psychologist Dr Angela Summerfield has developed a subtle technique of video analysis as an element in psychiatric rehabilitation. This technique, developed in conjunction with Dr Maurice Lipsedge (perhaps best known for his book *Aliens and Alienists*) at Guy's Hospital, could provide the foundation for collaborative work across Europe, linking psychiatrists in several university and medical sites with each other for teaching and diagnosis (using real time where necessary). People needing psychiatric help – guest-workers suffering as displaced persons, for example, and wanting both to be cured and fit for work – could be in touch in real time with the best-qualified psychiatrists, wherever they were based. Students in universities and hospitals everywhere could 'sit

Sectors of the educational systems

in' audio-visually on diagnostic sessions (encrypted) or sessions for teaching and training (which could be open to all possessing a dish).[11]

Planners and others would no doubt be wise to prepare a check list of criteria needing to be satisfied to justify the use of satellites for HACE. At Wye, the suggested criteria were that the use of the satellite should:

1 open up a new channel for delivery;
2 link education with European mobility and European interdependence;
3 upgrade professionals at their place of work;
4 to bridge the gap between training and reality;
5 establish links between institutions and professionals;
6 allow distance education to be recognized at a national and international level;
7 enable specialists and experts in different fields to link with each other
8 create a broader awareness and public involvement in general issues, and the ability to focus simultaneously on strongly felt issues in a number of countries or communities;
9 provide the opportunity to link expertise and specialist skills with other interest groups associated with particular themes or issues;
10 act as a catalyst.

In the euphoria of involvement with a new communications technology, it should also be noticed that, whatever educational, geographical and social justifications there may be for using the satellite, they have to be compatible with budgetary realities.

Visions, systems and frameworks

Such prudence can be overdone, however. It needs to be complemented by vision. The experience of high-quality networked broadcasting and the availability of broadcasting channels provided the basis for the vision which, starting as the University of the Air, became the Open University in the UK – widely recognized as an innovation of world significance. Similarly, it is the experience of such distance-teaching universities and the increasing availability of communications, including satellite communications, that has recently given rise to bold new educational visions such as the University of the North Sea and, on a even grander scale, the Commonwealth University.

As this is written (in 1988), the North Sea University as such is still an idea, although a potent one, made possible by communications and likely to be enhanced as a concept and in practice by making use of

Higher and continuing education

satellites. It already exists embryonically as the Electronisk Universitet Norge. Supported by the Norwegian Government and private enterprise, this has begun as an electronic mail network, intended to deliver education at a distance to people all over Norway, and possibly to link up with US and UK universities supplying courses in business, natural sciences, social sciences and the humanities. The hope now, which has been espoused particularly by the authorities and academics in Rogaland (in and around Stavanger on the west coast of Norway), is to extend the system through audio-conferencing and satellite. Among other objectives, they plan to unite universities with common academic interests, a shared geographical context and a common cultural inheritance in countries bordering the North Sea. The computer and oil industries in Norway, the UK and elsewhere are already showing interest.

The proposal to set up the University of the Commonwealth for Co-operation in Distance Education, to give it its full title, was made in 1987 by an 'Expert Group' chaired by Asa Briggs (Lord Briggs, Provost of Worcester College, Oxford, Chancellor of the Open University and official historian of the BBC) at the request of Commonwealth Ministers of Education and Commonwealth Heads of Government at their meetings in 1985. The Briggs Committee had been 'greatly impressed by the depth of Commonwealth experience in distance education and by the pace at which developments, spurred on by new break-throughs in communications technologies, are taking place. We have been equally impressed, however, by the range of needs and the as yet unrealised potential of distance education to meet them.' The experience to which the Briggs Report refers includes the Knowledge Network in British Columbia and TV Ontario mentioned earlier, as well as the Indira Gandhi Open University in India, the British Open University and many others. Satellite communication is thought to be 'a useful component of Commonwealth co-operation in distance education', although at present it would be realistic, because of the costs entailed, 'for education to share the use of a satellite with other agencies' rather than seek dedicated and exclusive facilities. Meanwhile, these same cost considerations have led the leaders of the Commonwealth to settle, at least for the time being, not for a new university, but for something more modest to be known as the Commonwealth for Learning.[13]

To be educationally effective such schemes will have to become the basis for new teaching–learning systems. Various models for such systems need to be imaginatively considered. This may not be easy at first, since most of us think of horseless carriages before we think of motor cars. Discussion of satellites for education tends at present to be dominated, in Europe at least, by a broadcasting model, with reference to 'programmes' and 'audiences'. Yet experiments on Olympus and

Sectors of the educational systems

elsewhere could more closely resemble video-conferencing, in which case the messages are not programmers and the participants are not audiences. Another model may be provided by the Open Univeristy itself with its sophisticated use of the postal service reinforced by broadcasting and other media in combination with some face-to-face tuition (in tutorials and summer schools). A satellite could be used as the lead medium in such a configuration of resources on a much larger geographical scale. It is to be understood therefore that a new form of educational communication is being created, having something in common with broadcasting or with tele-conferencing or with centralized teaching at a distance, but not to be confused with or reduced to any of them.

In addition to occasioning some surprise that it has an interest in the Olympus experiment, the UK Manpower Services Commission (MSC) has stimulated awareness of the significance of systems by outlining one of its won (although formal approval to proceed was awaited at the time of writing). The model in question was outlined at the Wye seminar by Mr Graham Cheetham. Satellite transmission is normally thought of as involving transborder communication or at least operating on a vast regional or subcontinental scale. However, a hugh organization, such as the MSC, with a massive budget, responsible for activities at thousands of large and small locations throughout the UK, could find that it made economic and logistical sense to send video messages and data by satellite from one to many sites within a single country. Cheetham envisages a three-tier system. A simplified account of this system starts with the inner tier which would enable participants both to receive broadcast video and to interact with each other through audioconferencing. The middle tier would consist of a larger number of people who could receive material and put questions or comments afterwards, by telephone, as in a radio phone-in. People in both tiers could already have received relevant documents, agendas, resource materials and so on by post or fax. The third tier could provide open sessions for a general public with access to the proceedings by receiving should and vision, but not necessarily or normally able to respond directly.[11]

This promising model can be adapted and applied in a variety of ways. It seems certain to inspire and provide a structure for the activities of SPACE, a consortium which has been allocated time on Olympus and which may serve as an illustration at this point. SPACE (Satellite Programmes for Adult and Continuing Education) is convened by the University of London Department of Extra-Mural Studies. As a department of adult education, this body is accustomed to partnerships which bring together university and non-formal educational organizations in a common enterprise. It this case the enterprise is national and international. The UK partners, of whom some already have European

Higher and continuing education

counterparts and others are seeking them, comprise academics from different parts of the University with interests in primary health care, veterinary science, architecture and planning, coastal zone management, and the professional education of adult and continuing educators, together with voluntary organizations concerned with education in mental health, human rights, religion and the European dimension in the curriculum of schools. These partners are a loose federation or cluster wishing to test the usefulness of Olympus for various kinds of education and training related to health and well-being in Europe (details can be obtained from the author).

They differ in their readiness to take part in such an experiment or, rather, they are all both prepared and unprepared in different ways. One may have ready access to video material which could be represented in a new format; another would have to commission video material from scratch. One already works with opposite numbers in European universities; another is only now identifying them, and so on. However, they all have in common an interest in facilitating communication between experts in different countries, and across professions and occupations in these countries, and between those elite groups – *les responsables* as the French would call them – and European citizens generally. It is being considered, for example, whether SPACE's experiment with Olympus will make a contribution to the major project sponsored in Europe by the World Health Organization (WHO) as part of its campaign to promote Health for All by 2000 – the Healthy Cities Project.[14,15]

Awareness of the Healthy Cities Project is to be enhanced by a television series featuring its progress in certain featured cities in different parts of Europe, including Liverpool (UK), Turku (Finland), Rennes (France) and Zagreb (Yugoslavia). The series, an international co-production, coordinated by Holmes Associates for Channel Four, will be the occasion for much educational follow-up in accordance with the channel's practice. However, something more may by needed to complement or reinforce this broadcasting initiative.

HFA 2000, as it is familiarly known to health educators, depends essentially on the notions that health is everyone's responsibility and that it is determined or conditioned by the environment (especially housing), as well as by each one of us individually and by no means solely by (national) health services as such. This WHO project will not become a movement unless *les responsables* learn to talk to each other – across departments and occupational demarcations – and also to involve a multifarious (and increasingly multi-cultural) general public in dialogue and decision-making. Something like the MSC – Cheetham model for Olympus use seems very suitable for serving such participatory objectives.

165

Sectors of the educational systems

Like much else in this chapter that relates to Europe, a good deal of this material about SPACE is speculative. The Open University course, already quoted, is right to prompt its students of education and communication to wonder where the money will come from to ensure that the satellite is used for education as seriously in Europe as it is in other parts of the world. The issue of finance – who will pay for what elements in the process and who will pay in due course for what will in the first years be free, i.e. time on the satellite – is closely related to the issue of frameworks. Indian use of satellite and other communications for HACE has the backing of the Indian Government and the Indian UGC. The educators and their media centres operate in an official framework as an integral part of the Indian system of higher education. In British Columbia, Knowledge Network and Open Learning Institute were devised and indeed required to amalgamate by provincial politicians and governments. On the other side of Canada, students of TV Ontario buy courses and support materials, but primary funding for the operations and capital expenditures of TV Ontario is provided by the Province of Ontario (through grants from the Ministry of Citizenship and Culture and the Ministry of Education). At the end of the fiscal year 1986–7, TV Ontario was in deficit.[5]

At present, there is no sign of any European analogues of these frameworks. There seems to have been no connection as yet between the ESA's work, which is fundamentally about technology and engineering, and either the European Community or the Council of Europe. Yet both the community and the Council have policies for the development of HACE, including programmes (such as Delta) intended to harness technology for European education. Unless these related issues of finance and of frameworks are resolved, so that 'programming' becomes an embodiment of policy, then Professor Bate's apprehension will be justified and an opportunity will be missed. The process of acquiring experience of using the satellite for HACE will lead nowhere. The experiments will turn out not to be experiments at all, but merely tentative pilot projects without issue.

These extraordinary means of communication are already powerfully and globally at the disposal of entertainment, of news and information exchange, and of commerce and of the military. Although its circumstances are so different from the Caribbean, the Pacific or North America. Europe also has educational needs that could best be met through harnessing these new resources. In this way, the communities of the world – intellectual, practical and geographical – could begin to share their knowledge and perhaps even to pool their wisdom.

References

1. Clemens, J. Change is in the air, Broadcast, 22 January 1988.
2. Syfret, T. Is this the year of the satellite? Broadcast, 18 January 1988.
3. Reddi, I.V. Satellite educational television in India, *Journal of Educational Television*, 13(2), 1987.
4. Stahmer, A. and Lopianowski, N. Satellite services and education: where do hopes and reality meet?, *Proceedings: Satellite Users Converence, Ottawa, Canada, 1987.*
5. Annual Report 1986–7; TV Ontario, Toronto, Canada, 1987.
6. Bates, A.W. The educational potential and limitations of satellite TV in Europe, *Journal of Educational Television*, 13 (2), 1987.
7. Blakely, J.R. *To Serve the Public Interest; Educational Braodcasting in the United States,* Syracuse University Press, New York, 1989.
8. Stevenson, J., *Satellite Education: An International Perspective,* Satellite Forum, Council for Educational Technology, London, 1987.
9. Bates, A.W. Educational television: In *Communication and Education,* Open University Press, Milton Keynes, 1987, Units 25/26.
10. Hughes, C.P. and Bartholome, P. The Olympus utilization programme, *E.S.A. Bulletin,* European Space Agency, Noordwijk, 1987.
11. Champness, B. and Groombridge, B. and *Satellite Communication for Education and Training: European Briefing and Progress Report,* Department of Extra-Mural studies, University of London, and C.S. and P. London, 1987.
12. Little, K. Open skies, grass roots. In *Communication and Education,* Open University Press, Milton Keynes, 1986.
13. *Towards a Commonwealth of Learning: A Proposal to Create the University of the Commonwealth for Cooperation in Distance Education,* Commonwealth Secretariat, London, 1987.
14. *Health for all by the Year 2000: Charter for Action,* Faculty of Medicine, University of London, 1986.
15. *The Liverpool Declaration of the Right to Health,* Deparment of Community Health, University of Liverpool, 1988.

Part IV

The realization of potential

Chapter ten

Resource systems for education

J. Stevenson

'What is the use of a book,' thought Alice, 'without pictures or conversations?'

(*Alice in Wonderland*, Lewis Carroll)

The apprentice and the student

If you want to learn to speak Italian then the best possible way to do so is to go and live in Italy. If you wish to learn about petrol engines and acquire the skills of engine maintenance and repair, then a year or two in a vehicle workshop should do the trick. The scientist learns skills at the bench with other scientists. Young goldsmiths learn from the master craftsman. The television director learns programme making as an assistant, a researcher, a carrier of film and coffee cans. Experience and professionalism is achieved on the job at the feet of those who have gone before. Our language, our behaviour and our skills are learnt through total immersion. This is the 'apprentice' route. It is the route which many of us have taken at least in part in order to achieve the positions in which we work.

Anyone involved in 'apprentice' learning is receiving inputs, and such inputs can be catalogued. Learning a language involves listening, looking, reading, writing, and talking. The people you talk to and listen to act as learning resources. Newspapers, television, radio, books, advertisements and street signs are similarly resources. Learning is continuous, random, interactive and multi-media. The master craftsman or engineer is a resource on which the young goldsmith or mechanic leans and interacts. The apprentice lives and works in a resource mixture – an environment of total learning.

Separate this apprentice learner from his/her learning environment and you have 'student' who works in a less than total learning environment. The student in the classroom has to rely on the teacher, the book and the practical demonstration as learning resources. He/she is a stage

The realization of potential

removed from the ideal. The teacher is a mediator, a translator of real experience and the student is already at a distance from the rich source of total learning. It is then inevitable that the resources of the classroom must be enhanced and increased as far as possible to re-create something of the intensity of 'apprentice' learning. The teacher's familiar cry for more resources is the recognition that a person in front of a class is not enough. There have to be books, wall charts, slides, videos, objects and activities, all brought in to enhance the learning. Order and linear learning has to replace the randomness of the workshop or laboratory. Lessons must have structure. Resources are marshalled in sequence. There are beginnings, middles and ends. There are high points, low points and assessments. Life becomes harder.

The third mode of learning is when the teacher is separated from the students. Imagine a lecture theatre in a university packed with people all listening and watching the teacher and demonstration. Suddenly the theatre is quite empty and the students are flung to the far ends of the country all in different directions. They are alone. They are 'distance' learners. Now they need their resources for learning as never before. They have no rich mixture in which to wallow. They have no time for random continuous inputs. They need pre-packaged learning resources. They need linear sequential stage-by-stage learning. They need access to primary source material and directions as to how to use it. They need as rich a variety of media as can be marshalled. Above all, they need communication systems of interaction, delivery, feedback and reinforcement. They need a network of specially designed resources.

Throughout life, the learning process seems to oscillate across these three types of learning (Table 10.1). Very young children are clearly apprentices. The formal classroom years follow, ending possible with a return to apprenticeship in work and higher education. Distance learning now characterizes much adult education. At each stage we can define our learning resources, but defining them is one thing and producing them is quite another.

Table 10.1 Relations between learners and learning resources

Learner types	Learning styles	Teacher ratios
Apprentice	Random/multi-media	1:1
Classroom student	Fairly structured, limited multi-media	1:10–100
Distance learner	Highly structured/linear, very limited media resources	1:100–1000

Hot and cold media

Watch any television programme or listen to any radio programme and try, a week later, to write down what was in it. It is a pitiful exercise. It is fairly difficult to do this a day or even an hour afterwards. The amount of information we take in from, say, a thirty minute television documentary or a news bulletin is only a tiny fraction of the whole. The same is true of a lecture or a classroom session. At this very moment, students are walking away from lectures, seminars and lessons all over the world with only a vague idea of what has gone on in the previous hour.

It is, of course, possible to be stimulated by a lecture or a television programme but the effect is much the same as listening to a piece of music. When the performance is over the memory is enjoyable but not detailed. So often, after following a brilliant lecture or programme, one says to oneself: 'That was interesting – I must get a book and learn about it'. For those who will learn as students the book is the hard learning resource. Anything else which cannot be re-accessed for repeated study is ephemeral. For the student, print is the equivalent of the apprentice's workshop. The apprentice learns from repetition of the technique. The student learns, in the main, from re-reading and regurgitating print; synthesizing, analysing and re-forming print.

When the Open University (OU) of the United Kingdom began teaching in the early 1970s it did so with carefully designed multi-media packages of which a small proportion (estimates varied between 5 and 10 per cent) was broadcasting. Much of the remainder was by print – attractively presented linear learning packages of booklets, papers, photographs and paper exercises. At the time only the science faculty had the courage to say that the television programmes were essential to study and an integral part of each science course. In fact the teams producing the science courses at the time deliberately cross-linked the media components of courses in order to ensure a real multi-media usage of the learning resource. Students had to keep pace with the broadcasts, and if they fell behind they began to miss out. The components would no longer gel together – a bit like reading a thriller with every fourth chapter missing. All other OU faculty areas regarded broadcasting as important but insisted that students could manage without them. This was particularly true in the arts area where a tradition of more random learning than in the sciences existed. The mathematics faculty, faced with a pre-natal criticism of its broadcasts and scepticism about the need to visualize equations, decided on the shotgun approach by peppering its students with the same material in print, radio and television to ensure that if you cannot knock it in through one medium then you might by another.

The realization of potential

Seventeen years later it is fascinating to see that the UK Open College (OC), which was set up with television teaching as a spearhead in its armoury, has decided that the programmes are not essential for students. They are, of course, highly desirable as adjuncts to the OC courses but they are apparently not integrated with the teaching to such an extent that a student missing them will be unduly disadvantaged. There is a recognition that the ephemerality of broadcasts has been the major disadvantage for their inclusion in multi-media learning situations.

This ephemerality is much less of a problem if the programmes are used as part of classroom sessions where the teacher mediates between the television or radio resource and the class with its other more tangible resources. If the teacher works skilfully the programmes can be well integrated into the teaching. Hence the undiminishing great success of school broadcasting in the UK. Programmes are designed to complement the curriculum and to give the teacher a resource which cannot easily be brought into the classroom. The programmes not only teach but can also provide a springboard to class discussion. However, the broadcasts, even if used in recorded form, are still ephemeral resources and do not lend themselves easily to hard learning, particularly that pressured learning associated with examinations.

It was McLuhan who first distinguished between the temperature of media. Television, in his terms, was hot – here today and gone tomorrow. Print was cold – for long repetitive learning, analysis and enjoyment. I once complimented a producer, of some renown, on a particularly beautiful programme he had made. He was pleased with it himself but said that the compliment was not necessary: 'It was only television'. Television, he felt, would hardly rate a footnote in the history of communication. However, this was before cassettes.

In education, the cheap video cassette and the even cheaper audio cassette have moved television and radio from 'hot' to 'cool'. The portable VHS-format video and the Walkman have opened two new technological avenues in which few in education have yet walked.

Convergence in media learning

In 1979 I was present at a demonstration of a future student's workstation. It consisted of a banana-shaped desk with a swivel chair, a television screen, a couple of loudspeakers, a telephone, a keyboard and a small bank of electronics. The student, or householder or indeed anyone, could call up a variety of media. Normal terrestrial television channels could be viewed in addition, of course, to video. There were audio channels and an audio cassette built into the banana and the keyboard was linked to a home computer and to data bases elsewhere.

Resource systems for education

Anything could be done: shopping, booking rail tickets, checking and buying shares. Data from a number of sources could be accessed, used and stored. The home could be programmed to keep out burglars, cats and the cold, all through the console. Book pages could be read on the screen. Everything could be obtained from that stool and the banana-shaped, futuristic desk.

I found the demonstration rather soul destroying, but it did illustrate one point very powerfully. If we need information we can now obtain it more easily than ever before and we can, if necessary, centre the receipt of information on one spot. It is not necessary to take the learner to the resource when the resource can be piped to the learner. This does not print to a new way of studying or new social behaviour. People will still learn lying on the floor, sitting in the park, on trains or in bed, but the possibility of harnessing the resources and taming and organizing them is with us.

Resources can be made to converge onto one console. In the field of tele-education, i.e. any educational material delivered electronically, technologies themselves are converging – IBM compatible, Astra compatible, PAL, SECAM and NTSC interconvertible. If it comes down a wire the black box will handle it.

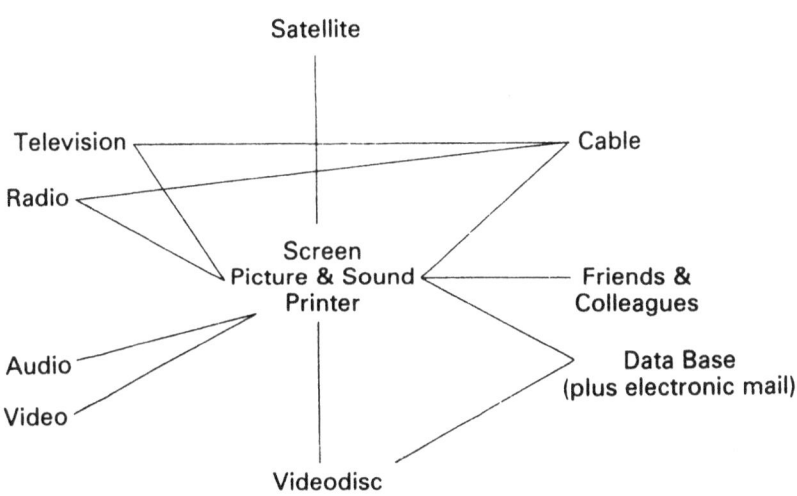

Figure 10.1 The convergence of resources

The realization of potential

Convergence within tele-education

What is fascinating in convergence is that all media are now electronically related. In education this relationship, coupled with the ability to store information electronically, like a book on a shelf, has opened an almost infinite variety of resource systems. Also, each separate medium has evolved or at least is in the process of evolution. Television has evolved into the video cassette and into the video disc. Print has evolved through the computer into data bases accessed through terminals. Telex and electronic mail have, in some places, replaced the letter or memorandum. As with biological evolution where apes, snakes and palms survive side by side with oak trees and people, inkwells, rooms of desks and consultative meetings still exist.

These new technical flexible media are only the framework on which we can hang our education. People do not learn better just because the resources for learning are delivered by cable or from outer space. For the student the reality of learning is still much the same. Lectures are often tedious. Books can still be turgid. Lessons on a hot afternoon invariably induce sleep. But because much electronic educational material – tele-education – is so public and often expensive, the educational standards of these resources have tended to rise. Exposure to high-quality learning resources has made people more critical. It is no longer sufficient to prop up a professor in front of a class and hope for the best. Because the new resources have to be properly structured and carefully aimed, with their words and pictures honed to perfection, there is a spin-off into conventional teaching. Poor teachers are less tolerated. Boring books are consigned to the waste bin. Dull computer software is cast aside. Teaching standards rise and evolve on the back of the new networks of electronic resource delivery.

Open learning/distance learning

No two buzz phrases have been more current in educational circles throughout the world in the past two decades than 'open learning' and 'distance learning'. They are different from each other and not to be confused, though it is true to say that the concept of open learning derives from the experience of distance learning.

Consider for a moment again my imaginary lecture theatre packed with students with a professor demonstrating at the front. If you remove all the students to the far ends of the country or to other countries, print everything that the professor is saying, make a video of his demonstration and design a small kit for the students to work with at home, you have distance learning – conventional teaching where the students are separated from the teacher by space and usually by time.

However, open learning has two meanings. First, it means open access. Anyone can join in irrespective of qualifications. It also means open in style; teaching resources are designed for use by the student at a pace dictated by the student rather than the system. This second use of the term is the one on which I shall concentrate.

The OU is a distance learning organization which uses open learning materials. However, students are paced in the OU not only by broadcasts but by the assessment system which demands student assignments on specific dates. It also uses a network of face to face tuition which is designed to ensure that students keep up. Therefore it is something of a hybrid between conventional university learning and distance learning. Time will tell, but it is possible that as technology progresses some of the face to face tuition might find its way to telephone teaching or tele-conferencing, but in the foreseeable future this is unlikely.

Open learning materials, in the main, must be capable of use by a student independent of time and place. Someone sitting on a train learning a language through a combination of book and audio cassette is involved in an open learning situation. Such learning resources are pre-packaged and usually modular. As I said earlier, they must be highly structured and complete in themselves if the student is to be prevented from becoming bogged down. Without being able to refer to a teacher, an isolated student needs learning materials of high quality.

More and more open learning systems are being developed. They can be used within a school classroom situation with a teacher relegated to a point of reference and guidance rather than the supplier of information. Industry in many countries uses open learning to train staff. The shelves of book stores in the West are filling up with open learning materials. The accent on learning throughout life and re-training is focusing more attention on such materials, and there are profits to be made. For example, a recently produced open learning package for business people visiting Japan consisted of some video cassettes about Japan and its people, some audio tapes and a book for elementary language acquisition. There was a booklet on standard forms of behaviour and business practices. It was genuine open learning – unique and very expensive.

Therefore open learning is very much a new and powerful approach. I anticipate that as the modules of open learning materials evolve, they will become more educationally and cost effective. Distance of learning will spread further using both open learning packages and live interactive distance teaching.

The multi-media package concept

Most modern open learning courses involve more than one medium. The book or correspondence course is clearly open learning but the trend is

The realization of potential

towards bi- or tri- or multi-media learning. It makes a lot of sense. Some aspects of the subject are highly visual and the moving image is an obvious choice; some, e.g. music, demand high-quality sound. The classic use of tri-media open learning is found in the BBC's language series *Get By In Arabic*. The leader is a radio series followed by a book and audio cassettes. *Buongiorno Italia!*, a basic course in Italian, leads with television and follows with a book and audio tapes.

When the OU started teaching in the early 1970s the accent was multi-media. There could be up to nine distinct media on a course, for example:

1 Science Foundation Course: print – course books, set texts etc.;
2 television programmes;
3 radio programmes;
4 tutor-marked assignments;
5 computer-marked assignments;
6 tutorials (face to face);
7 summer schools;
8 home experimental kits;
9 slides.

Later courses added audio tapes, disc recordings, computer programmes and telephone tutorials.

The characteristic learning pattern of many courses was linear, with each course component following in sequence, for example:

course book → reference book → TV home experiment → radio → assignment → tutorial

Other courses adopted a looser structure where components stood more alone. There was a recommended sequence but students could, in a way, browse in the learning framework. The linear approach demanded a harsh discipline and strict adherence to the timetable. Students fell behind and got the course components out of phase. No matter how beautifully you integrate the media, the student will disintegrate them.

Inevitably, the experience gained in mounting linear courses leads towards a de-coupling of media from each other. This protects the open learner from getting lost by being out of phase but throws more responsibility on the individual to marshal his/her resources. For each course a new strategy is required but it now seems that although a measure of linear studying is necessary with appropriate pacing, the less structured approach with a more flexible use of learning resources is potentially more powerful, especially if each resource cross references to the other (Figure 10.2). For broadcasters such de-structuring of linear multi-

Resource systems for education

media gives real problems. Transmission of programmes has to be at a defined time. For genuine open learning, broadcasts must be used in the recorded form. This means that video and audio designed *only* for open learning use demand a different production strategy to that employed with a conventional programme.

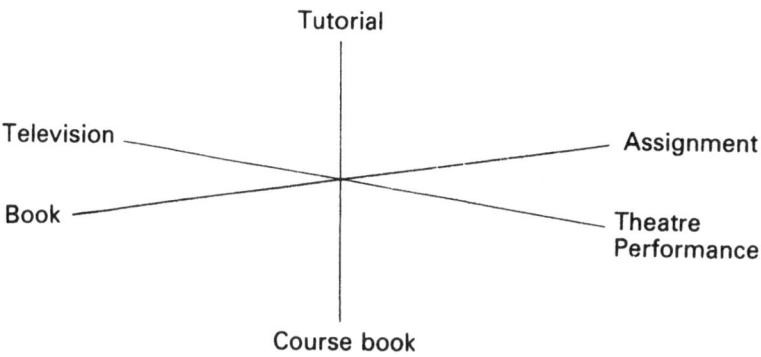

Figure 10.2 A framework for learning

Wrap-around materials

Educational broadcasts should never stand entirely alone. From the earliest days of school broadcasting in the UK teachers were supplied with notes and booklets. If you are to get the most out of a broadcast, you need to prepare beforehand and follow up afterwards. Many educational series generate a book for sale on the open market. As discussed above, in multi-media teaching involving broadcasts, there can be slides, tapes, booklets, computer software, kits and other activities. These non-broadcast resources are said to 'wrap around' the broadcast like a protective cocoon to ensure that the ephemeral messages are reinforced. 'Hot' broadcasts have 'cool' wrap-arounds.

It is worth looking at these materials in some detail. Suppose that a science teacher wishes to use television in the classroom. A sequence of events might be as follows.

1 Information: distributed free to the teacher by the broadcaster; teacher assesses programme intentions' discovers wrap-around materials available for sale.
2 Ordering: teacher orders notes, books, slides, computer software.

The realization of potential

3 Preparation: Using the notes/books the teacher prepares for the broadcast.
4 Class preparation: the teacher, using the wrap-arounds, prepares the class.
5 Broadcast: watching/listening.
6 Follow up: organization of post-broadcast activity involving wrap-arounds, e.g. software.

The teaching has been wrapped together with a combination of broadcasts and support materials.

For the student studying alone a related sequence of activities might be as follows:

1 casual viewing of a television programme stimulates interest;
2 information on screen or in the *Radio Times* indicates availability of support materials;
3 purchase of books/cassettes etc.;
4 continuation of viewing the television series with associated use of the non-broadcast materials.

Just as a novel, from which a television series is adapted, can be enjoyed without ever having seen the series, so wrap-arounds devised for use in conjunction with educational broadcasting can be used alone. Books teaching languages, written for a broadcast series, are used long after the series has finished. Slides purchased for use with an audio cassette can be shown in a different context. Programmes can be enjoyed without any wrap-around materials. The resources can be decoupled.

Leaders, integers and followers

Usually when someone begins systematically to study a particular subject, they have been stimulated to do so by an event. A visit to another country reminds you of your profound ignorance of the other's language and politics. How much more interesting the foreign news is in the daily newspaper after a tour abroad. Many people begin to study a language after a summer holiday, vowing to master it enough for an even more enjoyable visit the following year. Similarly the inputs through television are now so various and powerful that it has become the major source of information and stimulation in many homes in many parts of the world. I recall science documentaries about astronomy which have led to long neighbourly discussions about relativity. A programme in Britain about the microchip awoke the nation and the government to the development of the computer industry. The tragic scenes from Ethiopia awoke the world to the need to do something, to contribute and to learn about the causes and alleviation of poverty in the

Third World. These programmes are 'leaders' of thinking. They lead people to do other things. They introduce subjects. For the educationist they stimulate the desire to learn further.

This power of 'leader' resources has probably exaggerated the power of such resources actually to teach. It is one thing to stimulate a student to work – and quite another to set about teaching. Suppose that you want to teach mathematics. A television programme showing the houses of successful rich mathematicians with their life-style of yachts and sun-drenched beaches might stimulate someone to open the algebra book. Such a resource could be described as a leader. A programme designed through dramatic construction to explore drug abuse in teenagers might be used in the classroom to 'lead' the class to discussion. At university level such leader resources could introduce subjects, show their potential applications and stimulate further activity. They lead the teaching process. Recognizing the ephemerality of broadcasting, educational programme makers have adopted this philosophy for generations. Two things have altered this.

The development of distance and open learning systems in the 1970s encouraged the development of broadcasting resources which were integral to the courses. This different approach meant that the broadcasters had to shed, to some extent, the idea of programmes addressing a general audience of general ignorance. The first OU science television programme in the UK in 1971 began with the professor rolling a rubber ball down a sloping table. His first words were 'Well, I don't know how you've got on with this experiment at home ...'. There was an assumption that the target audience knew exactly what he was doing and had, in fact, been doing just such a thing themselves in their own back kitchens a few minutes earlier. The programme fitted snugly into a much larger study course. It made no concessions to an eavesdropping audience. It was television direct teaching, integral to the study. The only problem was that you could only watch it once. Then it had disappeared and the student was left with only the print component and a fuzzy memory.

The second alteration was the rise of the home recorder. These devices, whether for sound only or for pictures and sound, have totally changed the educational power of what was television and radio. But although their potential has only just begun to be explored, the potential for totally integrated media in multi-media courses is now with us.

'Followers' are more difficult to find. The assumption here is that the student has received both a major impetus to study and the study materials themselves from other sources and the 'follower' resource is added as the icing on the cake – for example, programmes of revision and explanatory support, programmes about the applications of knowledge etc. For instance, there might be a long course on general science

The realization of potential

accompanied by a series of radio lectures on the philosophy of science.

The radio resource would be an enrichment to the course – a follower, In a way followers are part of a circle and relate both to integers and leaders (Figure 10.3).

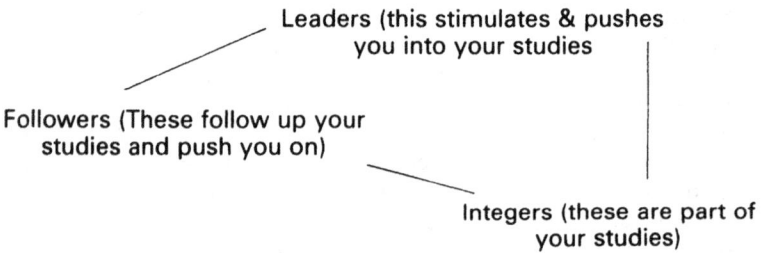

Figure 10.3 Followers as part of a circle

In designing any learning system it is as well to clarify this distinction between the positions of resources at the outset. For the development of new international learning systems across borders I believe that the accent will be on leaders and followers. Integrated programmes are more difficult to handle both in their production and the manner of their distribution.

Why satellites?

Before educationists look at any new technology it is important to define the territory and, because this chapter is about educational 'resources', we have to define what they are before we consider delivery systems and explore the potential of such new technologies as satellite broadcasting. It is also important at the same time to ride on the experience of using the old technologies.

Let me take a simple scenario. Scientist A produces a learning resource to illuminate and help the work of institution B. A and B are separated by a thousand miles. It does not really matter what the resource is, but assume that it is a video. A decides to uplink the video from his location to the distant institution. He negotiates with the cable company to link him to the uplink. He negotiates with the PTT for transmission of the signal. He negotiates with the satellite company for use of the transponder. His colleagues at B negotiate with the receiving company, lease a cable link to the institute and arrange for recording at

Resource systems for education

B. The time taken to arrange this will be several months and A will have approached a number of funding agencies to achieve adequate financial support. The chances are that he will have been on the telephone to his colleagues in B for many hours fixing it all up. The transmission takes place. Everyone is pleased with the success of the demonstration and they telephone each other again and a party is held to celebrate.

Why did not A stick a stamp on the video and drop it in the mail to B? The reason is that A and B have got carried away with the excitement of the technology. Space bridges are fun – the parcel post is not.

For a student using an educational resource it does not matter how it reaches him. In the example the satellite is only a tall transmitting tower – a highly complicated means to a simple end. The only important point is that delivery has taken place. The means are irrelevant. Therefore in seeking to use satellite systems for delivery a check list of questions always needs to be addressed.

For example, for a simple delivery of video, the check list might be

1. Is there another way in which I can deliver my resource apart from the satellite. Yes/No. If yes, go to 2.
2. Is the alternative delivery faster than by satellite? Yes/No. If yes, go to 3.
3. Is the alternative delivery cheaper than by satellite? Yes/No. If yes, give up the plan.

Answering no to any of these three questions immediately puts you in business and each question generates a subset of questions which also need to be answered, and each answer generates another subset. For example, suppose you have answered no to Question 1 – there is no other way of delivering the resource. The cynic will not believe you but it is worth pressing ahead anyway.

4. Why is there no other way? There is no other way for the following reasons.
   (a) Inadequate mail service. If yes, go to 5.
   (b) No terrestrial transmission. If yes, go to 5.
   (c) Terrestrial transmission all used up. If yes, go to 5.
5. OK, but what is the size of the audience?
   (a) Two people – forget it unless they are the President of the USA and the General Secretary of the USSR.
   (b) 200 people – worth thinking about.
   (c) 2,000 people – possible.

Audience size is one of the first criteria on which you have to make a decision and you can quickly calculate unit costs if the audience size is known:

The realization of potential

cost of resource production	x
cost of ground system A	y
cost of ground system B	z
cost of space segment	q
Total	t

$$\frac{t}{\text{audience size}} = \text{unit cost}$$

Therefore perhaps the first question to ask on the finance side is: 'What is the maximum I am prepared to pay to allow one student to use this resource?' The larger is the audience, the lower is the cost. It is a sobering question if the answer is given honestly. At a recent medical tele-conference in which some 10,000 physicians were linked together in a dozen countries with a system involving some seven satellites, it was estimated that it would have been cheaper to fly everyone to the USA to stay a week at the local Hilton than to conduct the seminar by satellite. But it was very exciting!

The other approach to take on the 'why satellite?' question is to see where educational satellite systems have already been successfully developed. Areas of the earth where the land is vast and rugged characterize such systems. It is not surprising that Canada, Australia, India, China, Indonesia and the Caribbean all have educational satellite services. Some of these operate a delivery-only service, but many are two-way interactive. In a developing country like India costs become secondary to the overriding educational needs. In these areas the unit costs have been calculated and found to be acceptable. In this respect it is not surprising that educational satellite systems which will soon be delivering much of our entertainment stimulate a different way of thinking. Needs are often met by new technologies, but technologies themselves stimulate needs. After all in 1920 nobody really felt they needed the soap opera *Dallas*.

Interactive systems

When we have all grown a good deal older we shall be able to talk and correspond with intelligent machines. We shall be able to 'interact' with them. There are currently no homo-technical interactive systems.

A colleague of mine, in discussing interactive learning systems, seriously put forward the view that in the act of switching on a light one was interacting with the light switch. He went further to postulate that the light switch knew when it was off or on. It is true that one has to be 'active' when using technology. Switching on a video cassette requires intelligent activity but it is not interaction. One does not interact with a data base. If one did, one could say that one interacted with a dictionary or a bicycle or an apple pie. 'Interaction' is something one does with other people, and to use the term with video or the videodisc or computers is confusing. However, I admit that I am likely to lose this particular nomenclature argument!

Project SHARE (Satellites for Health and Rural Education) is an unique series of interactive educational experiments on the international scale. Designed to foster the use of the satellite system for education and health-related topics, SHARE has, in the years between 1984 and 1988, demonstrated both the excitements and pitfalls of international tele-education. It has been a project of conversations, mainly between professionals. Physicians have talked to physicians, engineers to engineers and teachers to learners at the higher levels. Video, data, sound and still photographs have been successfully interchanged. Some forty countries have been involved and unique uses of the satellite system explored and in a few cases established permanently. Most projects have involved one-way video and two-way audio with the number of video receiving sites ranging between one and several hundred. Characteristically, the project has been adopted by widely separated groups who needed to talk to each other on a more or less equal footing. It has built professional bridges, generated new ideas and stimulated communications thinking. Interestingly, few of the SHARE projects were about delivery of prepackaged learning resources in only one direction.

One of the chief lessons learned has been that in the design of international learning systems it is easier to start at the professional or university research level than to attempt tele-education at a basic level. If global conversations are to develop using these technologies then it is likely to be at the business and professional levels where language and culture barriers are at a minimum. Ideas of using the satellite systems for global learning, although exciting, are still perhaps premature.

A pointer to future interactive systems at the institutional level can, however, be found in the local system of six London hospitals. Here a cable system has linked teaching hospitals in a star-shaped configuration in such a way that a lecture/demonstration can be delivered from any of the six and seen in the others. Furthermore, the lecturer can see and interact with all the students in each of the hospitals. The system is well used, up to six hours per day, and time and money are saved by the removal of the necessity to move people from place to place or repeat lectures/presentations in different hospitals. This system, which is part of London University's LiveNet project has been linked using Project SHARE to Harare, Zimbabwe, and Baltimore, USA. The same interactive principles which unite students and teachers across London

The realization of potential

can apply internationally for live teaching or exchange. In resource terms the SHARE and LiveNet projects are, in the main, more akin to the classroom learning mode than to the distance learner. It is the conversation which has become the resource, and the concept of the global classroom has moved a step closer.

Needs and resources to match

It is easy to describe a global or national educational problem, but quite a different matter to define a specific educational need. Most difficult of all is to put several needs in order of priority. Where does one start when faced with such overwhelming evidence as the starving children in Ethiopia? Better to send a grain ship than install uplinks for interactive video conferencing!

The first task of anyone involved in the provision of educational resources is to identify specific educational needs in their own country. It may well be that fundamentals are already catered for by conventional educational systems. If literacy is high, then there is no incentive to supply television resources on how to read. If literacy is low then one has to decide whether to tackle the young learner or the adult, and whether to attack the problem nationally or locally. In developed countries the objective is to find 'gaps' in the educational market, to provide the unique resource for a hungry audience and to be ahead in the competition for educational business. In the developing world it is more a question of selecting one area of urgent need and finding what resources and delivery systems are available.

For educational broadcasters 'success' is often associated with audience sizes and the sale of wrap-around materials. Broadcasting organizations spend significant amounts on audience research. We seek feedback from schools, colleges and students. We learn that, no matter how beautiful a programme is, it will be quite useless if the take-up is small, for whatever reason, and doubly so if the audience does not give a high 'appreciation index'.

To illustrate something of the complexity of needs matching resources, we give two hypothetical case studies. The first example is from the so-called developed areas.

It is widely recognized in Europe that business with Japan is highly desirable. Few people in Europe speak Japanese. There is virtually no established route in any European country to learn that language without a great deal of difficulty. Therefore a broadcasting company decides to address itself to the problem and produces programmes and booklets – *Japanese Without Tears*. The programmes are made and transmitted and the books appear in the bookshops. Many books are sold and the audience for the programmes is very large. Bingo! Success!

However, suppose that few books are sold and the audience is tiny. The need remains the same but the match with the resources is faulty. It is because (a) the programmes are dreadful, boring or too difficult, (b) the transmission times are too late/early or (c) the book is inadequate? Or is it because the target audience is very small anyway, and really only consists of the sales people of those firms currently operating in Japan? If this is so, then transmission the best delivery mechanism? Is there not another way?

A second case study might be agriculture – a widely recognized need in both the developed and developing world. An enterprising group devises audio cassettes to teach basic farming and sets up sales outlets in many countries. It is a flop. Is it because (a) the audio cassette medium is inappropriate to a visual subject like agriculture, (b) cassette replay facilities are not cheap or widespread in the target areas or (c) the technical/production quality leaves something to be desired? Or is it because learning about farming is all about conversations, and it is the teacher who should have been addressed rather than the students? How to teach agriculture to your students might well have been more appropriate than how to learn the subject as an individual farmer.

These examples lead us towards two rules. First, before embarking on any educational venture, particularly using the tele-educational techniques of audio and video transmission, it is necessary to analyse needs and resources carefully. Second, in order to do this time and money must be spent in feasibility studies with specific objectives. For international satellite proposals there are five matters to address in any feasibility study:

1 educational needs;
2 production of educational resources;
3 technical delivery systems;
4 legal and regulatory arrangements;
5 finance.

Again, it is possibly easier to see how such a study might be subdivided in a specific example. Suppose that it is felt that the subject of business management might benefit from the provision of specific learning resources.

1 Educational needs
   (a) What is the potential audience
      (i) within business?
      (ii) outside business?
   (b) What training provision is currently available and by what means?
   (c) Which needs are specific to one country and which are of general relevance?

The realization of potential

   (d) What immediate benefits can be identified after a programme of management training?
2 Production of educational resources
   (a) Which companies have experience in producing such learning resources?
   (b) What materials already exist?
   (c) What spare capacity exists in these companies?
   (d) What is the time-scale of production?
3 Technical delivery systems
   (a) Does the technology exist for
       (i) transmission?
       (ii) individual or institutional reception/recording?
   (b) When two or more alternative delivery systems are available, which is the most appropriate?
   (c) What hardware needs to be installed or developed in order to create an adequate system?
   (d) What is the measure of available technical capacity?
   (e) What international technical constraints, e.g. systems compatability, exist?
4 Legal and regulatory arrangements
   (a) Which organizations can be involved in transmission?
   (b) What national laws affect the direct transmission or reception of foreign signals?
   (c) What is the copyright position for providers and users?
   (d) Who will negotiate the deals?
   (e) What are the legal time-scales?
5 Finance
   (a) Where will the finance come from for
       (i) production?
       (ii) delivery?
       (iii) end use?
   (b) What is the relationship between initial finance and sustaining running costs?
   (c) What is the business potential for the system?
   (d) What are the costs to the end-users?

Matching educational needs with educational resources is no joke!

The design of international education

It is often very difficult to cross a national boundary. Educational broadcasts also encounter difficulties. Programmes made in one country for domestic consumption are usually very culture bound. It is sometimes only small things – dress, behaviour, environment – but more usually there are serious problems, language being the most obvious. The multiplicity of assumptions in one culture make it difficult for another to accept an educational product. There are obvious exceptions to the rule, but in the main there are in-built problems in transborder educational flow (TBEF). One only has to think of the subject of health. In some countries health is about survival; in others it is a question of choice. The potentially fairly neutral topics such as pregnancy, diet, stress, alcohol and sex would be treated one way in one culture and completely differently in another. Even in the pure subjects of mathematics, chemistry and philosophy, the curriculum differences at the lower levels and the cultural assumptions at the higher make programmes quickly lose relevance and therefore acceptability when used in a second culture.

Styles of teaching vary from one country to another. University professors are respected in some lands. In others it is the successful in business who attract admiration. Still others venerate the old. In Britain it seems to be the young who are admired. Teaching is traditionally didactic in some places; in others it has to be fun-laced and sugared.

Therefore in designing international resources we have to be careful to provide those which can be used without too much modification. Skills teaching is a good example. I once saw a film made in Venezuela for dentists about the technique of filling teeth. There was only one shot – an open mouth, with a drill going in and the badness coming out. It was simple and effective anywhere. Teeth are much the same in Bangkok and Milton Keynes. One can think of many examples of a similar nature. What is being provided is a fairly raw resource which can be used flexibly in another culture and context. The material can be used differently by different mediators. It does not stand alone nor does it have to fit into someone else's curriculum in its entirety.

The problem with TBEF is that there is no current pool of international tele-educational resources. Programmes are rarely made with an international usage envisaged. It is necessary to explore this area if we are to develop effective international education. An approach to this is to make an analysis of educational programmes sold overseas. Which subjects are most in demand? Which never leave our borders? When a programme fails abroad which factors are of relevance? What constraints are put upon buyers regarding re-editing and re-packaging?

Such analyses might be dispiriting especially when so much of another's culture can be enjoyed. Dramas cross national boundaries easily. Music travels even more easily. Sport is acceptable almost everywhere; even humour can transfer. So why not education? Certainly educational programmes from the UK are sold overseas, but the picture is confusing in that it is the wealthy countries who buy rather than those

The realization of potential

where the educational need is most apparent. However, it does seem to be the more technological subjects which appeal in another culture – a fairly obvious effect.

My own view is that education can cross national boundaries, but that we need to explore the design of international styles which minimize cultural fingerprints and maximize flexible end-usage. There is, however, a further development which, in terms of TBBF, has occurred more by accident than design. The traditions of educational broadcasting in the UK and the USA are quite different. Crudely, the difference is one of public service versus market forces and also a national network tradition in the UK with a more local and intimate approach in the USA. Perhaps also, because of the vast distances involved, the USA has been ahead in the development of individual tele-courses designed by one institution and used in another. The National Universities TeleCommunications Network now enjoys a membership of some 250 universities linked by satellite for the exchange of course materials for general benefit, both educational and economic. Designing contact systems, in both business and education, particularly higher education, is commonplace in the USA. It is rare in the UK. Tele-conferencing is fairly normal in the USA and is non-existent in the UK.

The tele-conferencing experience is leading towards the design of tighter learning packages in the USA with more emphasis on resource audio and video than before. It is as though the conference conversation, at first refreshingly open ended, is now being disciplined. In contrast the pre-recorded high-quality educational programmes in the UK are building in their own interactive components. It is not just the phone-in which has caught on, but the establishment of pre- and post-programme activities fixing the programmes in a jelly of real conversations. Therefore so if the educationalists in the USA are moving from conversations to structured programmes and those in the UK are moving from the cocooned programmes to the interactive, does this mean that we shall all meed in mid-Atlantic with a new product? Perhaps we shall, and the new era in TBEF will have begun.

Use of the media

By and large you can teach and learn using any medium – books, chalk, Morse code, beacon fires. The problem in this and the next decade is to select the medium to teach the message. The apprentice learner does not have this difficulty but everyone else, either in the classroom or at a distance, does. Each medium has unique characteristics, and if we have a mixture of media and alternatives we can be selective. Television has unique characteristics; so has radio. If both can be used, then it would be silly to use radio where a visual image was necessary and a waste of money to use television where a voice alone would suffice.

Satellites offer other unique advantages. They can cover a wide geographical area and they can carry high volumes of information. They offer increased numbers of channels, most easily seen with television, and the combination of cable and satellite must be the pattern of the future. However, the delivery system to both provider and user is irrelevant, and this chapter could have just as well been written as part of a book about cable as about satellite. In educational terms there are, in the tele-education bracket, only six media. They are television (video), radio (audio), data (line or portable), interactive television, interactive radio and interactive data. All can be delivered by satellite, cable or terrestrial link.

Project SHARE was about satellites using any medium. When it was devised it was thought that most users would opt for the simple data exchange. They did not. Almost all opted for video and, if possible, two-way video. Education was seen to be about pictures and sound. Interestingly, when we look at tele-education techniques they always involve two senses or two media: pictures and sound for television, sound and print for the audio cassette, sound and data for computer-synchronized audio, and pictures and data for video discs and data bases. The use of only one medium – pictures, sound or data – is generally too lonely for learning, too far away from the apprentice with his three-dimensional vision, directional hearing, touch, feel, sight, taste and smell.

In the selection of media one always has to ask fundamental questions. Why am I doing this on television? Why am I not telephoning instead? Why is this piece written when I can transfer it quicker with an audio cassette? For example television can (a) teach visually techniques in the physical manipulation of objects, (b) teach through visualization concepts which could be very difficult using any other medium, (c) bring the student into visual contact with his/teacher, and (d) show the students events and places far removed in space and time. None of these things can be done by radio. On the other hand, radio coupled with print or other materials can provide the student with a dual-sense input which releases the eye and brain for much wider and faster loading such as talking a chemistry student through equations, guiding the art student across a painting and talking the engineer through an engine.

These are simple rules. It is not difficult to think of others for other media. Each is unique and can do many jobs. In the right hands all media can be bent to teach, but for those in satellite tele-education some media are more equal than others. Therefore the order of events for those who would provide tele-education resources for satellite delivery is as follows:

The realization of potential

1. select the needs and fix priorities;
2. select the media and the teaching/learning technique;
3. find the production resources and cost them;
4. find the delivery resources and cost them;
5. assess the end-user costs;
6. sort out the legal hoops and climb through them;
7. assess the time-scale;
8. go back to 1 and see if there is an easier way.

It is all very simple really and certainly more fun than the parcel post!

Chapter eleven

Copyright and other legal issues

G. Crabb

In discussing the copyright and legal issues in a publication designed for an international readership, a problem arises which is not present in relation to the technical issues. Whereas the technical considerations will be common to all countries, the laws governing the use of satellites will vary from one state to another and so will the laws of copyright which will govern the extent to which satellite reception can be legally used for educational purposes.

It follows that in this chapter we cannot deal in detail with the legal issues but only explore them in a general way, leaving it to the reader to relate them to the local situation. For the purposes of illustration reference will be made to the relevant legislation in the UK where this might be helpful.

Reception of satellite signals

Many countries have legislation which relates to the use of apparatus for the reception of television signals. This may be for political, censorship or ideological purposes or, as in the UK, in order to raise revenue to finance part of the broadcast provision. It follows that, unless there are exceptions which provide otherwise, anyone receiving television signals will be legally required to comply with these statutory requirements.

In considering the implications for the reception of satellite signals the potential users must first discover whether, in their country, special permission or licences have to be acquired to cover satellite reception and whether any fees have to be paid. In the UK, for example, a licence is required to operate a television receiver legally, with the revenue going to the BBC to finance its radio and television channels. However, anyone wishing to receive satellite television signals requires a separate licence, obtaining at modest cost from a government department. The reason why such a licence is necessary is unclear since the revenue does not, as with the receiver licence, contribute to providing the service

The realization of potential

being received. It may merely be a bureaucratic ploy based on the principle that if an activity can possibly be controlled or licensed then there is no harm in doing so. Such enthusiasm for meddling in perfectly harmless activity can be observed in a number of countries as well as the UK.

However, in the UK it goes even further because the licence referred to permits only the reception of satellite television signals and not those from weather stations or from communication satellites such as Eutelsat or Intelsat. Here the situation becomes even more unclear because, although no licences are on offer, the appropriate government department will issue letters of authority without, apparently, being too sure of its statutory right to issue or withhold them.

Some states, including the UK, have in addition special regulations covering the operation of cable systems, where satellite signals are diffused over cables to subscribers or others who wish to receive them. Although of most relevance to the commercial cable providers, educational establishments which operate closed-circuit systems in order to distribute material round a campus or to split sites, should check whether their systems qualify as cable systems in their national legislations. In the UK this is not the case, and so universities and other establishments require no special authorizations in order to operate campus cable systems legally.

Finally, there may be national or local restrictions on the erection of satellite dishes or other receiving equipment. Certainly in the UK planning permission is needed before practically any structure can be erected, and permission is frequently refused where the proposed site is environmentally or scenically sensitive.

Copyright

Unlike the general legal issues dealt with above, the copyright implications of using satellites have an international rather than a national or local dimension. This difference exists because, whereas governmental controls on the reception of broadcasts by way of licences or on the erection of aerials by way of planning controls is a purely domestic affair, copyright is an international concept which is recognized by most states and which to some extent is formalized within international forums.

However, there is no such thing as 'international copyright' in the sense that there is a commonly accepted law which relates to every country. Those countries which include copyright law in their legislations compile them to reflect the social, cultural, educational and industrial needs of that country, and so a state which has a large and valuable media industry will have copyright law which will protect that

Copyright and other legal issues

industry whilst a country which has little in the way of publishing or audio-visual production will give greater emphasis to the need of the population to use materials imported from other countries.

It follows that the copyright laws will vary from one state to another and this will occur even with those which are signatories to one of the major international agreements, the Berne Convention and the Universal Copyright Convention. The user of satellite broadcasts for educational purposes has no need to understand the ramifications of these arrangements but only to comprehend one important rule which applies to all countries. It is that where material from an overseas country is protected, it will be protected to the same extent and under the same rules as that of the domestic product. For example, since the UK is a member of the Berne Convention, French material will be protected in the UK because France is also a member. However, it will be UK copyright law which will apply, not French. Similarly, UK material will be protected in France but under the provisions of French copyright law.

From the foregoing paragraph it will be evident that the extent to which broadcasts, and satellite broadcasts or transmissions, will be protected will depend on the law of the state where the signals are received. Anyone receiving these transmissions for educational purposes needs to acquire some familiarity with the copyright law of their country so that the extent of permitted use can be ascertained. Such information cannot be given here, but a summary of the features which occur in all legislations may help readers in their explorations of their own law. This summary is the subject of the following section.

The bare bones of copyright

Copyright is that part of the legal framework which is based on the principle that those who create or produce certain materials should have a right of ownership over and above that in the physical product. In other words, if an author writes a novel he should have the right to control certain actions by others and, if that is his wish, to negotiate terms and conditions under which others may utilize his material. This is not just in recognition that we should own what we create, but also that in being able to exploit creative material for gain authors, composers, artists etc. will be encouraged to produce more for the general benefit of society.

Most of the developed countries have copyright law which originated many years ago, in the case of the UK back in the early 1700s. Originally, the intention was to give to authors the sole right to copy or publish their writings, but over the years the range of protected material has been extended as has the number of 'restricted acts' which only the creator or producer can legally undertake or authorize. Therefore in many countries the law of copyright not only applies to written material

The realization of potential

but also to music, artistic works, sound recordings, films, broadcasts and typographical layouts, computer programs and folklore.

Categories of protected material

In investigating the law of copyright in his country, the user will first require to know the range of materials protected. Almost all will protect the 'traditional' types such as written works, music, dramatic works and artistic works such as paintings and drawings. Some, like the UK may also protect more modern materials such as photographs, sound recordings, films and broadcasts, while other states may not do so. It can generally be assumed that each type of material is protected in its own right even where combined with another which will in turn be protected. Therefore, if photographs and paintings are protected by copyright, then a photograph of a painting will represent two distinct copyright elements each protected in its own right and, possibly, subject to different rules and regulations in the copyright legislation.

Conditions for protection

Second, what conditions are necessary before material can be protected? It is a principle of the Berne Convention that copyright is automatic without any kind of registration or formality, but some states outside the Convention stipulate registration procedures which must be followed. All states will require that the material must be original, that is not copied from something which already exists, and that it must exist in material form and not just as an idea or concept. Usually the creator or producer must be a national of the country concerned but, as already indicated, membership of international treaties or other international agreements usually means that the products of other countries will be protected in the same way and to the same extent as the home product.

Ownership of copyright

Third, copyright legislation will usually describe who is to be the first owner of the copyright which in the case of literary, dramatic, musical and artistic material is usually the author, composer, dramatist or artist. Some countries, including the UK, make special provisions so that the copyright in material produced by employees belongs to the employer whilst others accept that the author has an overriding claim to the copyright even though paid a salary to produce it. The ownership of copyright in sound recordings, films and broadcasts shows more variation between states, as some take the view that those who pay the production costs should own the copyright whilst others try to ensure

Copyright and other legal issues

that all those who make a creative contribution share the copyright between them.

Duration of copyright protection

All legislations will provide that copyright protection will, in respect of each type of material, continue for a certain period and will then expire. In the case of literary, dramatic, musical and artistic works this is usually calculated from the author's death but may also be influenced by the date of first publication. Sound recordings, films and broadcasts are usually treated differently, as there is no 'author', and the duration of copyright is usually calculated from the date of first publication or transmission. Where material is covered by the Berne Convention the minimum period of protection is 50 years, and in fact the 50 year period is increasingly becoming the standard for protection although some states give a shorter period for sound recordings, broadcasts and typographical layouts.

Concessions for copyright users

Finally, and perhaps most importantly in the present context, the law will usually describe a number of concessions whereby the use of material in a way which is restricted by the copyright may be legal in certain circumstances or for specified purposes. For example, although all legislations will provide that making copies is a restricted act, some may also permit copying under certain circumstances by way of concessions to users. These users may include newspapers or reviewers, whilst other provisions may be made for those engaged in private study or working in libraries. A number of legislations will also make provision for copying in schools or other educational establishments. The effect of these concessions is that if copying or other specified use is for the purposes covered by the concession the courts, in any action for infringement by copyright owners, must accept and recognize that the copying was for a permitted purpose and no infringement took place.

Performer's protection

Brief mention must be made of another area of law which, in many countries, has a bearing on the use of satellites for educational purposes. In the UK, for example, the law of copyright does not give any rights to performers, those who sing, play or act. These contributors are protected by a special act which provides that it is illegal, otherwise than for private purposes, to record, film or broadcast a performance without the prior written permission of the performer. The effect of this legislation

The realization of potential

is to add another legal restraint which users of satellite broadcasts in the UK must consider and which must also be checked by those using satellite broadcasts in other countries.

The main points of copyright which will, in one form or another, be found in the copyright law of every country are summarized in the previous sections. Mention has also been made of the separate but related issue of performer's protection. It now remains to relate these legal provisions to the use of satellites as a means of both receiving signals and distributing them.

Using satellites

We should first consider the reception of satellite signals. It is probably true to say that in no country is the reception of signals an act which can infringe copyright. Such reception might be illegal or restricted for political or ideological reasons but mere reception would not have any copyright implications. However, most educational users will wish to make a recording of the signal for repeated study and it is the act of copying which may be restricted by the national copyright laws.

Receiving signals other than television

Where signals consist of material which is not protectable by copyright, then copying will not require permission. An example would be remote sensing by way of a transmission which is 'live' and not by way of a signal which has been recorded first. However, weather forecasting data might well be protected as literary material and maps and diagrams which are included as artistic material. Establishing the copyright status of such material might be difficult, as might the person or body owning it, but in the UK the use of remote-sensing and weather information for educational use appears to be accepted as a reasonable use and, if copyright does exist in the material, the owners of it have not tried to enforce their rights as far as educational use is concerned.

Receiving television transmissions

The reception of satellite television broadcasts is quite another matter. Here there is likely to be a mix of many types of protected material such as scripts, music, artistic material such as photographs and video extracts. In addition, the programme is likely to be protected as a film or video, and the broadcast itself may also attract copyright protection. The extent to which this is the case will, of course, depend on the national law but in the UK off-air recording of a satellite broadcast would not be permitted without prior permission because, leaving aside the status of the broadcast itself, the various parts of it would be protected. Even where the broadcast originated in a foreign country the various elements such as literary, musical or artistic material and sound recordings and film will be protected under UK law because of treaty obligations with that country.

The copyright law of most countries will, to a greater or less extent, similarly protect elements in the broadcast from unauthorized copying. However, there may be considerable differences in the extent to which the broadcast may be copied, either for private or for educational purposes. In the UK the present law would make it illegal to record off-air a programme which contained sound recordings or film/video, even if the copy was made in the home for private use. Similarly, educational establishments are not permitted to record and replay such programmes unless the appropriate permissions have been obtained. The UK law which protects performers would also make it an offence to record a performance off-air for other than private purposes.

In practice, however, such illegal off-air recording is difficult to stop, especially in the home. The broadcast authorities and the copyright owners of the various elements in the broadcast tend to ignore private and educational off-air recording, provided that the resulting use is limited and is for non-commercial purposes. The various interests do offer licensing schemes which permit off-air recording of certain programmes either free or in return for fees, but much unauthorized recording still goes on.

Checking the national situation

It will be apparent that anyone wishing to receive and/or record satellite transmissions should make a number of checks before doing so. The first is to ascertain to what extent the national law protects satellite signals and the component parts of the information which is transmitted. The second is to check the extent to which television broadcasts, including satellite broadcasts, are protected both as a separate category of material and as component parts such as music, sound recordings etc. The third is to check if the national law permits the off-air recording of material for educational use and under what conditions. Finally, if off-air recording is not permitted under statute, it must be ascertained if there are any licences available which would authorize the copying. If, after all these steps have been taken, it is evident that the off-air recording of satellite signals and transmissions cannot legally proceed either because there is no statutory provision allowing it or authorization is not forthcoming from rights owners, then the most difficult decision of all has to be taken. This is whether to forgo the advantages of off-air recording or to record illegally. The decision will depend on the views

The realization of potential

of the user as well as an assessment of the likelihood of legal action resulting.

The use of satellites for distribution

The second way in which education may wish to use satellites is in order to transmit visual material, including video material, to a wide audience. It has already been emphasized that the extent to which such transmissions may be legally used will depend on the law of the receiving country and not that of the country where the broadcast and material originates. A similar situation exists for the sending of material. Since copyright law is territorial, it follows that a transmitter in space cannot be covered by the copyright law of any one state. Although there is much international debate amongst experts about the appropriate law for satellite transmission it may be assumed for the time being that the law governing the transmission will be that of the country where the uplink of the transmission is located.

This is the case in the UK, and so any educational producer wishing to use an uplink based in the UK will, in effect, be making a broadcast of the material. Whether a broadcast is also made from the satellite is one of the matters for international debate, but for all practical purposes the producer of a video for satellite use need only be sure that the elements which make up, say, the video presentation have been cleared for use over the appropriate satellite. In other countries it may be the case that a transmission to a satellite does not constitute a broadcast and, in law, no permission to broadcast will be necessary in order that the transmission may legally take place. However, in the present uncertain state of the legal position it is suggested that, whether legally necessary or not, the appropriate permissions are first obtained.

New material

Taking a video presentation as an example, most will consist of video material specially shot by the producer and, of course, no copyright permission is needed here. Most will also contain a script which is likely to be protected as a literary work. This will probably have been specially written and the right to transmit over a satellite should form part of the initial agreement. Care should be taken where a member of the academic staff of the producing institution is the author, as the institution may already own the copyright if the script was prepared as of the duties of an employed academic. This would be the case in the UK but not in all countries.

Copyright and other legal issues

Music and sound recordings

A musical sound track may be specially composed, in which case the same conditions apply as for the script. The use of existing copyright music either recorded from a live performance or dubbed from a recording will be more likely. In both cases the permission of the copyright owner of the music will be required, and this is often available through a licensing agency such as the Mechanical Copyright Protection Society in the UK. If dubbed from a record, the prior permission of the record company will also be required in countries where recordings are protected. Sometimes this is not forthcoming, and it is less troublesome to use mood-music libraries which provide a wide range of recorded music especially designed for dubbing purposes. When applying for licences to copy it should be made clear that the video is to be transmitted via satellite so that the appropriate rights are transferred.

Performers

It should also be remembered that where, as in the UK, performers are protected, their permission may be legally required before the recording of their reading of a script or the performance of music may legally proceed, and here again the inclusion of the right to transmit the result over a satellite must be made clear. The inclusion of other existing items, the copyright of which is owned by third parties, will similarly need to be cleared if the national legislation protects them. These include dramatic works and artistic works such as photographs as well as sound recordings, film clips and video material.

Implications for producers

Although the agencies which collect fees for the use of their materials will be fully familiar with the implications of satellite use, individual copyright owners may not be aware of just what they are agreeing to when granting the right of satellite transmission. It is therefore recommended that, to save subsequent ill-feeling, the producer explains that granting the permission will mean that the material will be transmitted to all those territories within the footprint of the satellite and, through overspill, to a number of others which cannot be specified. It should also be explained that the extent to which the video and the material in it may be legally copied or otherwise used will depend on the legislation of the country where transmission is received. This could range from being illegal to record off-air even for private use, as in the UK, to being legal to copy for educational purposes without any restraint. More

The realization of potential

importantly, the producer should include in any agreement with contributors that he is not liable to take or be joined in any legal action on behalf of contributors in respect of any infringement, or alleged infringement, of copyright or performer's protection which may occur.

Royalty fees

A knotty problem may arise when negotiating the royalty fees for satellite use. The collecting agencies, such as the Mechanical Copyright Protection Society in the UK, will have a scale of charges which will include one for the satellite use of the musical works in their repertoires. Many individual copyright owners will have little idea of what to charge. In theory the royalty should be linked to the number of people able to receive the broadcast, and in the case of a satellite transmission covering a whole continent this could be many millions. In practice only a small minority will have the equipment necessary for reception and the royalty may be reduced where the broadcast is to be encrypted to limit reception to an identifiable group. This introduction of a 'box office' element enables a quite sophisticated royalty calculation to be made.

From the producer's point of view it is generally preferable to pay a single sum for the right to transmit over satellites rather than pay for each transmission. This avoids complicated accounting procedures and the need to make returns to the contributors. The exception may be where the transmissions are encrypted and here the contributor may insist on a 'payment per viewer' arrangement. Where material is specially commissioned for inclusion in the presentation, then he is advised to make it a condition that he acquires the complete copyright and then no further accounting to the originator is needed. In some countries, including the UK, the commissioner of certain types of material will acquire the copyright of law unless there is some agreement to the contrary with the originator.

Agreements between producers and contributors

All agreements between the producer and contributors should be in writing and should constitute a legally binding agreement. The various agencies which license the use of material will have standard licence forms, but for specially commissioned material and existing material in which the copyright is owned by individuals the appropriate document will need to be drawn up. As with all the other aspects the law of the country concerned will regulate the conditions to which legally binding contacts must adhere. The best advice is to seek advice locally either from textbooks on the subject or from a qualified lawyer.

Summary

It may be useful to summarize the salient points of the foregoing which is of necessity only a brief review of a most complex subject. Readers should regard it as merely an introduction, providing signposts to the areas of enquiry they must address.

The national law of the country where a satellite transmission is received will govern its use.

Receiving a satellite broadcast may require authority or a licence from a government department or ministry.

Erecting a receiving dish may require national or local planning permission.

Recording a satellite transmission off-air may require permission under copyright or performer's protection legislation.

The national law of the country where the satellite signal is received will govern the extent to which it may be legally used.

Producers of material for transmission over satellites should acquire from all contributors of material and from performers the permissions necessary under the law of the country from which the transmission is to be made.

Producers should explain to contributors that the extent to which their contributions may be legally used will depend on the laws of the country in which the signals from the satellite are received.

All agreements should be in writing and conform to the statutory provisions covering contracts of the country from which the transmission is made.

Finally, and most importantly, check the national laws to see how, and to what extent, they influence the practical application of the information contained above.

The future

The use of satellites, especially for television transmission, is in a very early stage and many of the legal issues raised have still to be resolved. It is usually the case that, whilst the progress of technology is rapid, the corresponding changes in the law are tortuous and lag behind. This is certainly the case with copyright which is constantly having to cope with new developments such as computers, information technology and now the use of satellites to disseminate material which may be subject to copyright protection.

The international bodies such as the Berne Convention have spent many hours debating how the copyright laws of member countries should affect satellite use, but so far no agreement has been reached. Those countries in the European Economic Community have also

The realization of potential

discussed how the transmission of signals over a wide area relates to the principle of a free market and how in turn this can be reconciled to the traditional exploitation of copyright on a territorial bases. The Council of Europe has also been considering the matter, and it is inevitable that not all these various organizations think alike.

Therefore it will be many years, if ever, before an international view of satellites and copyright evolves. In the meantime those wishing to receive and copy satellite transmissions for educational purposes and, especially, those producers who see it as a means of wide dissemination, must endeavour to keep abreast of developments both nationally and in the wider international legislations.

Chapter twelve

Research and development on satellites in education

John Gilbert

The current situation

From the pioneering work at Kettering Grammar school in the 1950s and 1960s, activity in the field of satellites in education grew slowly. Enthusiasts built their own ground-stations and collected data, sometimes just to show that the equipment actually worked. However, the pace of new initiatives and the general level of activity has risen sharply since the early 1980s. This can be traced to a number of influences. The evolution of a truly global system of telecommunications has focused attention there, and within the UK, British Telecom has developed a series of well-produced materials to explain the basis of its enterprise. Public news broadcasts have made increasing use of cloud-pattern photographs in weather forecasting and of pictures of the earth's surface to show ecological events, both of which are produced by remote sensing satellites.

These and other highly visible public events have encouraged equipment manufacturers to produce user-friendly prefabricated ground-stations at relatively low cost. Individuals have raised the money to purchase such equipment, are introducing the equipment and the data so collected into the curriculum, and are gradually establishing networks with those who are like-minded. So far it is all *ad hoc*. The wheel is re-invented daily. Equipment is purchased and then not used for the benefit of students. Opportunities are lost. Good practice goes unapplauded and without emulation. Bad practice continues, unnoticed or unremarked. There is, in short, a grave shortage of appropriate research and development.

Research on 'satellites in education' might ask such questions as: Who is doing what, how, with whom, to what effect? What consequences has this activity for the curriculum for teaching, for learning generally? Development, which might proceed concurrently or consecutively with research might produce and test resource packs for different groups of teachers, so that they can exploit the potential of satellites when using varying teaching styles, e.g. project work or supported self-study, within their subjects, produce computer software with which to analyse and present data in differing ways, and produce in-service education materials and courses with which to disseminate good practice.

Whilst the need for research and development (R&D) would be unquestioned in an industrial context, the lack of a tradition of systematic R&D in education requires that it be justified in terms of the interests of participating groups. For teachers and their students, in whatever part of the educational system, this should lead to more appropriate and effective teaching and learning. For those charged with curriculum development, the place, value and methods of conduct of satellite-related work can be demonstrated. The legion of informal educators, in museums, zoos and the media, might see a value for satellites within their activities which do so much to influence public attitudes to science and technology. The hidden army of radio amateurs might see where their contribution may best be made, for they have in-depth relevant experience. Satellite engineers may be inspired to render their creations more educationally user friendly. Equipment manufacturers may see what is really required to support worthwhile education. Why, then, is so relatively little R&D currently taking place?

To some extent, the reason must include the nature of the satellite engineering industry. It is necessarily hardware driven, with the emphasis placed on the optimum design and production of electronic systems to undertaken specific tasks. It often seems to overlook, or ignore, the software or human aspects of its artefacts. The introduction of any new piece of technology, e.g. the car cell-phone, does carry with it implications for changes in how people manage their lives, e.g. for safe and effective use. Anything to do with social science, including education, is neglected, perhaps because it is seen as soft, i.e. incapable of multiple reproduction in identical form. This is to be very much regretted, not least because the abrasive encounters that citizens have with new technology does colour their inclination to support the funding of new ventures of the same kind. Another major contribution to the reason must stem from a lack of awareness of how satellites, and their data, can contribute to the main educational trends of our times. Educationalists either do not propose appropriate features to satellite designers or, where these are included, do not exploit the potential thus made available. I shall attempt to rectify these issues in what follows, drawing both on contemporary documents and on the implications of earlier chapters in this book.

Satellites and the new education

Throughout the world, and certainly most markedly in the UK, the recent trend in educational reform has been to attempt to make it directly supportive of industrial development or regeneration. These reforms are sometimes referred to as the 'new education'[1] and have a number of loosely associated attributes. The first of these is a move to provide an 'education in technology' which will have the following three aims:[2]

1. the development of an awareness of technology and of its implications as a resource for the achievement of human purposes and its dependence on human involvement in judgements and decision-making;
2. to develop in pupils, through personal experience, the practical capability to engage in the central task actions of the processes of technology;
3. to help pupils learn to acquire those resources of knowledge, of physical and intellectual skills, of personal qualities and of experience which need to be available for calling upon when engaged in the task actions of technology.

A second attribute of the new education is a greater reliance on experiential learning, especially that which involves out-of-institution activity, including work within the general community. This links directly to the third attribute, a greater emphasis on vocationalism, meaning either a preparation for the world of work or as viewing industry as an opportunity for study. A fourth attribute involves a shift in teaching methods away from didactic exposition (chalk and talk) towards participative techniques with an emphasis on active learning, including the use of group work. The valuation placed on problem-solving techniques of teaching and learning raise it to the status of a fifth attribute. The placing of these trends within a modular design of the curriculum so that students can perceive a clear relationship between goals accepted and their realization, (the sixth attribute), the reliance on criterion-referenced forms of assessment (the seventh attribute) and a greater involvement of the students themselves, their parents and the community generally in the organizing of opportunity and the negotiation of curricular choice (the eighth attribute) complete the profile of the new education.

Satellites, ground-stations, and the reception, storage, processing, display and interpretation of data collectively offer a valuable route to the realization of the new education. I now consider each attribute in turn.

The realization of potential

The provision of education in technology

Satellites as such are the product of technology. Handling the data that they produce offers opportunities to students, likely to be seen as very relevant to today's world, to engage in the processes of technology. Whilst the younger among them may begin by constructing models of satellites, older students may construct ground-stations from circuit drawings or bring commercially available kits into use. As was argued in Chapter 7, data produced or merely transmitted by satellites offer a window into modern computer-managed information technology. In short, a broad awareness of space, space science and the development of space technology can be readily provided.

The use of more experiential learning

The general use of telecommunications within society, whether the well-established international network of telephones or the rapidly emerging continent span of television reception, as well as the use of weather maps, e.g. by farmers and fishermen, offer a wide diversity for experiential learning involving satellites in commerce and industry. In addition to multi-national and major national companies, many small enterprises now exist within the service sector of industry. Many are approachable for educational support: the problem is to avoid overloading those that are willing to provide opportunities for teachers and students.

Greater emphasis on vocationalism

The decision by the UK Government in 1987 not to increase its financial commitment to the space industry may lead it to a relative or absolute decline. It may be that the financial institutions of the UK will provide substitute investment. In any event, other European countries, the USSR and the USA are increasing their investment, and this will lead to the creation of more jobs in satellite engineering, communications and remote sensing. These are strong enough pointers to justify recommending to young people that they consider entering the relevant fields of employment, and of giving them a flavour of what is entailed during their formal education. Satellite engineering is, of course, an excellent advertisement for modern engineering practice generally; engineers of all types are constantly in demand.

The use of more active methods of learning

As has been constantly reiterated in Chapters 4–10 of this book, the data transmitted or generated by satellites offer a wealth of material which can be stored, processes, displayed, analysed and interpreted by students working alone or in groups with a teacher as a manager of resources and as a consultant. Certainly students must not be allowed to drown in the sea of highly encoded data that satellites generate or the undifferentiated flood of television programmes or opportunities for telephone conversations that they make accessible. A graduated and structured introduction will be needed. However, once basic skills have been acquired, there is much to say for a progressive introduction to the wild excess of informational possibilities that exist. After all, skills of differentiation, selectivity and evaluation are at the core of life in today's communication-rich environment.

The development of problem-solving skills

As the Third Industrial Revolution has produced information at an exponential rate, much of which may make a claim for inclusion in educational provision, the search has begun in earnest for generative skills – ways of locating, structuring and deploying information of all types in order to answer questions posed or needs identified. This has crystallized into a call for the teaching of 'problem-solving skills', and generalized algorithms for this activity set have appeared. Whilst I am far from convinced that humans use only one way of solving problems, or indeed that the concept of 'problem' is capable of a single definition, such ambitions are worthwhile, if only because factual information is treated as a route to an answer and not as the answer in itself. Satellite-related data, as we have already seen, are capable of being utilized to address a wide variety of questions in analysing a plethora of contexts and situations and thus are capable of making a valuable contribution to an exploration and development of problem-solving skills.

Inclusion of technology in the curriculum

The Secondary Science Curriculum Review[3] observed that technology can be included in the curriculum in four ways: as a single subject; as an enrichment and extension offered to traditional subjects; within an interdisciplinary topic approach; within open-ended project work. Modularization, i.e. the cutting up of a theme or subject into short periods of instruction, e.g. 1 hour per week for 10 weeks, framed between aims for achievement and the assessment of learning, is compatible with any of these approaches. Indeed, until the potential of satellites is more fully realized their contribution may be confined, in many subject areas, to a few modules. However, there are plentiful opportunities for cross-

The realization of potential

curricular activities, and satellite-related work may make its greatest contribution in this way.

The introduction of criterion-referenced forms of assessment

The only unusual contribution that satellites can make in the evolution of assessment procedures from being norm referenced, where an individual's performance is graded within an anticipated structure of response from all students, to being criterion referenced, where an individual effectively competes with him/herself, is that they can produce or communicate large quantities of unique data. Thus the question set can always be based on novel information, so as to preclude the deployment of unwanted memorization skills by students.

A broader participation in the curriculum

As many parents now work in the communications or other satellite-related industries, it can be anticipated that there would be an increased willingness to support satellite-related activity when local control over the implementation of the curriculum is exercised. Indeed, the possibility of satellite-related work offers many parents and industrialists the opportunity for contribution to decision-taking in education on the basis of their own expertise.

If satellites have a broad potential for contributions to contemporary views of the desirable curriculum, how far is this being realized?

Current research on satellites in education

In a study conducted in 1987 by Gilbert *et al.*,[4] and undertaken by questionnaire and interview, to explore the needs of local education authorities (LEAs) with respect to in-service training (INSET) related to satellite work and to identify ways in which this INSET might be most advantageously provided, a 38 per cent response was obtained to a questionnaire sent to 380 science and humanities advisers and Technical and Vocational Education Initiative (TVEI/TVE) Coordinators. The picture that emerged was one of satellite-related work just getting under way in many LEAs with some pockets of relatively advanced activity being identified, a view substantiated by interviews and correspondence with twenty-three enthusiasts in the field. An auxiliary enquiry into the use of a television receive only (TVRO) system in ten schools with a project mounted jointly by the British National Space Centre and the Royal Signals and Radar Establishment showed a similarly uneven pattern of response.

The main enquiry, where data were collected between September and

December 1987, showed that 218 schools were active in 98 LEAs, although the distribution of activity was very uneven: Dyfed had twelve active schools (perhaps due to the presence there of Annette Temple, co-editor of this book) whilst 34 LEAs had no activity recorded. Much of the work was reported to be in its infancy. The curriculum areas of geography, the sciences, modern languages and computer studies were those where satellite work was being most frequently pursued. However, over forty subject areas/themes were cited in replies. Those mentioned by 10 per cent and over are listed in Table 12.1. Whilst cross-curricular initiatives were mentioned, e.g. within a 'technology for all' course aimed at lower secondary pupils, the pattern of satellite systems from which data was received is revealing (Table 12.2). It would seem that many schools are still only using data from one type of satellite. The early stages of development of satellite-related work is revealed in the 106 replies to a question on the type of activity being pursued (Table 12.3). Whilst the level of project work is encouraging and interschool communication networks are being set up, many schools are still bringing equipment into use and trying to make sense of data received; the issues of curriculum exploitation have not yet been extensively addressed.

Table 12.1 Subject areas in which satellite work was pursued

Area	Mentioned, as percentage of all replies
Geography	53
Information technology	48
Physics	47
General sciences	41
Computer studies	32
French	22
General studies	21
German	19
Mathematics	13
Modern languages (overall)	10

The amount of support needed for the potential of satellites to be realized is shown by the figures on INSET activity: only 32 per cent of replies reported that INSET was underway. In order of decreasing contribution, the providers of INSET were LEA advisory staff, school teachers, higher-education based, British Telecom sponsored, provided by data base, conferences, commercial demonstrations and through

The realization of potential

teacher secondment. In a similar order the preferred methods of delivery for such INSET were distance learning materials, consultancy to local working groups, day-length courses and weekend courses.

Table 12.2 Satellite systems from which data was received by schools

Satellite system	Mentioned, as percentage of all replies
Weather (NOAA, Meteosat)	89
Scientific/educational (UoSAT)	42
TVRO (Eutelsat)	32
Imaging (Landsat, SPOT)	25
Amateur communications (JAS)	15
Weather, scientific, TVRO	15
Other (Cosmos)	1

Table 12.3 Types of activity being pursued in satellite-related work

Activity type	Mentioned, as percentage of all replies
Building systems from commercial equipment	71
Collecting and interpreting weather/surface images	64
Collecting and interpreting scientific data	38
Project work on satellites	38
Reception of TV broadcasts	35
Construction of equipment from plans	33
Collecting and interpreting all types of data	13
Communication with other schools	9

The TVRO enquiry produced mixed results. It was evident that the equipment provided was not appropriate given the levels of technical support available in schools or the uses to which it was put. Nevertheless, edited versions of newscasts and other items were used in modern language classes to good effect, providing authentic examples of contemporary pronunciation within the context of current social and political issues. The editing was thought necessary by the teachers not only to make best use of class time, but also to allow for appropriate language levels and to remove material thought undesirable on other grounds.

Research and development

Future development work

On looking back over the chapters of this book, it is evident that three types of development work, taking that phrase in its broadest meaning, are needed.

1   Plentiful supplies of data of an appropriate type should be made available when and where required.

The commercial equipment manufacturers are now producing ground-stations which are both relatively cheap and user friendly with which to collect data from scientific research satellites, e.g. UoSAT, and from weather satellites, e.g. NOAA. Appropriate TVRO equipment is still under development. There is a clear market for cheap high-resolution earth-observation images, e.g. from Landsat, which are related to curriculum needs, as opposed to what is available as a by-product of scientific and commercial research. The management of resources will present problems if opportunities are to be fully grasped. The TVEI-related in-service training (TRIST) project 'Satellites in Education' at the University of Surrey in 1987 showed that one controlling factor in satellites work was access to microcomputers and VDUs: all too often these are held, with excessive security precautions, in one place, e.g. the 'resources room', or by one special interest group, e.g. the mathematicians. It will be necessary either to locate satellite ground-station equipment where the microcomputers are stored, which will have the disadvantage that curriculum integration of satellites work may be hindered, or vice versa, which is only possible if schools have a plentiful supply of microcomputers so that they are readily available to all subject departments.

The use of real-time data, i.e. that directly collected from a satellite at the time of use, is attractive because the relationship between transmission and reception is reinforced, and because large quantities of data are readily available. However, this does present difficulties for schools either because satellites do not transmit during the school day, e.g. the French station TV5, or because the school timetable will not allow students and signal come together. In these circumstances, schools may wish to rely on recorded signals, which will imply editing, or even, *in extremis*, that video/audio cassettes are carried from a central reception point,.e.g. at a Teacher's Centre.

2   The analysis of examination syllabuses must be undertaken to show how satellites can contribute to education provided.

At school level, Cooper and Underwood[5] have analysed public examination syllabuses for a mention of satellites or satellite-derived data. Whilst some examination requirements, particularly at A level, e.g.

The realization of potential

physics, geography and electronics, do mention satellites, many current syllabuses do not where they might. Certainly, many GCSE syllabuses refer to aspects of data handling, and there is unpublished evidence that training and vocational education (TVE) schemes, e.g. in Surrey, and joint support activity (JSA) schemes, e.g. in Dyfed, are including work that is satellite related. However, the full range of possibilities has not been fully identified.

3 Teachers should be aware of the potential contribution of satellites to education and their skills developed in order to realize that potential.

How do teachers, in general, find out about new ideas and gauge the relevance and practicability of innovations to their professional circumstances? The evidence is that the two main mechanisms are being involved in the primary development of ideas or of having the opportunity to see how innovations have worked out in practice in other institutions. How this might be done is discussed in the last section of this chapter. There is a clear need for materials, both printed and in the form of videos, to support satellite work across the curriculum. Given the universal use in schools of worksheets as the main medium of support for individual and small group work, there will be a ready market for such an output. However, worksheets are usually very highly structured, and there is also a need for a more open-ended type of material, e.g. a collection of satellite data sheets, articles on the theme from popular journals and magazines and outlines of projects suitable for school realization. The pack might include some industry-related materials, i.e. those showing the background to industrial satellite activities, and also videos of actual satellites and their support agencies, for these will not normally be accessible to students.

Future research work

Many interesting questions for future research are embedded within the previous section. In some ways this is as it should be: innovation and evaluation proceeding hand-in-hand within a model derived from engineering practice. In other ways this is not so healthy: the current climate, both within the UK and elsewhere, which presents enquiry as a luxury, is not favourable for long-term development. Strategic research is necessary to ensure that appropriate opportunities are identified and addressed in an efficient and effective manner. From a plethora of possibilities, I will set out an agenda based loosely on the five features of satellite use put forward by Jim Stevenson in Chapter 10.

Research and development

1. (a) What population might usefully be involved with 'satellite education'?
    A review of the earlier chapters in this book leads to clear conclusions: secondary school pupils and higher and continuing education students. Yet one could equally well ask: What might primary school pupils obtain from satellite education? How might technical college students benefit? What might that vast majority of the population not involved in any formal education or training derive from it?
   (b) What is actually learnt during satellite-related activities?
    If, as has been advocated, students have direct access to satellite-derived data, what psychomotor skills are developed during such work? As much activity will be based around the computer, the whole field of 'research into the processes of information technology education' is opened up.
   (c) What satellite-related work is currently taking place?
    Given the rapid pace of developments in the field, a continuous monitoring procedure is needed.
   (d) What similarities and differences exist between the satellite-related education and training provided in different countries?
    The moves to integrate fully the economic systems of the EEC countries and the underlying trend towards the global village point to a need for enquiries into Stevenson's idea of trans-border educational flow.

2. The production of educational resources
   The questions here flow into each other: What resources currently exist? How can existing resources be made more widely available? What additional resources are needed? How can new resources best be produced? Whilst this book has addressed these issues throughout, systematic enquiry is needed.

3. Technical matters
   Assuming that signal transmission is in the hands of satellite engineers, the questions to be asked thus include: How can ground-station equipment systems be evaluated? What technical support is needed for equipment to be fully exploited over a long period of time? What computer software is needed?

4. Legal and regulatory arrangements
   Geoff Crabb's analysis of this theme in Chapter 11 is so incisive as to make further comment unnecessary. This key set of issues must be addressed, at national and international levels, if extensive progress is to be made. Moreover, the outcomes of such deliberations

The realization of potential

must be presented to those active in the field in simple language. The question here is: How might this be done effectively?
5 Finance
The questions surrounding the financing of satellite-related work are really a subset of those involved in the broader context of education and training generally. However, as satellites are a prime example of high technology, and therefore problematic in many countries, the question may be: How can satellite-related educational activity be so presented as to relate to the legitimate values and aspirations of influential citizens who have knowledge bases other than in the sciences?

The conduct and organization of research and development

Enquiry into the educational implications of satellites falls squarely into the area of educational or applied social science research. Controversy has raged for many years about the most appropriate view of knowledge on which to base such research. On the one hand, it is argued that, in order to be researched in a valid and reliable way, social phenomena must be defined such that they reflect an assumption of an invariant occurrence throughout humanity, e.g. the notion of intelligence quotient (or IQ). This leads to enquiry procedures being adopted which mirror those thought appropriate for the study of the physical world as conceived by Newton, i.e. the isolation of variables and their manipulation against each other in an experimental manner. Whilst there are some social phenomena which have an uncontested physical reality, e.g. numbers of individual people, experience of conducting social research in this manner has led to many doubts about whether the results obtained have a predictive value, i.e. can be used as a basis for guiding future action. The alternative view of knowledge recognizes the infinite plasticity of the human mind, and accepts that the most worthwhile perceptions are those of the perceivers, and that these preceptions are almost certain to change over time, if not rapidly. This set of assumptions leads to the study of 'cases', whether of individuals or naturally occurring groups, by means of observation and interview. This type of research has been found to influence the future actions of teachers, not by direct emulation, but my metaphorical transfer to new circumstances.

From the point of view of enquiry into satellites in education, questionnaires are an appropriate way to establish obvious facts, e.g. the amount and type of equipment held by an institution and the quality and type of data captured by ground-stations. The case study approach, based on observation and interview, is appropriate for context-dependent phenomena, e.g. the contribution of satellites to the curriculum, the teaching styles which most appropriately present learning opportunities and the learning styles that students adopt. Notions of 'good practice' approaches, which seem to yield an educationally valuable process or outcome, emerge from all this.

The skills of educational research, like those in any field of enquiry, take time and the concentrated application of effort if they are to be mastered such that high-quality outcomes are to be obtained. This certainly means that enquiries into satellites in education must be associated with individuals who are skilled educational researchers – a relatively rare breed, nearing extinction in the current intellectual climate. However, it would be entirely appropriate for practising teachers, perhaps on full- or part-time secondment, to carry out some, if not all, of the research. Their own experience will yield a ready capacity to identify important features of an educational situation, although safeguards against prejudice will be needed.

Traditionally, most education development work has been conducted on a 'centre-to-periphery' model. A few experts, gathered in one place, constructed a development of the basis of their perceptions of what was needed by teachers. This was then tested by teachers, modified by the experts and disseminated to teachers by means of highly structured courses, the intention being that the innovation was adopted and implemented *in toto*. Alas, painful experience has shown that this model is flawed: the experts misjudge the requirements of the educational system, teachers do not see the underlying assumptions of the innovation and introduce them in such a way that the novelty is nullified, and schools vary enormously in their circumstances and requirements. The alternative, or 'periphery-to-centre', model allows for a loose guidance by experts, fully negotiated with teachers, with the latter actually undertaking the development. The Secondary Science Curriculum Review in the UK was an example of this approach, where both process and product had considerable influence on the development of science education. It is argued that this 'periphery-to-centre' model is the most appropriate for 'satellites in education' work.

Turning, finally, to the financing and management of work on satellites in education', it is obvious that the immediate outlook is dismal. Within the UK there are relatively few government agencies that fund research and development work in educational matters. Of late, these have been priority driven, i.e. they will only fund work in areas of their own initiative and choice. Given the plethora of other demands on a miniscule R&D budget, satellites are unlikely to achieve a high priority. However, other alternatives do exist. Industrial companies may be brought to see that such educational work encourages the emergence of a constituency of support for satellite engineering, telecommunications and remote sensing. Additionally, pan-European initiatives, e.g.

The realization of potential

the Olympus satellite, will produce opportunities for education-related funding. Perhaps the overriding need is to ensure, by normal professional networking augmented by conferences which draw together diverse groups, that funding agencies are mutually aware and willing to work cooperatively in support of broad ventures.

What seems to be needed is a few centres specializing in satellites in education. These would be lightly staffed, but over a sufficient period to ensure stability for sustained research and development, and augmented by a core of consultant experts. These centres could form a focus for teacher secondments, with the outcomes of work being disseminated within a cascade model driven by the use of data bases, e.g. National Education Resource Information Service (NERIS), distance learning materials, mobile practical work units, and access to practitioner – consultants. Several such centres exist within the UK: the National Resource Centre on Satellites in Education, the Dyfed Satellite Education Project Centre and the Lancashire Satellites in Education Centre. Based on the energy of enthusiasts, they need a small, but continuous, dose of financial fertilizer to realize the enormous potential of the educational opportunities afforded by the exciting technological advances which seem likely to be sustained well into the twenty-first century.

References

1 Tomlinson, J. Changes in education. In I. Jamieson and D. Blandford (eds), *Education and Change*, CRAC, Cambridge, 1986.
2 Manpower Services Commission, *Technology for TVEI*, Manpower Services Commission, London, 1987.
3 Secondary Science Curriculum Review, *Technology and Science in the Curriculum*, Secondary Science Curriculum Review, London, 1987, p.5.
4 Gilbert, J., Underwood, C. and Sweeting, M. *The Report of a Feasibility Study into the Development of Models of INSET Concerning Earth-Orbiting Satellites in Education and Training*, University of Surrey, Guildford, 1988, p.30.
5 Cooper, A. and Underwood, C. *Satellites and Current Examination Syllabuses*, National Resource Centre on Satellites in Education, University of Surrey, Guildford, 1987.

Index

communication satellites
 Eutelsat series 73–6
 Intelsat series 64–71
 use in higher and continuing education 156–67
 use in information technology education 139–40
 use in language teaching 91–102
copyright issues 193–203
 categories of protected material 196
 conditions of protection 196
 duration of protection 197
 music 201
 ownership 196
 royalty payment 202
 signal distribution 200
 signal reception 198
 summary of issues 203

environmental science
 use of satellites in teaching 79–89

geography
 use of satellites in teaching 79–89

higher and continuing education 156–67
 Commonwealth for Learning 163
 criteria for use of satellites in 160–2
 Healthy Cities Project 165
 Project Share (Satellites for Health and Rural Education) 185

SPACE (Satellite Programmes for Adult and Continuing Education) 164
 use of satellites in Canada 157; Europe 159, 164; India 156; Indonesia 158; West Indies 158

information technology (IT)
 as a separate school subject 129–30
 communication satellites in 139–40
 in English 131
 in geography 131
 in history 130
 levels of education in 135–6
 in mathematics 131
 meaning of 128
 remote sensing satellites in 136–9
 in science 131–3

language teaching 91–102
 addresses 101–2
 benefits of satellite use 91–2
 Olympus 99–101
 programme material types 94–8
 sources of material 92–4
 teacher's role 98–9

named satellites (by major country of origin)
 'European': Eutelsat series 73–6; Meteosat 41–2; Olympus 99–101, 159–60

219

Index

France: SPOT-1 to -3 53–4
India: Bhaskara 1 and 2 49; Insat 1A to 1D 42
Japan: FUJI-OSCAR-12 6, 8–9; GMS-1 to -4 42; MOS-1 54
UK: UoSAT-1 5, 6, 12–22; UoSAT-2 5, 6, 22–35;
USA: Discovery-36 4; Echo 62; ESSA series 43; Explorer-1 3; GOES (NOAA) programme 40–1; Heat Capacity Mapping Mission 47–8; Intelsat I and II 64; Intelsat III 65; Intelsat IV 66–7; Intelsat IVA 68–9; Intelsat V 69–70; Intelsat VA and VB 70; Landsat 1 to 3 44–7; Landsat 4 and 5 51–3; Landsat 6 and 7 55–6; OSCAR-1 4; OSCAR-2 to -8 5; OSCAR-9 5(see also UoSAT-1); OSCAR-11 5; (see also UoSAT-2); Score 62; Seasat 47–8; TIROS series 38, 43; TIROS-N series 43–4
USSR: RS-1 5; RS-2 5; RS-3 to -8 5; RS-10 and -11 5, 9–10; Sputnik-1 3, 4
West Germany: AMSAT-OSCAR-13 6–8

orbital types
  geostationary 39; uses of 40, 62–76; satellites in 40–2, 62–76
  polar 39; satellites in 42–4

radio amateur community 3, 4, 6
remote sensing satellites 38–61
  categories of: earth resources 39, 44–9, 51–7; meteorological 39, 40–4; multi-purpose 49–51
  educational use: equipment purchase 149–50; in geography and environmental science education 79–89; in information technology education 139–40; of Landsat images 81–9; in school education generally 148–50; in science education 105–9

sensor types 38
satellites
  developing the educational use of 187–90, 191–2, 207–10, 213–18; educational place in multi-media packages 182–5; in-service education and training 153–4; learning styles in respect of 172; research into educational uses of 210–18; school course based on 110–12; teaching styles in respect of 152–3
science education 103–27
  benefits of satellites in 103
  use of remote sensing satellites in 105–9
  use of satellites in development of scientific process skills 112–25

technical descriptions of satellites
  ERS-1 56–7
  Eutelsat series 75
  GOES (NOAA) 40–1
  Heat Capacity Mapping Mission 47–8
  Intelsat IV 66–7
  Intelsat IVA 68–9
  Intelsat V, VA and VB 69–70
  Meteosat-1 and -2 41–2
  MOS-1 54
  OSCAR-12 8–9
  OSCAR-13 6–8
  Landsat 1 to 3 45–6
  Landsat 4 and 5 51–3
  Landsat 6 and 7 55–6
  Seasat 47–8
  SPOT-1 to -3 53–4

Index

SPOT-4 and -5 56
UoSAT-1 12–22; Digitalker experiment 20; HF propagation experiment 21; objectives 12; radiation experiment 19; remote sensing from 19; SHF beacons experiment 20
UOSAT-2 22–36; digital communications experiment 31, 34; Digitalker Experiment 33, 35; earth-imaging experiment 32; objectives 22; particle–wave experiment 32, 34; space dust experiment 33, 35

UoSAT series
educational use in the classroom 112–27, 150

For Product Safety Concerns and Information please contact our EU
representative GPSR@taylorandfrancis.com
Taylor & Francis Verlag GmbH, Kaufingerstraße 24, 80331 München, Germany

www.ingramcontent.com/pod-product-compliance
Lightning Source LLC
Chambersburg PA
CBHW061442300426
44114CB00014B/1797